THE HEALTH CARE SUPERVISOR

LAW

Edited by
Charles R. McConnell
Vice President for Employee Affairs
The Genesee Hospital
Rochester, New York

AN ASPEN PUBLICATION®
Aspen Publishers, Inc.
Gaithersburg, Maryland
1993

Library of Congress Cataloging-in-Publication Data

The health care supervisor on law/
[edited by] Charles R. McConnell.
p. cm.
Includes bibliographical references and index.
ISBN: 0-8342-0367-7
1. Health facilities—Employees—Legal status, laws, etc. —United States.
2. Health services administrators—Legal status, laws, etc.—United States.
3. Supervisors—Legal status, laws, etc.—United States.
4. Health facilities—Law and legislation—United States.
I. McConnell, Charles R. II. Health care supervisor.
KF3580.H4H425   1993
344.73' 0321068—dc20
[347.304321068]
93-6695
CIP

Editorial Resources: Barbara Priest

Library of Congress Catalog Card Number: 93-6695
ISBN: 0-8342-0367-7

Printed in Canada

1 2 3 4 5

Contents

Part I   General Legal Concerns

    Few jobs are completely without risk, but the job of the health care supervisor carries with it a sometimes significant risk of legal liability against which the supervisor's conscious awareness is the best defense.

    Many new supervisors quickly discover the existence of state and federal laws that require them and their organizations to report certain events, occurrences, and circumstances to various government agencies.

    More than simply a business fad of the 1980s and 1990s with which the supervisor may seem to be helplessly swept along, corporate reorganization has been addressed by many health care organizations as necessary to preserve their flexibility in an ever more restrictive operating environment.

    Although establishing pay grades and rates of compensation may remain "something that the personnel department takes care of," the supervisor who understands the broad basis for most compensation decisions will be in a better position to deal effectively with employees on pay issues.

    Emerging strongly in the 1980s, ethics committees continue to proliferate in the 1990s as supervisors spend an increasing amount of time attempting to deal with conflicts arising between and among matters of medicine, legality, and morality.

    The legal, moral, and ethical issues surrounding the refusal and withdrawal of medical treatment are increasing in number and complexity at least as rapidly as medical technology is advancing.

Part II Employment and the Supervisor

Part III AIDS, Drugs, and Employee Rights

Part IV Organized (and Organizing) Labor

Preface

INTRODUCTION

The Health Care Supervisor is a cross-disciplinary journal that publishes articles of relevance to persons who manage the work of others in health care settings. This journal's readers, as well as its authors, come from a wide variety of functional, clinical, technical, and professional backgrounds. Between the covers of a single issue of *HCS,* for example, you can find articles written by a nurse, a physician, a speech pathologist, a human resource specialist, an accountant, a nursing home administrator, and an attorney. These authors, and the numerous others who write for *HCS,* write with a single purpose: to provide guidance that all health care supervisors, regardless of the occupations or specialties they supervise, can use in learning to better understand or fulfill the supervisory role.

In the late twentieth century it seems as though life is becoming increasingly more complicated on a number of fronts and in a number of ways. Foremost among modern life's growing complexities is the extent to which an increasing number of federal and state laws of generally expanding scope are affecting health care delivery and employment relationships in general. Today's health care supervisor must be aware of the legal implications of most aspects of supervisory behavior. In *The Health Care Supervisor on Law* we have assembled 18 articles intended to heighten the supervisor's awareness of the major areas of supervisory conduct or involvement that have experienced significant change because of legislative action.

GENERAL LEGAL CONCERNS

In "Liability and the Supervisor," Robert Miller defines the concept of liability from the supervisor's perspective and contributes to a healthy awareness of potential legal pitfalls. Margeurite Mancini, in "Mandatory Reporting Laws: A Supervisor's Introduction," supplements the previous article's theme by highlighting the legal responsibility for external reporting.

With "Corporate Restructuring: The Whys and Wherefores," Laura Kalick puts into perspective the recent two decades' apparent preoccupation with corporately reorganizing health care organizations.

In "The Supervisor's Role in Matters of Pay Equity" Jerry Norville and Karen Swisher review points of basic wage and hour law and clarify the supervisor's relationship to them.

Bowen Hosford takes on the application and value of ethics committees in "Bioethics Committees: The Panacea of the 1980s?" and brings this issue well into the 1990s, Ilene Goldberg and Ira Sprotzer round out a concern for ethics with Life, "Death, and Liability: Duties of Health Care Providers Regarding Withdrawal of Treatment."

EMPLOYMENT AND THE SUPERVISOR

"Surviving the Employment Documentation Jungle" leads the supervisor through the maze created by the legal and practical need to document a growing number of dimensions of the employment relationship. Further documentation having expanding legal implications is examined by Joan Gratto Liebler in "Job Descriptions: Development and Use."

Seeming now as a harbinger of things to come as practical advice for the supervisor, "Sexual Harassment: A Problem for the Health Care Supervisor," by Gayle Goldberg and Janet Thompson Reagan, contains thoroughly sound and fully applicable advice for the supervisor although it was written well before the sudden national prominence attained by the topic in 1991.

In "Wrongful Discharge and Discipline," George Pozgar reveals how to get the supervisory job done with awareness of legal requirements and with in consideration of individuals' rights. With "Managing a Discrimination Case," Marion Blankopf adds an attorney's perspective to the editor's in offering supervisory guidance based on experience.

AIDS, DRUGS, AND EMPLOYEE RIGHTS

One of the most critical areas of legal concern for the foreseeable future is at the heart of three consecutive articles. "The AIDS Epidemic: Implications for Health Care Employees" (Karen Henry), "Privacy Rights and HIV Testing in the Hospital Setting: A Medicolegal Quagmire for Administrators" (Lee Mann and Thomas Wise), and "The Right to Know and the Right to Privacy: HIV Testing and Health Care Management" (David Wyld, Sam Cappel, and Daniel Hallock) address various dimensions of the critical issue of the rights of the individual versus the needs of the many. Related to this, in "Substance Abuse in the Workplace: Drug Testing and the Health Care Industry," Karen Henry and Stephen Parrish further explore the rights and safety issues related to drug and alcohol testing of existing or prospective employees.

ORGANIZED (AND ORGANIZING) LABOR

With "Health Care Organizing: Guidelines for Supervisory Conduct," Karen Henry clearly delineates the essential role of the supervisor in an organizing situation. To this perspective Andrew Banoff, in "Issues Concerning an Employee Strike," adds clarification of the supervisor's role and responsibility during a strike. Finally, in "From Grievance Through Arbi-

tration: A Supervisor's Perspective," Donald Petersen rounds out our coverage of organized labor with a complete picture of the supervisor's continuing relationship with a legal bargaining unit.

CONCLUSION

In the not-so-distant past the supervisor had few concerns with legal matters and could operate day to day with little chance of running afoul of the law. This is no longer the case; day-to-day operations are filled with potential legal traps and pitfalls, and the coming few years will bring even more legislation into the supervisor's arena.

Nobody realistically expects the typical supervisor to become a "sidewalk lawyer," fully up to date on legal decision making. However, today's health care supervisor must be sufficiently knowledgeable of the potential traps and pitfalls to know when a certain position or course of action might be risky and to especially know when to request professional advice and assistance.

Acknowledgments

It would not have been possible to assemble this volume without the active involvement of the members of the guiding boards, past and present, of *The Health Care Supervisor*. As of this writing some of these valued advisors and authors are well into their second decade of service to *HCS*.

Our sincere thanks to the following past members of the *HCS* Editorial Board, the present *HCS* Advisory Board, and the present Board of Contributing Editors.

Past Members of HCS Editorial Board

Steven H. Appelbaum, Zeila W. Bailey, Claire D. Benjamin, Marjorie Beyers, Philip Bornstein, Leonard C. Brideau, Robert W. Broyles, Joy D. Calkin, Kenneth P. Cohen, Joseph A. Cornell, Darlene A. Dougherty, Kenneth R. Emery, Valerie Glesnes-Anderson, Lee Hand, Allen G. Herkimer, Jr., Max G. Holland, Bowen Hosford, Charles E. Housley, Loucine M. D. Huckabay, Laura L. Kalick, Janice M. Kurth, Marlene Lamnin, Joan Gratto Liebler, Ellyn Luros, Margeurite R. Mancini, Robert D. Miller, Joan F. Moore, Victor J. Morano, Harry E. Munn, Jr., Michael W. Noel, Rita E. Numerof, Samuel E. Oberman, Cheryl S. O'Hara, Jesus J. Pena, Donald J. Petersen, Tim Porter-O'Grady, George D. Pozgar, Ann Marie Rhodes, Edward P. Richards III, James C. Rose, Rachel Rotkovich, Norton M. Rubenstein, Edward D. Sanderson, William L. Scheyer, Homer H., Schmitz, Joyce L. Schweiger, Donna Richards Sheridan, Margaret D. Sovie, Eugene I. Stearns, Judy Ford Stokes, Thomas J. Tenerovicz, Lewis H. Titterton, Jr., Dennis A. Tribble, Terry Trudeau, Alex J. Vallas, Katherine W. Vestal, Judith Weilerstein, William B. Werther, Jr., Shirley Ann Wertz, Sara J. White, Norman H. Witt, and Karen Zander

Present HCS Advisory Board

Addison C. Bennett, Bernard L. Brown, Jr., Karen H. Henry, Norman Metzger, I. Donald Snook, Jr., and Helen Yura-Petro

Present Board of Contributing Editors

Donald F. Beck, Robert Boissoneau, Jerad D. Browdy, Vicki S. Crane, Carol A. Distasio, Charlotte Eliopoulos, Howard L. Lewis, R. Scott MacStravic, Leon McKenzie, Jerry L. Norville, Stephen L. Priest, Howard L. Smith, and John L. Templin, Jr.

Our sincere appreciation as well to those who, in addition to the persons mentioned above, participated in creating the articles that make up this book:

Andrew Banoff, Sam D. Cappel, Gayle L. Goldberg, Ilene V. Goldberg, Daniel E. Hallock, Lee S. Mann, Stephen W. Parrish, Janet Thompson Reagan, Ira Sprotzer, Karen N. Swisher, Thomas N. Wise, and David D. Wyld.

Part I
General Legal Concerns

Liability and the supervisor

Robert D. Miller
Assistant to the Director
University of Iowa Hospitals and
*   Clinics*
Adjunct Assistant Professor
Graduate Program in Hospital and
*   Health Administration*
University of Iowa
Iowa City, Iowa

EVERYONE INVOLVED in the delivery of health care is acutely aware of the potential for patients or their families to make legal claims demanding money because of injuries they believe were caused by malpractice or other wrongful conduct. Some of this concern for potential liability claims exists because of personal experience or the experiences of colleagues. However, much of the concern is caused by the uncertainty and mystery surrounding legal liability and the legal process. This article is intended to take away some of that mystery by helping supervisors to understand their own exposure to liability and the exposure of the employees they supervise. By developing a basic understanding of liability principles, supervisors can help to minimize claims and facilitate proper handling of claims that are made.

Health Care Superv, 1983,1(2),59–72
© 1983 Aspen Publishers, Inc.

THE DIFFERENCE BETWEEN LIABILITY OF INDIVIDUALS AND LIABILITY OF EMPLOYERS

There are two basic kinds of liability, liability for the consequences of personal acts and liability for the consequences of employees' acts. The liability for the consequences of personal acts is nearly always based on the principle of fault. To be liable, the person must have done something wrong or must have failed to do something he or she should have done. There are a few exceptions for which there is strict liability for all consequences of certain activities regardless of fault, but they rarely apply to individuals.

In the second type of liability, employers can be liable for the consequences of their employees' job-related acts regardless of whether the employer is at fault. This legal doctrine is called *respondeat superior,* which means "let the master answer." Under this doctrine, the employer can be liable for any consequences of an employee's activities within the course of employment for which the employee could be liable. The employer need not have done anything wrong. Thus, for example, if a nurse employed by a hospital injures a patient by giving the wrong medication, the hospital can be liable even if the nurse was properly selected, properly trained and properly assigned the responsibility.

The liability of the employer under *respondeat superior* is for the benefit of the person who is injured, not for the benefit of the employee. The liability of the employer does not mean that the employer must provide the employee with liability protection. It means that the person who is injured can sue either the employee or the employer or both. If the employee is individually sued and found liable, the employee must pay. If, as usually occurs, the employee is not individually sued, and the employer is, then the employer must pay. Technically, the employer can sue the employee to get the money back, but this is almost never done perhaps because it can have negative effects on future recruiting efforts.

Many employers provide individual liability protection for their employees. For example, governmental employers in Iowa are required to provide employees with liability protection for acts committed in the scope of employment and are prohibited from suing employees to get the money back. This does not mean that the employer must buy commercial insurance. Many employers choose to self-insure, and many others provide individual liability protection either through commercial insurance or through self-insurance.

Before deciding what additional liability protection, if any, to secure, an employee should determine the coverage provided by the employer. Most employers who provide liability protection cover only job-related activities, so some employees with this type of coverage elect to purchase coverage for their outside activities, such as volunteer services, which are not covered by the insurance arrangements of the agency for which the person is providing the services.

LIABILITY OF SUPERVISORS

The supervisor is not the employer. The supervisor is an employee. *Respondeat superior* does not impose liability on the supervisor. Supervisors are liable only for the consequences of their own acts or omissions. Of course the employer can also be liable for those acts or

---

The acts or omissions for which a health care supervisor can be found liable include improper supervision and improper provision of care.

---

omissions under *respondeat superior*. The acts or omissions for which a health care supervisor can be found liable include improper supervision and improper provision of care.

The liability of a supervising nurse for the actions of supervised nurses was discussed in a California court decision, *Bowers v. Olch*.[1] The case involved a needle left in a patient's abdomen during surgery. The patient sued the physicians, the hospital and the supervising nurse. The court ruled that the supervising nurse could not be sued because she had done nothing wrong. She had assigned two competent nurses to assist with the surgery, and she had not been present, so she had had no op-

portunity to intervene. The court ruled that *respondeat superior* did not apply to the nursing supervisor because she was not the employer.

The actions that can lead to liability of supervising health professionals are discussed in more detail in a New Jersey court decision, *Stumper v. Kimel*.[2] The case involved a surgeon who had ordered a resident physician to remove a tube being used to extract a patient's gastric contents. The patient's esophagus was perforated in the process. The court ruled that the supervising surgeon was not liable for the acts of the resident. The court said that the supervising surgeon could be liable only if (1) it was not accepted medical or hospital practice to delegate the particular function to someone with this level of training, (2) he knew or should have known that the individual resident was not qualified to perform the task with the degree of supervision provided, (3) he had been present and had been able to avoid the injury or (4) he had a special contract with the patient that he did not fulfill. Since none of these circumstances was present, the supervising surgeon was not liable.

In some states the courts apply a different legal doctrine to supervising physicians, the "borrowed servant" doctrine. This doctrine applies only to supervisors who are independently practicing professionals; the "borrowed servant" doctrine does *not* apply to supervisors who are also employees of the same employer. When the "borrowed servant" doctrine is applied, the courts say that the supervising physician has borrowed the employee from the regular employer, and the law will consider the supervising physician to be the employer, so *respondeat superior* can be applied to make the supervising physician liable for all acts of the borrowed employee while working under the direction of the supervising physician.

Another case that illustrates the potential liability of a supervising nurse is *Laidlaw v. Lions Gate Hospital*,[3] which was decided by a Canadian court in British Columbia. In this case, the court found both the supervising nurse and her employer, the hospital, liable for injuries to a woman who was not observed often enough in a postanesthetic recovery room. The patient had a cholecystectomy (excision of the gallbladder) without complications and was transferred to the postanesthetic recovery room. The hospital had provided two nurses for the area, which the court accepted as adequate staffing, but the supervising nurse had permitted the other nurse to leave the area for a coffee break just before three patients were admitted to the area. One of the patients suffered a respiratory obstruction, which was not observed until the lack of oxygen caused permanent brain damage.

The court ruled that the supervising nurse was liable for permitting the other nurse to leave the area at a time when she knew that the operating schedule would result in several admissions to the unit. The court

went on to say that even if the supervising nurse had not known the operating schedule, she would still be liable for not knowing the aspects of the operating schedule that applied to the staffing needs of the area she supervised. The supervising nurse, who was also providing direct nursing care to the patients in the area, was also liable for failing to personally observe the patient more frequently. The court ruled that the nurse who left the area would also have been liable had she been included in the suit, because she should have known the aspects of the operating schedule that applied to the staffing needs of the area in which she worked. The hospital was also liable for the acts of both nurses under the doctrine of *respondeat superior*.

The foregoing case was followed two years later by a very similar case, *Krujelis v. Esdale*,[4] in the same province of Canada. A ten-year-old boy who had undergone plastic surgery for overprominent ears suffered cardiac arrest, which resulted in a permanent coma of nearly four years until his death. The cardiac arrest occurred in the postanesthetic recovery area while three of the five nurses assigned to the area were on a coffee break. The hospital was found liable for the same reasons liability was imposed in the *Laidlaw* case.

In a New York case, *Horton v. Niagara Falls Memorial Medical Center*,[5] a patient who was disoriented had been found on a balcony outside a second-story window. After the patient was returned to the hospital room, the physician told the staff to arrange to have the patient watched. The charge nurse called the patient's family to tell them to arrange to have someone watch the patient. The family said someone would be at the hospital in 10 to 15 minutes. By the time the family member arrived, the patient had fallen out of the window and was severely injured.

The hospital was found liable for failing to move the patient to a secure room, apply additional restraints or find someone to watch the patient for 15 minutes. There was one charge nurse, one new registered nurse in orientation, one practical nurse and one aide on a unit with 19 patients. The court found that all except the aide had been engaged in routine duties that could have been delayed for 15 minutes and that the aide had been permitted to leave for supper during the period. The court said that this was evidence that there had been sufficient staffing to provide continuous supervision for a patient in known danger for 15 minutes. The failure of the supervising nurse to properly allocate the time of the available staff was one of the grounds for finding the hospital liable.

Although the reported court decisions involve liability of supervising nurses and physicians, the same general principles apply to other supervising health care professionals. In summary, a supervisor can be liable if any of the following events occur:
- The supervisor assigns a subordinate to do something that the supervisor knows or should know

the subordinate is unable to do.
- The supervisor does not provide a subordinate with the degree of supervision the supervisor knows or should know the subordinate needs.
- The supervisor is present and fails to take action when possible to avoid the injury.
- The supervisor does not properly allocate the time of available staff—for example, by permitting breaks from areas in which there are critical needs—at times when the supervisor knows or should know that the staff will be needed.

TYPES OF CIVIL LIABILITY

Civil liability is liability imposed through mechanisms other than the criminal law. There are two types of civil liability: liability that is based on contract and liability that is not based on contract. The latter is called tort liability. Liability based on contract will not be addressed in this article.

A tort is a wrongful civil act that is not based on a violation of a contract. Tort liability is almost always based on fault; that is, something was done wrong or something that should have been done was not done. This act or omission can be intentional or the result of negligence. There are some exceptions to the requirement of fault, but these rarely apply in suits against individual health care providers, so they will not be discussed.

Intentional Torts

Liability for intentional torts is a serious concern. Intentional torts include assault and battery, defamation, false imprisonment, invasion of privacy and the intentional infliction of emotional distress.

Assault and battery

An assault is an action that puts someone in apprehension of being touched in a manner that is insulting, provoking or physically injurious without lawful authority or consent. No actual touching is required; the assault is simply the credible threat of touching in this manner. If actual touching occurs, then it is called battery.

Assault or battery can occur when medical treatment is attempted or performed without lawful authority or consent. Assault or battery can oc-

---

Assault or battery can occur when medical treatment is attempted or performed without lawful authority or consent.

---

cur in other circumstances as well, such as in attempts to restrain patients who are competent and oriented without lawful authority.

Defamation

Defamation is wrongful injury to someone's reputation. Written defamation is called libel, and spoken defamation is called slander. A claim of defamation can arise from inappropriate release of inaccurate medical records or from untruthful statements being made about staff members. However, courts have recognized the importance of communications concerning a staff member's performance to supervisory staff and on up through the organizational structure. Thus such communications are protected by a "qualified privilege" when they are made in good faith to the persons who need to know. This means that liability is not imposed for defamation, even if the communication is false, as long as the communication was made without malice. Supervisors and employers must be careful to keep communications regarding employees within appropriate channels, because discussions with others will not be protected by the qualified privilege.

Some courts have also recognized a qualified privilege for assessments provided by a former employer to a prospective employer. The foregoing is illustrated by *Wynn v. Cole*,[6] in which the director of a department of health that had employed a nurse was found not liable for providing a prospective employer with information concerning the nurse's abilities. The court ruled that the qualified privilege applied, and no malice had been shown. The better practice, which many institutions follow, is to refrain from releasing information regarding former employees unless a written request for the release is received. This reduces the need to rely on the court to decide that the qualified privilege applies. Of course there still could be liability for untruthful information released with malice. This policy will not reduce the availability of important information to the prospective employer, because the prospective employer can and probably should require a release.

False imprisonment

False imprisonment is the unlawful restriction of someone's freedom. Holding a person against his or her will by physical restraint, barriers or even threats of harm can constitute false imprisonment if not legally justified. Claims of false imprisonment can arise from inappropriate detention of a patient in a hospital or from a challenge by a patient to commitment for being mentally ill.

Hospitals do have the common law authority to detain patients who are disoriented. There is also a legal procedure in all states to secure authorization to detain the mentally ill, substance abusers and those with contagious diseases. When a patient is oriented, competent and not legally committed, hospital staff should avoid detaining the patient unless authorized to do so by an explicit institutional policy or institutional administrators.

Invasion of privacy

Claims for invasion of privacy can arise from unauthorized release of information concerning a patient. However, not all releases of information violate the right to privacy. For example, in the case of *Koudski v. Hennepin County Medical Center,*[7] the Minnesota court found that even though the patient had explicitly requested that the information not be released, it was not an invasion of privacy to orally disclose the fact that the patient had been discharged from the hospital and that she had given birth, as long as the information was in response to a direct inquiry concerning that patient. The better practice would be to attempt to avoid release of discharge and birth information when the patient requests nondisclosure, but it is reassuring to know that at least the Minnesota courts did not impose liability for releasing admission and discharge information in these circumstances.

Obviously, institutional policies concerning confidentiality need to be followed, because some courts will impose liability for failure to follow institutional rules. One exception to the rule concerning admission and discharge information concerns information about substance abusers. Federal regulations (42 C.F.R. Part 2) prohibit disclosure of information concerning patients being treated for substance abuse or substance-abuse–related conditions unless one of the exceptions in the regulations applies. This prohibition extends to disclosing whether or not the patient is in the institution. Staff who are involved with substance abusers should be familiar with these regulations and know how to comply with them.

Intentional infliction of emotional distress

Intentional infliction of emotional distress is another intentional tort. This includes some of the most outrageous conduct. It should be easy to avoid this tort by remembering to treat patients and their families in a civilized fashion. This was apparently forgotten in the following two examples involving actions after the death of patients.

The case of *Johnson v. Woman's Hospital*,[8] concerned a mother who had sought the body of her baby who had died in the hospital. A hospital staff member gave the body to her preserved in a jar of formaldehyde. A second example of intentional infliction of emotional distress is the case of *McCormick v. Haley*,[9] which dealt with communications after death. A woman died, and a month later her family physician's office sent a notice for her to come in for a periodic checkup.

The court said that this first reminder was an excusable error. Her husband sent the physician a letter explaining that she had died. The husband later sued the physician for malpractice in her death. After the suit was filed, the physician's office sent two more reminders for the dead woman to come in for a checkup, one of which was addressed to the youngest daughter of the deceased. The court said that the second and third reminders could be the basis for liability.

Negligent torts

The most frequent basis for liability of health care professionals is the negligent tort. Fortunately, negligence by itself is not enough to establish liability. There must also be an injury caused by the negligence. Everyone makes negligent errors and is lucky enough to cause no injury. There are four elements that must be proven to establish liability for negligent torts: (1) duty (what should have been done), (2) breach of duty (deviation from what should have been done), (3) injury and (4) causation (the injury was legally caused by the deviation from what should have been done).

There is a "fifth element" in negligent torts that the courts do not discuss, but supervisors should remember—there must be someone willing to make a claim. Health care providers who maintain good relationships with their patients before and after incidents are less likely to be sued. If a supervisor suspects that an incident may have occurred, the persons responsible for risk management in the institution should be notified promptly so that steps can be taken to minimize the chance of a claim.

Duty

If a claim is made, the first element that must be proven is the duty. This is sometimes called the standard of care. What should a reasonably prudent health care provider engaged in a similar practice have done under the circumstances? This is proven in one of three ways. First, the technical aspects of care can be proven through expert testimony, usually by other health care professionals. Sometimes the health care provider's out-of-court statements can be used against the provider as an admission, so care must be taken in what is said or written after an incident. When in doubt, a health care provider should seek the advice of the institution's administrators or attorneys.

Second, nontechnical aspects of care can be proven by nonexperts. Some courts will permit juries to use their own knowledge and common sense when the duty is considered common knowledge. For example, many courts consider one of the nontechnical aspects to be how a disoriented patient should be protected from falling from a bed. Those familiar with this clinical care problem may question how nontechnical it is, but they should be aware of how the courts perceive it.

Third, some courts will look to published standards, such as institutional rules and accreditation standards, to determine the duty. Thus it is important for staff members to be familiar with the written rules of the institution applicable to their areas of practice. When the rules are impossible to follow, steps should be taken to modify them—instead of ignoring them.

The proof of duty can become confused when there are two or more accepted approaches to a situation. The courts have attempted to resolve this through the "respected minority" rule. If a health care professional follows the approach used by a respected minority of the profession, then the duty is to properly follow that approach. The courts will not permit liability to be based simply on the decision not to follow the majority approach.

Examples of the duty of supervisors include having a general knowledge of the capabilities of staff members, assigning staff members to functions within their capabilities, providing necessary instruction or ensuring that arrangements are made for instruction, providing or arranging for the appropriate degree of supervision, informing superiors of staffing needs and appropriately assigning available staff.

Courts will sometimes impose a new duty not previously recognized by the profession. In such cases, the court says that the whole profession is lagging in its standards, so the court imposes a more stringent legal standard. The classical case did not arise from health care. The case of *The T.J. Hooper*[10] concerned a tugboat that sank along with two barges in a storm off the Atlantic Coast in the early part of this century. Warnings of the impending storm had been sent out by radio from the U.S. Weather Bureau. If the T.J. Hooper had had a radio, it could have heard the warning and safely entered a port. The owners of the barges sued, claiming that the owners of the tugboat were negligent for not having a radio on board. In their defense, the owners of the tugboat claimed that few tugboats had radios, so they had not violated any industry standards. The court said the entire industry was negligent and imposed liability on the owners.

Occasionally, courts have also imposed stricter standards on health care providers. For example, in *Tarasoff v. Board of Regents*,[11] when parents sued for the death of their daughter, the court found the employer of a psychiatrist liable for his failure to warn the daughter that his patient had threatened to kill her, even though other psychiatrists would have acted in the same manner.

Breach of duty

In a negligent tort, after the duty is proven, the second element that must be proven is the breach of this duty. Thus it must be proven that there was a deviation in some manner from the standard of care. Something was done

---

In a negligent tort, after the duty is proven, the second element that must be proven is the breach of that duty.

---

that should not have been done, such as letting the nurse take a break at the wrong time in the *Laidlaw* case, or something was not done that should have been done, such as observing a postanesthesia patient every five minutes in the *Laidlaw* care.

Injury

The third element of a negligent tort is injury. The person making the

claim must demonstrate physical, financial or emotional injury. With few exceptions, courts will not allow suits to be based solely on emotional injuries. In most malpractice cases the existence of the injury is very clear by the time there is a suit, although there still may be disagreement concerning the dollar value of the injury.

Causation

The fourth element of a negligent tort is causation; that is, the breach of the duty must be proven to have legally caused the injury. For example, a treatment may be negligently delayed (which is a breach of duty), and the patient may die (which is an injury), but the person suing must still prove that there was a substantial likelihood that the patient would have lived had the treatment been given sooner. Thus causation is often the most difficult element to prove.

The difficulty of proving causation is illustrated in *Lenger v. Physician's General Hospital*.[12] A nurse gave a patient solid food immediately after colon surgery (which is a breach of duty), and eight days later the ends of the sutured colon came apart (which is an injury). Because of the time lag, the patient was not able to prove causation.

Causation has been proven in many cases, however, such as *Schnebly v. Baker*.[13] A baby was born with Rh blood incompatibility. An outdated reagent was used for the tests of the bilirubin level in the baby's blood, so the tests erroneously indicated a safe level. By the time the error was discovered, the baby had suffered severe, permanent brain damage caused by the high bilirubin level in his blood. The hospital and pathologists were liable, because accurate tests would have led to timely therapy, which probably would have prevented the brain damage.

Res ipsa loquitur

There is a major exception to the requirement that the four elements of a negligent tort be proven. This is the doctrine of *res ipsa loquitur*—"the thing speaks for itself." In England in the nineteenth century the courts were confronted with cases arising from barrels flying out of upper-story windows and hitting pedestrians. When a pedestrian tried to sue the owner of a building, the owner claimed that the four elements had to be proven. Of course, the person suing could not find out the specifics of what went wrong in the upper-story room, so the case would have been lost. However, the courts said the owner could not take advantage of the rules to escape liability in cases in which someone had clearly done something wrong, so the courts developed the *res ipsa loquitur* doctrine.

In the doctrine the courts said all that has to be proven is (1) the accident is of the kind that does not occur in the absence of negligence, (2) the apparent cause is in the exclusive control of the defendants, (3) the person suing could not have contributed to the difficulties, (4) evidence of the true cause is inaccessible to the per-son suing and (5) the fact of injury. Courts have frequently applied this rule to two types of malpractice cases: (1) sponges and other foreign objects unintentionally left in the body during surgery and (2) injuries to parts of the body distant from the site of treatment, such as a leg laceration during eye surgery.

Liability is not automatic in *res ipsa loquitur* cases, however. The persons being sued may attempt to explain why the injury was not the result of negligence. This can successfully be done in some circumstances; for example, if a physician can prove that a sponge was left in a patient because the patient had to be quickly closed on an emergency basis to save the patient's life, and there was no time for a sponge count.

Defenses

There are several defenses that are sometimes available to individuals sued for negligent torts. One defense is the statute of limitations, which specifies the time period in which suits must be started. Suits are barred after that time period has expired. The time period varies depending on the nature of the suit and which state's law is applicable. The rules are complicated in many states. It should be remembered that there is a time limit, but in some states it can be quite long, especially for injuries to children. In most states, minors may sue up to one year after becoming adults. This means that suits arising out of care of neonates may be filed nearly 19 years later. Since few people have memories that long, it is important for health care providers to thoroughly document the care given to patients. The records will be the only way to prove what was done. Most courts assume that if it was not written down, it was not done.

Another defense is a release. As part of the process of settling a claim, the claimant is usually asked to sign a release of all future claims arising from the same incident. In most cases, if such a release has been signed, it will bar a future suit based on the same incident.

An exculpatory contract, an agreement not to sue or an agreement to limit the amount of the suit, is different from a release and is not a successful defense. Some providers have asked patients to sign an exculpatory contract before providing care. Courts have refused to enforce these contracts on the grounds that they are against public policy. For example, in *Tatham v. Hoke*,[14] the federal courts refused to enforce an agreement to limit all claims to $15,000.

However, in some states, a patient can sign a valid agreement to arbitrate any claims, instead of taking them to court, as long as the agreement does not place other limits on the claim. If a patient has signed a valid agreement to arbitrate, courts will refuse to accept the case except for limited review of the arbitration process after it is completed.

Contributory negligence is a defense to a claim of a negligent tort. Contributory negligence occurs when the patient does something

wrong that contributes so much to the injury that the health care provider is not responsible for the injury. In other words, the patient is unable to prove the fourth element, causation of the injury by the provider's error.

Whenever providers begin to feel that the patient has no responsibilities, they should look at the cases in which there was a successful contributory negligence defense. Examples of contributory negligence on the part of a patient include failing to follow clear orders by failing to return for a follow-up visit; walking on a broken leg; getting out of bed and falling; lighting a cigarette in bed while unattended; and deliberately giving false information during the taking of the history, leading to the wrong antidote being given for a drug overdose.

The success of the contributory negligence defense depends on the intelligence and degree of orientation of the patient. Obviously, a patient who does not appear to be able to follow orders cannot be relied on to follow orders, so contributory negligence would not be a successful defense against a claim by such a patient. Some states do not use the all-or-nothing contributory negligence rule. Instead, they apply comparative negligence, which means the percentage of the cause attributed to the patient is determined, and the patient does not collect that percentage of the total amount of the injury.

• • •

There is a difference between liability for the consequences of personal acts and the liability of the employer under *respondeat superior* for the consequences of an employee's acts. Supervisors are not the employers, so they are liable only for their personal acts. These acts can include improper supervision through negligent assignment, negligent failure to provide personal supervision or negligent failure to intervene when present.

Civil liability is divided into contract and tort liability. The torts that most frequently involve health care providers are intentional torts and negligent torts. Intentional torts include assault and battery, libel and slander, false imprisonment, invasion of privacy and the intentional infliction of emotional distress.

To establish liability for a negli-

The torts that most frequently involve health care providers are intentional torts and negligent torts.

---

gent tort, four elements must be proven: duty, breach of duty, injury and causation. An unwritten "fifth element" is someone who is willing to make a claim, so it is important for health care providers to maintain good relationships with patients and their families. One exception to the requirement to prove the four elements is when the doctrine of *res ipsa loquitur*—"the thing speaks for itself"—applies. There are several defenses to suits, including the statute of limitations, releases, agreements to arbitrate and contributory negligence.

REFERENCES

1. Bowers v. Olch, 260 P.2d 997 (Cal. App. 1953).
2. Stumper v. Kimel, 260 A.2d 526 (N.J. App. Div. 1970).
3. Laidlaw v. Lions Gate Hospital, 8 D.L.R.3d 730 (B.C. Sup. Ct. 1969).
4. Krujelis v. Esdale, [1972] 2 W.W.R. 495 (B.C. Sup. Ct. 1971).
5. Horton v. Niagara Falls Memorial Medical Center, 380 N.Y.S.2d 116 (App. Div. 1976).
6. Wynn v. Cole, 284 N.W.2d 144 (Mich. App. 1979).
7. Koudski v. Hennepin County Medical Center, 317 N.W.2d 705 (Minn. 1982).
8. Johnson v. Woman's Hospital, 527 S.W.2d 133 (Tenn. App. 1975).
9. McCormick v. Haley, 307 N.E.2d 34 (Ohio App. 1973).
10. The T.J. Hooper, 60 F.2d 737 (2d Cir. 1932).
11. Tarasoff v. Board of Regents, 551 P.2d 334 (Cal. 1976).
12. Lenger v. Physician's General Hospital, 455 S.W.2d 703 (Tex. 1970).
13. Schnebly v. Baker, 217 N.W.2d 708 (Iowa 1974).
14. Tatham v. Hoke, 469 F.Supp. 914 (W.D. N.C. 1979).

Mandatory reporting laws: a supervisor's introduction

Marguerite R. Mancini
Director of General Assistance
Department of Income
*   Maintenance—Connecticut*
Hartford, Connecticut

DOCUMENTATION occupies a considerable percentage of a health care supervisor's time. Some, if not most, of the supervisor's documentation involves reporting to agencies outside the health care institution.

Reporting laws are applicable to a number of situations encountered in the health care setting. The purpose of requiring that reports by health care professionals be submitted to public officials is to facilitate detection of problems and to help determine appropriate action needed to ensure the health and safety of the entire community.

FEDERAL AND STATE DISTINCTIONS

Because of the system of government maintained in the United States, most reporting laws in effect

Health Care Superv, 1983,2(1),66–76
© 1983 Aspen Publishers, Inc.

are those enacted by the individual states. There are some federal reporting laws that every health care supervisor should be knowledgeable about, but there are many more important state laws.

The major distinctions between federal and state laws are few, but they are important to understand. The first distinction is that federal reporting laws are basically uniform in their application from state to state. The application of a federal reporting law will be the same in New York as it is in California. The corollary to this is that state reporting laws are applicable only within the borders of the state in which they were enacted.

The health care supervisor must be familiar with both state and federal laws and must appreciate that state laws may be quite different in another, even neighboring, state.

The health care supervisor must be familiar with both state and federal laws and must appreciate that state laws may be quite different in another state.

A second important distinction is the impact of the reporting laws. Since most of the reporting laws are state laws, it might be logical to conclude that a supervisor will spend more time on issues involving state laws than on data needed to report to the federal government. This may sometimes be true, but it is not always so.

A look at the subjects addressed by reporting laws illustrates this distinction. Most cases to be reported to state officials are those involving communicable diseases, suspicious and unattended deaths, violent wounds, and cases of suspected abuse of the elderly and minors.

Federal regulations cover the maintenance of medical records of patients who are the beneficiaries of medical coverage through either Medicare (Title 18 of the Social Security Act) or Medicaid (Title 19 of the same act) as a condition of participation in these programs by the health care institution.

The time a health care supervisor spends on federal regulations dealing with Medicare and Medicaid may well be none if the health care institution does not participate in those programs. However, if the institution participates and has a large number of Medicare and Medicaid patients, then the supervisor's reporting time may be significant.

There are some areas of overlapping jurisdiction, in which an activity may be covered by federal and state laws. It is important for health care supervisors to be aware that in cases in which federal and state laws apply, both must be followed. If there are such cases and a discrepancy exists the federal rule will generally prevail, so long as the rule deals with a practice governable by federal law as specified in the U.S. Constitution. Two major areas of concern dealt with by the federal government, in addition to Medicare and Medicaid, are drugs and handicapped patients.

USE OF DRUGS

Both state and federal laws regulate the use of drugs and mandate drug-related reporting by health care institutions. There are two federal laws concerned with drugs. One is the Comprehensive Drug Abuse Prevention and Control Act of 1970, more commonly called the Controlled Substances Act. Before this law was enacted, most states had adopted some version of the Uniform Narcotic Drug Act. Since 1970 the states have been repealing their narcotic and depressant-stimulant laws and replacing them with the less comprehensive "mini" controlled substances acts. The new state laws occasionally vary somewhat from the Uniform Narcotic Drug Act, so state law must always be consulted.

Controlled substances

The Controlled Substances Act defines what constitutes narcotics, depressants, stimulants and hallucinogens. It covers the distribution systems used in hospitals, rehabilitation programs under community mental health programs, and research in and medical treatment for drug abuse and addiction. It also covers importation and exportation of controlled substances.

Section 802 of the Controlled Substances Act requires that only practitioners dispense or conduct research with controlled drugs. Under the act, the term *practitioners* is limited to those who are duly licensed or registered to dispense drugs. It includes hospitals and pharmacies as well as physicians, dentists and veterinarians. In accordance with this act, each practitioner must register with the federal government.

An actual inventory must be taken by each registrant every two years. Although a separate inventory is required for each registered location and for each activity that is registered, it is not mandatory to keep a perpetual inventory. Along with the inventory record, each practitioner who has registered with the federal government must maintain correct and complete records of all controlled substances received and distributed.

Under the act, all registrants must implement effective procedures to control these drugs and protect them from theft or misuse. Central storage should be controlled by the chief pharmacist of the health care institution. When these substances are kept in several locations, they should always be under lock, and access should be limited to authorized personnel of the institution.

Penalties under the Controlled Substances Act, as they apply to registrants, include a civil fine of not more than $25,000 for the first infraction. If the violation was committed knowingly, the person may be sent to prison for a maximum term of one year in addition to being fined. A violation committed knowingly after one or more prior convictions exposes the offender to a maximum prison term of two years, a fine of $50,000 or both.

Food, drugs and cosmetics

The Federal Food, Drug and Cosmetic Act applies to the purity, labeling, potency, safety and effectiveness of drugs and devices used in health care settings. This act, together with the Comprehensive Drug Abuse Prevention and Control Act of 1970, was passed by Congress with the intent of creating two complementary checks on the production and marketing of new drugs.

During the production and pre-marketing stage of a new drug, the Food and Drug Administration has primary responsibility for labeling potency. Once a drug is cleared for marketing, by way of new-drug application approval, and the drug is determined by the Food and Drug Administration to be a controlled substance, permissible distribution falls under the jurisdiction of the Justice Department. Penalties administered under the Federal Food, Drug and Cosmetic Act are much less severe than those administered under the Controlled Substances Act.

The difference between a drug, device and cosmetic is important in health care institutions because so many kinds of products are regularly used in health care. A number of items, not seeming to be drugs at first, have been held to be such under this act. These items include antibiotic sensitivity discs used in laboratory procedures to determine the inhibiting ability of various antibiotics on sample microorganisms, certain sutures used for tying off blood vessels during surgical procedures, whole blood and the bags used to store blood and other intravenous substances.

Although certain provisions of the Federal Food, Drug and Cosmetic Act specifically apply to intrastate commerce of drugs, at various times Congress has specifically provided for the applicability of state law. Therefore, most states now have laws based on the Uniform State Food, Drug and Cosmetic Act. State laws vary in some specific details from the Federal Food, Drug and Cosmetic Act and the Uniform Narcotic Drug Act. Therefore, state laws must be consulted in determining whether a specific course of conduct is in compliance with all applicable laws.

TREATMENT OF THE HANDICAPPED

The Rehabilitation Act of 1973 mandates equal access to the handicapped in obtaining health care service. The regulations that implement Section 504 of this act cover all health care institutions that employ 15 persons or more *and* receive funding from the Department of Health and Human Services (HHS). Such institutions must take positive steps to ensure that handicapped persons will have access that is equal to that of the nonhandicapped in obtaining health services. These regulations, which became effective in 1977, forbid hospitals to deny or limit health or social services to the handicapped.

To repeat, an institution must employ 15 persons or more *and* be the recipient of federal funding through HHS in order to be subject to their laws and regulations. The funding will usually be that received as a result of the treatment of Medicare and Medicaid patients, but it could also be from grants, contracts or construction funds.

The definition of a handicapped person under this act is extremely broad. A handicapped individual is defined as: (1) a person who has a physical or mental impairment that substantially limits one or more major life activities, or (2) a person who has a history of such a condition or is thought by any others to have such a condition. In addition to persons with sensory impairments and deprivations, the definition includes those suffering from mental retardation, emotional illnesses or an addiction to drugs or alcohol.

The salient features of the Rehabilitation Act of 1973 are as follows:

1. Health care institutions are required to notify handicapped persons of a nondiscriminatory practice toward the handicapped in admission, treatment or access.
2. Health care institutions are required to consult with handicapped persons on ways to remedy the effects of past discrimination and on ways to amend policies and procedures

that fall short of compliance. For at least three years, the facility must maintain a file of those handicapped persons consulted, the remedial procedures to be followed and the policies and procedures that were discussed. The file must be open to the public.

Health care institutions found to be discriminatory to the handicapped could, under the regulations, be mandated to develop remedial action plans. Loss of federal funds is the penalty for continued failure to conform to the regulations.

STATE LAWS

As noted, most reporting laws that a health care supervisor deals with most often are state laws. All states have enacted laws requiring the reporting and documentation of incidents and cases as a means of protecting the health and safety of the community at large. Also required is statistical reporting.

If considered simply as data, the need for such reporting could be questioned. However, if one looks at what the figures *mean*, much more can be learned. One can see the trends shown by the figures (i.e., a decrease in the birth rate or an increase in life expectancy). The more data available, the more one can learn. Although a report that a birth or death has taken place is informational, it does not have the same significance as reports showing an increase in premature births or a decrease in a specific disease as a cause of death.

Health care supervisors should bear in mind that reporting is required by legislation concerning many activities other than health care. All should be keenly aware that obtaining data is part and parcel of society's recognition of the need to improve the quality of life for its citizens. For example, states often re-

> *Obtaining data is part and parcel of society's recognition of the need to improve the quality of life for its citizens.*

quire court reports on divorces granted, ages of those obtaining a divorce, number of children, educational level of the parties and number of times each party has been married.

There have been legal challenges to some reporting laws on the basis of invasion of a patient's privacy and infringement of the right to confidentiality. However, the courts have upheld the right of a state to require reporting, even reporting involving specific patient information, when the state is able to demonstrate a compelling and overriding interest and has also shown that it has used the information only for the stated purpose.

Child and elderly abuse

Ignoring a reporting law is a risk that should not be taken lightly. Fine examples of this point may be found in the relatively new requirements for reporting suspected cases of child abuse. The reporting of suspected cases of child abuse is new in the United States; almost every state law covering child abuse has been enacted since 1970. The laws vary somewhat from state to state as to the age limits of the children for whom incidents should be reported, who must and who may report, to whom the reports must be made and the penalties involved for failing to report.

Typically, the laws cover those individuals who have not reached their eighteenth birthday. Incidents must be reported by those who are most likely to discover them, such as social workers, nurses, physicians and teachers, but incidents may be reported by anyone. Reports are usually made to a state's department of social services, and the penalty for failure to report is usually not severe.

A 1976 California court case demonstrates clearly, however, the risk taken by failing to report suspected cases of child abuse. The same risk is inherent in other reporting laws as well. In *Landeros* v. *Flood*,[1] the California Supreme Court ruled a hospital liable for subsequent injuries sustained by a battered child whom it improperly released to the care of its parents.

In this case, an 11-month-old child charged, through her court-appointed guardian, both the institution at which she was treated and one of its physicians with negligently failing to order X-rays or to report her condition as required by law. The report, under California law, was to have been made to the police or to the juvenile probation department.

The court ruled that because "battered-child syndrome" had become an accepted medical diagnosis, it was proper for the patient to show by expert testimony that the physician should have known how to diagnose and treat this condition. In addition, the physician's and hospital's exculpatory claim that they had not legally caused the patient's injuries subsequent to their examination of the child was, the court ruled, without merit. The court reasoned that the patient was entitled to prove that it was reasonably forseeable at the time of her release that her parents were likely to resume abusing her physically.

Had the case been reported as the law required, the hospital and the physician would have avoided liability. California, along with the majority of the states, provides immunity for reporters. All states provide protection from civil suit for anyone making a good faith report, and most states also provide protection from criminal liability.

Reporting suspected cases of elderly abuse is an even more recent phenomenon than that of child abuse. At this time, only a minority of the states have enacted protective laws, but more such statutes will probably be enacted as life expectancy continues to increase. No cases have been reported in which a health care professional has been held liable or penalized for not reporting a suspected case of elderly abuse. However, this is to be expected considering the recent development of this facet of the law.

Criminal acts and communicable diseases

Two areas in which states require reports by health officials are criminal acts and communicable diseases. Police are legally empowered to acquire reports on criminal acts for the safety and health of the community as a whole. The reporting of specific diseases is directed more to the health of the community.

Typical state statutes addressing the reporting of criminal acts cover injuries inflicted with lethal weapons, explicitly covering wounds inflicted by firearms and stab wounds. The statutes require that reports be made to local police authorities.

All states require the reporting of specific diseases. State law commonly requires that reports be made to the public health department, sometimes centrally for the state and sometimes locally.

The reporting of diseases is not a stagnant activity. Some diseases, such as polio and diphtheria, which were once common, are now rarely seen. Conversely, venereal diseases are being seen more commonly and may be reaching epidemic proportions.

It is through reporting the occurrence of these diseases that public health officials can assess whether efforts at controlling a specific disease have been effective. Reporting also alerts public health officials to unusual increases in specific diseases, which then need to be treated and eradicated, if possible, to protect the health of the general population.

Reporting laws concerned with communicable diseases usually specify prompt reporting. Immediate reporting by telephone or telegraph may be required for highly contagious diseases such as smallpox or yellow fever. These diseases, although highly contagious, are rarely seen in this country now, but the reporting requirements remain in force. Statutes and regulations requiring reporting of these diseases usually specify that reports are to be made by physicians or other health care personnel. However, some laws specify reporting by *any person* having actual knowledge of an individual with a disease presumed to be communicable.

In addition to the protection of the health of the population, an economic concern must be acknowledged. The public funds required for the care of people afflicted with communicable diseases could become greater than those reserved for preventing such diseases.

LEGAL PROCESS

Health care supervisors, like other professionals, are capable of doing a better job if the rationale for what they must do is clearly understood. Supervisors must recognize that re-porting laws basically exist for the protection of the health and safety of the community.

Health care facilities must function within the law. All hospitals, whether private or public corporations, or proprietary or nonprofit, are subject to state licensing and reporting laws as well as to many other state laws. If they are recipients of federal funding, they are also subject to federal laws and regulations. It is important for supervisors to understand how reporting laws are enacted and how they are implemented. Once this is understood, supervisors should be able to have some influence and involvement in the process.

Enactment

Unlike policies, which are internal rules of an institution, laws and regulations are enacted and enforced *outside* the health care institution. Reporting laws are statutory laws (i.e., acts of the legislative departments of governments) declaring, commanding or prohibiting something. State laws are enacted in each state by the state legislative body, often referred to as the General Assembly. Federal laws are enacted by the U.S. Congress, which as the federal legislature comprises the Senate and the House of Representatives.

Regulations are promulgated by federal or state agencies; although they are made by neither judges nor legislatures, they have the force of law. Regulations of a governmental agency are rules with respect to a specific area in which the agency acts. The regulations are promulgated by the agency head through power delegated by the legislative body responsible for the enactment of the law.

This power is delegated by law, and most states use the Uniform Administrative Procedures Act. The Uniform Administrative Procedures Act states clearly what procedures agency heads must follow to establish regulations that will then implement law.

The purpose of regulations is to specifically define areas of the law and thus to implement them. It is axiomatic that a regulation cannot exist without a written law for a legal basis. It is also true that a regulation can never include subject matters not included in the legislation that it is defining and implementing. Although it might appear that attempts to do this would be rare, they occur frequently.

Should a question ever arise as to what takes precedence, the law is clear. If there is a discrepancy between a law and a regulation, the law governs. If there is a conflict between a regulation and a policy, the regulation governs. Therefore, in distinguishing between laws, regulations and policies, the health care supervisor can understand the distinction as to effect insofar as all three can, and often do, legally coexist.

Reporting laws include statutory laws and implementing regulations. The statutory law may be so specific that it can stand on its own. More often the enacting legislation is broad, and regulations are needed to define it. For example, a law might mandate reporting communicable diseases to a state health department and give that department the power to promulgate regulations for implementation. The regulations would then define communicable diseases, specify when and to whom reports should be made, specify forms to be used for reporting and define the penalty for failure to report. Failure to report would include not reporting in a timely manner as specified by regulation.

As noted earlier, the reporting of diseases, crimes, accidents, stillbirths and deaths is not a stagnant area. Laws and regulations are revised and updated periodically to meet constantly changing needs. This is as true in the area of reporting laws as it is in any dynamic area of the law.

Implementation

Regulatory agencies cannot arbitrarily create or change regulations without notifying the public. On the federal level, the normal notification procedure is to publish a proposed change in regulations in the *Federal*

Regulatory agencies cannot arbitrarily create or change regulations without notifying the public. The normal procedure is to publish the proposed change.

Register. Under the Uniform Administrative Procedures Act, state agencies normally notify the public, through a specific publication similar to the *Federal Register*. These documents are not often seen by the average citizen, but the health care supervisor can obtain the appropriate documents at a public library.

The regulations themselves, as opposed to the notifying documents for proposed regulations or amendments, under the Uniform Administrative Procedures Act, are on file in the Secretary of State's office in each state. Federal regulations can be obtained from the Superintendent of Documents, U.S. Government Printing Office, Washington, D.C. 20402. Libraries in large health care institutions often contain copies of appropriate regulations and, of course, they are always obtainable from the state or federal agency that has the power to promulgate and enforce them.

Federal and state agencies often hold public hearings on new regulations and also on proposed amendments to existing regulations. Similarly, federal and state legislatures often hold hearings on proposed lawmaking, both new and amendments to existing legislation. At these hearings, any member of the public is free to testify orally and is invited to submit written testimony. Health care supervisors might be interested in attending such hearings when they involve matters such as reporting laws or other health care–related topics.

The best way for health care supervisors to become knowledgeable about appropriate regulations is to familiarize themselves with what exists and the procedures for implementation in their respective states. Supervisors should also familiarize themselves with members of state regulatory agencies who are responsible for enforcement. For example, an inservice education program could be arranged to include a state official who could clearly explain reporting laws and regulations.

Penalties

The penalties for not reporting vary in severity. In fact, exacting penalties for failure to report is very rare. However, as in *Landeros* v. *Flood*,[2] the hospital and physician would have avoided civil liability and monetary damage in court had the case of child abuse been reported as required by California law.

Certainly, this was an indirect penalty (i.e., not one specified by the statutory law or regulations). Had the hospital and physician reported as required by law, thereby avoiding liability, the onus would then have fallen on the local agencies (in this case the police or juvenile probation department).

Apart from penalties exacted, it should be clear to any health care supervisor that the health of the whole community is often at stake in the careful adherence to mandatory reporting laws. Many diseases eradicated in the United States flourish in other parts of the world. Concurrently, there is an increase in some communicable diseases (i.e., venereal diseases). The incidence of communicable diseases, particularly Herpes II, is frustrating because there is currently no known cure. However, it is the reporting of it, albeit probably underreported, now that could lead to government involvement in research and cure.

CONTINUING DEBATE

In these days of increasing controversy over the broad question of government regulations, the subject needs to be looked at with an open mind. Can U.S. society afford less regulation in such major concerns as health and safety? There is clearly no easy answer to this question. However, the question may be easier to deal with when the reporting of communicable diseases is considered apart from regulations governing access to health care by the handicapped. The same would apply in comparing the reporting of criminal acts with regulations to protect the handicapped. Handicapped regulations protect only the handicapped segment of society, and their impact is thus fragmented. But communicable-disease reporting holds implications for the total population.

Individuals' attitudes will influence how they answer such questions. Is society to protect all of its members by passing regulations that protect specific segments, or does this constitute overregulation? If this is seen as overregulation, then there may eventually be some lessening of government regulation of health care facilities. However, such lessening is more likely to occur on the federal level than on the state level.

REFERENCES

1. Landeros v. Flood, 131 Cal. Reptr. 69, 551 P. 2d 389 (Cal. Sup. Ct., 1976).
2. Id.

Corporate restructuring: the whys and wherefores

Laura L. Kalick
Tax Manager
National Tax Division
Coopers & Lybrand
Washington, D.C.

IF YOU WORK IN a restructured hospital (which is more and more likely to be the case) you have probably noticed changes going on around you as a result of the restructuring. Consider what your role has been in bringing about these organizational changes. Has the implementation of a new corporate structure left positive or negative impressions? After exploring the reasons that led to restructuring and its attendant changes, you can then consider whether the restructuring has accomplished the objectives intended at its beginning.

Any of several reasons may have been the one providing impetus for undertaking corporate restructuring at your hospital. One main objective involved in most hospital reorganizations has been to enable a hospital to take excess funds that had accumulated over the years and deposit them in a parent holding company that could use those funds in the future to

Health Care Superv, 1986,4(2),71–79
© 1986 Aspen Publishers, Inc.

capitalize new subsidiaries, both taxable and tax-exempt, for the future expansion of health care activities. These new subsidiaries would provide the additional diversification and flexibility needed in the 1980s and into the twenty-first century for maintaining the viability of the hospital institution.

GOVERNMENTAL REGULATION: A SIGNIFICANT FACTOR

In some instances, the reason behind corporate reorganization may have been to avoid the arduous and uncertain process of certificate-of-need (CON) review. Having a new parent organization undertake a new capital, nonprovider project such as a parking garage or medical office building has given rise to instances in which the state health planning authority has not required a full-blown CON review.

Especially in the era that preceded diagnosis related groups (DRGs), maximization of reimbursement was also a significant reason for restructuring. Nonreimbursable activities were identified from cost reports. General and administrative costs were being allocated to these nonreimbursable cost centers, thus reducing the potential reimbursement of the hospital. Where it made sense to isolate these nonreimbursable cost centers and put them in separate nonprovider corporations, such was done.

For example, nonpatient, nonhealth care rental property could be put into a separate properties corporation, exempt from federal income tax pursuant to §501(c)(2) of the Internal Revenue Code (IRC). The purpose of the properties corporation is to hold title to income-producing property, collect income therefrom, and turn over the net proceeds (less the expenses of operation and debt service) to the parent organization.

Putting hospital-owned non-health care assets into a properties corporation can accomplish two results. First, prior to the use of DRG reimbursement, administrative and general expenses of the hospital would no longer be allocated to these nonreimbursable cost centers, thus maximizing reimbursement. Second, separating the non-health care, income-producing assets from the hospital provides a vehicle to get money into the parent organization. These funds can then be used to subsidize the projects of other subsidiaries, whether any particular subsidiary was the hospital or one of its siblings. If this move of the rental property was not made, not only would the administrative and general expenses be allocated to the hospital, but also the income earned from the property would be reflected on the hospital's financial statements, possibly providing an interest-income offset against one of the hospital's capital projects.

IMPROVED MANAGEMENT THROUGH REORGANIZATION

Other reasons for restructuring can be found in hospital organizations in which more than one hospital exists in the corporate structure. Here, the guiding impetus may be more centralized management. Consider, for example, a religious-order hospital system in which the church owns and operates three different hospitals in diverse locales. A parent organization juxtaposed between the church and the hospitals can provide the centralized management necessary for the efficient operation of all three hospitals. By having the chief executive officers (CEOs) of each hospital employed by the new tax-exempt parent, the hospitals are ultimately managed by the parent because the parent has the final authority over the rewards and penalties accorded the CEOs.

The salaries of the reorganized hospitals' CEOs will still be reimbursed by third party payers under the home-office expense concept. The books and records of the parent will be open to the third party payers because of the reimbursement requirements. Therefore, it is probably not the best of ideas to retain excess funds from the hospitals and other subsidiaries in the parent management company. A separate capital formation company should be established to collect and raise funds for the hospital. In this way, it should be possible to avoid any interest-income offsets.

DIVERSIFICATION: TAX CONSIDERATIONS

Another significant reason for corporate reorganization has been to provide hospitals with a flexible legal and tax structure so that activities that may be profitable, but may not exist in furtherance of the hospital's charitable purpose, will not affect the tax-exempt status of the hospital.

Primary purpose test

The Internal Revenue Service (IRS) has a rule called the primary purpose test. This test is used to determine the extent to which a hospital may carry on nonexempt activities without jeopardizing its exempt status. As long as the exempt activities are more than 50 percent of a hospital's activities, the exemption should not be affected. The 50 percent can be measured by a combination of receipts, expenses, and employee activities.

The Internal Revenue Service (IRS) has a rule called the primary purpose test. This test is used to determine the extent to which a hospital may carry on nonexempt activities without jeopardizing its exempt status.

Because of the primary purpose test, it may be necessary for a hospital to set up taxable subsidiary organizations to enter into activities unrelated to its exempt purposes. For instance, the health care provider with extra capacity from its fine dietary center may want to go into the business of catering banquets, weddings, and bar mitzvahs. By fitting the catering business into a separate entity, not only is the tax-exempt status of the provider protected, but the provider corporation is also protected from any of the liability from claims arising from the operation of the catering business and vice versa.

Some hospitals with an active laboratory or pharmacy that serves many nonhospital patients have moved these activities into separate taxable corporations. Sometimes, however, and especially when the nonpatient activity does not even approach 50 percent, it may be more bother than it is worth to take an existing activity and sever it from the hospital. The only adverse effect, if there is no threat to the primary purpose of the hospital to serve hospital patients, is the earning of some unrelated business income. Of course, if this occurred in a for-profit taxable corporation, the income would also be taxed.

Exempt versus taxable organizations

It is especially important to understand the difference between the tax treatment of expenses in an exempt organization and a taxable organization. In an exempt organization, only those expenses that are directly tied to the generation of unrelated business income (UBI) can offset the UBI in deriving the net taxable income.

On the other hand, in a taxable corporation, expenses from all activities are netted together to offset gross income in order to derive a net taxable income figure. For this reason it may make sense to put both profitable and unprofitable taxable activities into the same corporation.

Typically, a medical office building is a taxable venture. Because of depreciation deductions in excess of carrying expenses, the medical office building will usually generate tax losses, at least in the initial years of operation. Therefore, if there is another activity that will generate taxable income, it may make sense to place that activity in the corporation that includes the medical office building.

Consolidated tax returns

If it does not make sense to combine more than one activity in a single corporation because of managerial difficulties or because it does not indicate a good mix of risks, then the same result can be achieved by having an affiliated group of taxable corporations file a consolidated tax return. In order to file consolidated tax returns, the corporation must belong to an affiliated group within the meaning of §1504 of the IRC.

An affiliated group is defined as one or more chains of includable corporations connected through a parent, whereby each corporation is 80 percent owned directly by one of the other corporations in the group. For example, if corporation A owns all the stock of corporation B and corporation C, then they can all file a consolidated tax return. Likewise, if corporation A owns all the stock of corporation B, which in turn owns all the stock of corporation C, they can all file consolidated tax returns.

EFFECTUATING A NEW ORGANIZATION

The new structure is typically effected by first incorporating a new corporation under the nonprofit laws of the state. This new corporation will be the parent. Articles of incorporation and bylaws must be written for the new parent corporation, and a board of directors must be elected for the parent.

Control of the affiliated group

The board of the parent is typically elected by the board of the hospital. Usually there are various members of the board of the hospital who also serve on the parent board. In many cases, a majority of the parent board is made up of members who also serve on the hospital's board. Overlapping boards ensure that the hospital will have continued control over the parent corporation so that it can never "run off with the hospital's assets."

It is probably inappropriate to have completely overlapping boards. When this is the case, the overlap simply supports the argument that the parent is the alter ego of the hospital and that the acts of one should be considered the acts of the other. However, even with complete board overlap, the corporate veils usually will not be subject to piercing as long as there is no indication of fraud or abuse. One way to avoid overlapping boards while keeping control of the parent in the hospital is to have the CEO of the hospital serve on both boards, ex officio, or without vote.

The parent corporation has legal control over the hospital corporation if the parent is the sole corporate member of the hospital. The sole corporate member usually has the power to appoint and dismiss the board of the hospital, the ultimate control that can be exercised. With this system of checks and balances, some interesting legal paradoxes are created. For example, if 51 percent of the parent's board comes from the hospital, the IRS will deem the parent to be supporting and controlling the hospital. A special public charity status will be afforded the parent by the IRS for this reason.

On the other hand, because the parent legally controls the hospital (the parent can appoint or dismiss the hospital's board), the hospital's financial statements need not disclose, except perhaps in a footnote, the parent's existence (although major transactions must be reported). The consequence of nonconsolidation is that earnings on amounts held by the parent will not offset the interest expense of the hospital that is reimbursed by third party payers.

Tax-exempt status

For the tax-exempt hospital, a tax-exempt parent is essential both under federal tax laws and state laws governing charitable organizations. As an IRC §501(c)(3) exempt organization, a hospital's assets must be dedicated to charitable purposes, even at dissolution. This means that it would be impossible for the hospital to make a "gift" to a taxable corporation other than one that it owned. In other words, it would be permissible for an exempt organization to make a contribution to capital proportionate to its stock ownership interest in a taxable corporation because it is a mere change in the form of ownership.

Public charity status

Not only is it necessary for the parent to have tax-exempt status, but it also is essential for the parent to be classified as a public charity pursuant to §509 of the IRC. The consequence of not being classified as a public charity is that the parent would be considered a private foundation. Private foundation status carries with it more complicated reporting requirements and distribution requirements as well as excise taxes. For example, a 2 percent excise tax is imposed on the investment income of a private foundation. In addition, charitable contributions to a private foundation are limited to 30 percent of an individual's adjusted gross income as opposed to the 50 percent limit for contributions to a public charity.

There are three basic ways of meeting the public charity requirements. The first is for the organization to be of a type that is publicly supported (for example, a church, a hospital, or a community fund) or to numerically prove it is publicly supported, sometimes bolstering the numbers with certain facts and circumstances. The

second route for public charity status is for an organization to normally receive at least one third of its support from its exempt activities and not more than one third of its support from investment income. The third way is to establish public charity status as a supporting organization.

In order to qualify as a public charity through the supporting organization test, the organization must be operated exclusively for the benefit of, or to perform the functions of, another organization that qualifies as a public charity under either one of the first two tests, and the supporting organization must be operated, supervised, or controlled by or in connection with the organizations it supports.

As a supporting organization, the organization will receive a definitive ruling from the IRS at the time of its application for exemption as a public charity. However, for the first two tests the IRS may review the numbers and facts three to five years after the advance-ruling period has expired. Except under special circumstances, donors can rely on the public charity status of the corporation during the advance-ruling period.

Transfer of assets

After the parent has applied for and received a determination letter from the IRS that it is exempt from tax under IRC §501(c)(3) and is a public charity pursuant to IRC §509, it is appropriate to effectuate a transfer of assets to the parent.

In some states, such as Pennsylvania, the formation of the exempt parent corporation and the transfer of assets is effectuated in one step by a "division" of the hospital corporation. The division, which is like an amoebic reaction, can be a division into two or more exempt corporations. For example, a single hospital entity could divide itself, relinquishing some of its assets to be deposited in a parent holding company and other assets, like real estate, to be held in an IRC §501(c)(2) properties corporation. By using a plan of division, the 2 percent real estate transfer tax imposed by the state of Pennsylvania is avoided.

Because of the requirement of perpetual dedication of an IRC §501(c)(3) exempt organization's assets to charitable purposes, a parent holding company structure is sometimes used to effectuate the sale of a hospital facility or nursing home to a for-profit entity. For example, where there are two affiliated hospitals and one will be sold to a for-profit entity, the proceeds from the sale can be given to a new parent holding company. The parent can then distribute funds to the remaining hospital on an as-needed basis.

AFFILIATED GROUP: NEW PLAYERS AND ACTIVITIES

In addition to the hospital subsidiary, other corporations are usually created in the parent holding company structure. For example, a related nursing home may become a subsidiary of the parent by making the parent the sole corporate member of the nursing home. A new ambulatory care center or surgery center may be incorporated under a parent member. Sometimes an exempt real estate title-holding company may be established to hold title to real property, turning over net revenues to a parent corporation. Often a taxable subsidiary is also incorporated.

Provision of capital

Initially it is the hospital that funds the existence of the parent. The parent in turn can provide capital for the projects of the new subsidiaries. The new subsidiaries will in turn be providing additional revenues for the entire hospital structure. To the extent that one subsidiary is in need of capital, different arrangements can be worked out to provide that capital. This can be done either in terms of a loan or a guarantee on a loan. A parent in control of a taxable subsidiary can cause that subsidiary to declare a dividend to the parent. Similarly, it would be within the parent's discretion to cause different subsidiaries to make loans or contributions to other sibling subsidiaries.

When a dividend is received by an exempt organization, it is not subject to tax in the hands of that organization because it is deemed to be passive income. Only unrelated trade or business income is taxable, and passive income is left out because of the absence of the activity required for a trade or business.

Unrelated debt-financed income is an exception to the rule requiring an active trade or business to trigger taxation of unrelated income. Unrelated debt-financed income could arise if, for example, the parent borrowed the money it used to contribute to the funding of a taxable corporation. If all the money was borrowed, then the entire dividend could be taxable to the parent. For less than total borrowing, however, only an amount in proportion to the total amount borrowed would be taxed.

A restructured hospital may choose to have a subsidiary of the parent serve as general partner in various joint ventures, either with private individuals or other corporations.

Partnerships

A restructured hospital may choose to have a subsidiary of the parent serve as general partner in various joint ventures, either with private individuals or other corporations. At one time, the IRS prohibited an exempt hospital from serving as general partner in a partnership where individuals were limited partners. The rationale behind the prohibition was that a general partner's responsibility is to further the profit-making objectives of the partners, a goal inconsistent with the charitable purposes of the exempt organization. The assets of the general partner are subject to the liabilities and claims of creditors

of the partnership, thus putting the charity's assets at risk to the inurement of private individuals.

Although the IRS has changed its position and will now, in limited situations, allow an exempt organization to serve as general partner in a partnership, the industry has also changed its position. Now it is much more common to find a taxable subsidiary of an exempt parent corporation serving as general partner in a partnership or joint venture. Profits and losses from the partnership or joint venture will be passed up to the corporate general partner with a tax imposed only at the corporate level. Then dividends can be passed up to the parent on a tax-free basis, and if the partnership generates tax losses, these can be used in the taxable corporation to offset any net profits in that corporation.

Compensation incentives

Through a taxable management subsidiary, a restructured hospital may be able to provide better compensation incentives than under the old structure. Better incentives attract better people and improve the system as a whole. For example, profit-sharing plans may be less cumbersome to administer in a for-profit entity than in a large nonprofit hospital where one must be concerned with the concept of private benefit. It is always important to remember, however, that if an individual is employed exclusively by a taxable corporation that contracts with an exempt organization to provide management services, the employee of the taxable entity will probably not be eligible for an IRC §403(b) annuity. Present benefits should be carefully reviewed before major changes are made by management.

Although private benefit is a concern in providing profit-sharing incentives in a tax-exempt hospital, there is IRS precedent that appears to approve of the concept. It may be necessary, however, not only to provide rewards but also to provide a penalty for less efficiency in order to avoid any threats to tax-exempt status.

Risks

Without a new structure, it would be difficult for the hospital to enter into new activities. One of the reasons is that new activities carry with them a certain amount of risk. To undertake these new ventures through the hospital itself would cause additional risk of liability that the hospital's assets, heavily burdened with existing debt service, could not bear. For example, if a hospital and a nursing home are housed within the same corporate shell and a fire in the nursing home was not completely covered with insurance, any claims resulting from the nursing home fire could be satisfied from the assets of the hospital. This is not good risk management.

•   •   •

In the DRG era, it now has become even more evident that restructuring is worthy of serious consideration.

Non-health care and outpatient activities are adding significant revenue to the whole parent holding company structure. In Washington, D.C., health care providers are now seeing the possibility of another shoe dropping on the hospital industry; recent U.S. Treasury Department proposals on tax reform may have a significant impact on the hospital industry. Of greatest significance would be the virtual elimination of tax-exempt financing for hospitals, except those that are government owned. Under the Treasury proposals, for-profit corporations are faced with corporate tax-rate increases, less favorable systems of depreciation, and repeal of the investment tax credit. These could cause significant financial dents in a hospital's armor.

Restructured hospitals have made significant strides into joint-venturing projects. Partnerships and real estate investment trusts are just some of the vehicles that have been used to capitalize on the new, flexible structures.

In summary, the reasons for restructuring were and are to make the hospital institution more financially sound. However, one has to appreciate that just creating new corporations does not in itself solve the problems. The hospital supervisor must work to put meat on the bare legal bones; this is the true role of the hospital supervisor in restructuring. Whether participating in meaningful dialogues or writing reflective reports, the employee is always the building block of the structure—and the restructured structure.

The health care supervisor's role in matters of pay equity

Jerry L. Norville
Professor/Director
Graduate Program in Health
* Services Administration*

Karen N. Swisher
Assistant Professor of Health Law
Department of Health
* Administration*
School of Allied Health Professions
Medical College of Virginia
Virginia Commonwealth University
Richmond, Virginia

ATTRACTING AND retaining a high quality, productive work force while maintaining desired service levels and quality within acceptable cost parameters are perhaps the greatest challenges faced by the nation's health care services managers. Addressing this challenge requires that both executive managers and health care supervisors focus attention on the institution's human resource policies and practices. Policies and practices relating to establishing jobs and determining their relative worth to the organization need special attention. Intuitive, often arbitrary methods of determining job content, job specifications and relative pay rates are no longer acceptable. Failure to objectively and systematically determine the value of a job in relation to other jobs in the organization has been condemned by today's more knowledgeable employees, by advocacy groups, by labor

Health Care Superv, 1985,3(4),1–16
© 1985 Aspen Publishers, Inc.

unions and by the courts. The issue of pay equity is therefore an important concern of health care supervisors. Knowledge of pay equity issues, an understanding of applicable law and skill in the application of effective methods for determining wage rates have become essential to effective performance as a supervisor.

PAY EQUITY ISSUES

Issues of equal pay for equal work and equal wages for jobs considered to be of comparable if not equal value to employers are at the forefront of challenges facing health care supervisors in human resource management. Recent court developments raise a number of important questions, indicate several potential problems regarding how pay decisions are presently made and focus on how future pay decisions might be made in hospitals and nursing homes. Insight can be gleaned from these decisions and applied in fulfilling the supervisory role.

Why is the issue of pay equity of importance to health care supervisors at this time? A number of key indicators lead to the conclusion that both employee grievances and litigation relating to matters of pay equity will increase if careful attention is not given to the manner in which pay rate decisions are made. Processing grievances and defending against employee suits are both costly and dysfunctional to the health care institution. Preventive measures by supervisors and executive management are therefore essential.

In seeking to redress perceived discrepancies in the manner in which pay rate decisions are made, employees will use the courts to challenge the job evaluation programs and other techniques that form the basis for deciding the relative value of jobs. Job evaluation and supporting job analysis techniques will be attacked as subjective and arbitrary. Market analysis techniques designed to find competitive rates in the community, performance appraisal systems designed to identify and reward merit and the objective judgments of experienced health care supervisors may all be challenged in court by employees seeking equal pay for equal work or comparable pay rates.

One school of thought defines pay equity as equal pay between the sexes for equal work. Others, who champion the theory of comparable worth, argue that pay equity means equal pay for jobs that are dissimilar in content but of comparable value to the employer and society in general. The quintessential question is one of pay equity between men and women. Has the organization satisfied both the law and its moral obligation by ensuring equal pay for jobs that are equal, or must the organization ensure that men and women receive equal pay for jobs that are not truly equal but are considered to be of comparable worth?

The argument is deceptively simple. Comparable pay means that people in different jobs that are not equal but are of equivalent worth to an employer should get the same wage or salary. The Equal Pay Act of 1963 requires equal pay for equal work only when men and women perform the same job.[1] Since men and women often do not perform the same job, proponents of comparable worth argue that existing legal protections are inadequate and should be extended to include a requirement that pay rate decisions be based upon the equivalent worth of different jobs to an employer.

Though problems exist in the manner in which wage decisions are made in many health care institutions, many of these problems simply reflect the broader problems inherent in establishing sound compensation policies and practices. The broader problems of pay equity can be viewed from their underlying philosophical, social, political, economic and legal dimensions with special emphasis on the economic, legal and social questions and on the health care supervisor's role in pay equity matters.

DETERMINING WAGE AND SALARY LEVELS

It is generally agreed that the ideal employee compensation program would be: (1) *adequate* to meet all legal requirements; (2) *equitable* in ensuring that each employee is paid fairly; (3) *balanced* with respect to pay and benefits; (4) *cost effective* by functioning within the limits of what the employer can pay; (5) *security oriented* to meet employee security needs; (6) *incentive providing* in that it serves as an element of extrinsic motivation; (7) *acceptable* to employees; and (8) *defensible* to labor organizations or the courts should it be challenged.[2] Notwithstanding such noble goals, achieving these wage and salary program objectives is difficult. Pay inequities and dissatisfaction are ubiquitous. Attempting to achieve total equity is tantamount to rolling the Sisyphean stone, but employers must strive to do so.

Although the other dimensions of pay equity are considered important, employers tend to be realists, recognizing economic realities and paying what they must pay to attract and retain employees. The economic dimension is thus a paramount consideration, but the methods used to make pay rate decisions are being challenged more frequently.

In deciding the relative pay rates for different jobs, employers typically give major weight to both the specific job requirements and the prevailing rates of pay for related jobs in the particular market. Although other factors such as supply and demand, the organization's ability to pay, the existence of a collective bargaining agreement and changes in the cost of living may be considered, the relative worth of one job to the organization when compared to other jobs in the organization remains the cornerstone of sound pay rate decisions if internal equity is to be achieved. The ideal overall objective is to keep wages both competitive in the marketplace and internally equitable.

Stated simply, the traditional approach to pay decisions involves first developing wage ranges and then establishing general guidelines for paying and advancing the pay of individual employees within their respective wage ranges. Developing wage ranges is usually accomplished by employing job evaluation methods which result in establishing a hierarchy of all jobs according to their relative value to the organization. Market survey methods are then used to determine related wage rates in the community.

Job evaluation

The essence of job evaluation is the application of a systematic, formal process for evaluating and rating jobs and placing these jobs in a hierarchy with respect to their relative value or worth for pay rate purposes. The purposes of job evaluation are to establish the relative worth of various jobs in the organization, to establish a basis for a fair wage scale that accounts for differentials among jobs and to correct any existing pay inequities while preventing additional inequities.[3]

As a systematic, formal approach to determining the relative money value of jobs within a particular organization, a comprehensive job evaluation program includes: (1) the analysis of each job to determine principal duties and responsibilities; (2) delineation of job specifications that state the human qualifications necessary to do the job; (3) preparation of a job description which usually states duties, responsibilities, qualifications and job conditions; and (4) establishing the relative value of positions in a hierarchy of wage or salary grades or levels.[4]

For many years the four principal job evaluation methods commonly used have been the ranking method, grade-description or classification system, the point system and the factor comparison method. Although the personnel department ordinarily provides the expert guidance needed to administer a job evaluation program, health care supervisors need a fundamental knowledge of the relative strengths and weaknesses of the array of job evaluation methods commonly used.

Nonquantitative methods of job evaluation include a simple *ranking* of positions in terms of their perceived value as judged by a group of competent persons and a *classification system* which divides the job hierarchy into pay groups and then assigns each job to a particular pay grade based upon the written definitions for each grade. Quantitative methods of job evaluation include the use of *point systems* and job *factor comparison systems*.[5] Of these four common methods, the point-factor combination system is most commonly used and is most accurate for job evaluation in the majority of health care organizations.

Because of its widespread use, health care supervisors need a working knowledge of the point-factor system of job evaluation. This quantitative approach first entails development of a detailed job description and a definitive set of job specifications for each job. Job factor categories including skill, effort, responsibility and working conditions are then used to establish a framework for specific job factors such as required education, judgment, mental effort, hazards and perhaps many others for a particular job. Numerical point values are then assigned to each job factor. All jobs in the organization are thus evaluated based upon the total of points. By evaluating each job description in relation to predetermined job factors that are assigned point values, salary ranges can be systematically determined for each salary grade.

A job evaluation program is more likely to serve its intended purpose as a credible means of determining the relative worth of jobs if job evaluation is preceded by a thorough analysis of the job, if care is taken to evaluate the job rather than the employee, and if the evaluation represents the combined judgments of several persons using a systematic approach. While it is not exact, job evaluation is a systematic, logical means of setting relative rates of pay for a job.[6]

While it is not exact, job evaluation is a systematic, logical means of setting relative rates of pay for a job.

Although a job evaluation program is useful in establishing the relative value of jobs in the organization, it does not serve to provide a basis for determining individual wage rates. This determination is usually made through use of a merit system, a longevity system or a combination of both. With the use of a merit system, an employee receives higher pay usually based upon the supervisor's judgment of his or her relative achievements in performing the job. The longevity system provides for pay increases based upon length of service only.

When the job evaluation process is used to determine the relative value of jobs in an organization, a number of important assumptions are made. For example, the use of quantitative job evaluation techniques assumes that the underlying basis upon which wages are determined can be explicitly stated and objectively measured. It is implicitly assumed that the collective judgment of those selecting the factors and points and those doing the actual ratings of jobs will tend to neutralize any specific biases or misjudgments by any one individual involved in the process. While value judgment is always present, the system is assumed to be bias-free. These underlying assumptions are being challenged by the courts.

Questions about the reliability and validity of job evaluation methods also abound. A job evaluation process is reliable if it consistently produces the same results with a given set of factors. It is valid if it accurately measures the relative differences among jobs. But even if both validity and general reliability are high, the existing potential for judgmental discrepancies could yield a resultant error of two or three salary grades.[7] Job evaluation is being challenged as an appropriate method of deciding questions of pay equity on the grounds that it is far from being an exact science.

Wage surveys

Establishing job pay differentials based upon differences in job content through the use of job evaluation techniques is a necessary but not, on its own, sufficient measure to determine job pay rates. While job evaluation techniques address questions of internal pay equity, wage information obtained from secondary sources and wage survey information gathered by the employer from the community-at-large provide the principal means by which managers can determine whether the organization's entire wage level curve is proper. It is of little value to have equity among wage rates if the entire range of rates is not sufficiently competitive to attract high quality employees.

Although setting the level of the organization's wage curve according to supply and demand factors found through wage surveys and labor market analysis can be rationalized economically, opponents of setting rates based upon surveys argue that jobs have a social or intrinsic value apart from market forces. They contend that market surveys do not reveal the true value of jobs. They also reason that using "going rates" in the marketplace to set pay rates in the organization actually perpetuates past discrimination against women that is inherent in the marketplace.

LEGAL CONSIDERATIONS

Wage surveys and job evaluation techniques have served for decades as vital and distinct elements of corporate employee compensation decisions. Wage surveys have served to provide a rationale for setting the level of wage curves to ensure that wages are competitive. Job evaluation has become the corporation's most valuable tool for rationalizing the internal equity of the employee wage structure. Both techniques have shortcomings that have recently become a frequent subject of debate in the courts.

Historically, legal questions focused on equal pay for equal work. More recently, the concept of comparable worth has been widely argued. Both are questions of pay equity between men and women. Both questions are important to the health care supervisor.

The arguments, which have gained and held national attention for the past five years, are deceptively simple. Proponents of comparable worth argue that the worth of male and female jobs should be evaluated in making decisions about wage discrimination. If jobs have the same relative worth, although they are dissimilar, then everyone in the jobs should receive the same pay. Arguments regarding whether pay inequities between women and men can be resolved using the existing law that requires equal pay for equal work or whether such inequities should be addressed using the theory of comparable worth are not new.

Equal pay

Despite the legal protection provided for women by the Equal Pay Act of 1963 and the Civil Rights Act of 1964, the earnings gap between women and men has increased.[8-11] Women's average income is only about 60 percent of men's average income. What has caused this disparity, and is comparable worth theory the answer to reducing the wage gap?

The concept of equal pay for equal work became law with passage of the Equal Pay Act of 1963.[12] This statute stipulates that if jobs require equal skill, effort and responsibility and if working conditions are equal, then employers must pay men and women performing those jobs the same pay. For example, if aide and orderly jobs require equal skill, effort and responsibility under equal working conditions, then persons of different sexes performing those jobs must be paid the same wage rate unless the employer can establish that the difference in rates is based upon a seniority system, merit program, measures of quantity or quality or differentials in pay based on any factor other than sex.

As originally drafted, the Equal Pay Bill would have guaranteed women equal pay for work of comparable character. This wording was specifically rejected by Congress, however, since it failed to take into account a job's particular value to the employer.[13] The scope of this Act is quite narrow and does not protect employees unless the four criteria of equal skill, equal effort, equal responsibility and similar working conditions are fulfilled. The result of this limited scope has been that the courts have generally denied relief under a comparable worth theory because of insufficient evidence that the jobs being compared involved "substantially equal work."[14]

The Supreme Court of the United States has interpreted the Congressional intent of the Act as being based in part on the idea that if employers use "well-defined and well-accepted principles of job evaluation . . . wage differentials based upon bona fide job evaluation plans would be outside the purview of the Act."[15] Thus, even when drafting the Act, Congress was aware that employers compared the content of the jobs as a basis for determining hierarchical wage rates.

The Equal Pay Act also requires that both men and women being compared must be employed by the same employer and be in the same location or establishment.[16] The whole concept of comparable worth, however, necessarily involves comparing dissimilar jobs among dissimilar institutions, prompting employees to begin litigating comparable claims under the broader antidiscriminatory provisions of Title VII.

Title VII

Title VII of the Civil Rights Act of 1964 is broad ranging in that it forbids discrimination in all aspects of employment on the basis of race, sex, religion and national origin. The statute specifically forbids discrimination in hiring, discharge, compensation, terms, conditions and privileges of employment.[17] Before 1981, federal courts were divided on the issue of whether Title VII's prohibition against discrimination was, in composition, broader in scope than the provisions for dealing with sex discrimination under the Equal Pay Act. The courts were not sure whether employees even had cause of action under Title VII when the Equal Pay Act purported to address compensation discrimination. Questions of pay discrimination based upon differences in sex were thus pursued under the Equal Pay Act.

The link between these two statutes is found in what is known as the Bennett Amendment of Title VII. This one-sentence amendment states that it is not a violation of Title VII for an employer "to differentiate upon the basis of sex in determining the amount of the wages or compensation paid . . . if such differentiation is authorized by the provisions of The Equal Pay Act."[18]

Prior to 1981, the courts were confused as to the interpretation of this amendment. It was not clear if the amendment indicated that employers would be immune from legal attack under Title VII unless their conduct also violated the Equal Pay Act, or if the amendment only meant that the defenses available to an employer under the Equal Pay Act were also available to an employer defending a claim under Title VII. This question was finally resolved in 1981 when the United States Supreme Court decided *County of Washington v. Gunther*. In this case, the Court ruled that compensation claims brought under Title VII are *not* restricted to claims of equal pay for "substantially equal work."[19] Pay equity disputes can now be pursued either under the Equal Pay Act or under Title VII of the Civil Rights Act.

Because the case dealt primarily with the administration of compensation claims rather than their merits, the Supreme Court did nothing to quell disagreements regarding comparable worth when it rendered what has been referred to as a "marvelously murky" opinion in *County of Washington v. Gunther*.[20] Although the Court in the *Gunther* case dodged the real issues of comparable worth, its ruling cracked open the door for advocates of comparable worth by looking at the market value of women's jobs. Many cases are likely to be brought forth; health care institutions are highly vulnerable to this type of litigation unless preventive measures are taken. An understanding of the various types of possible discrimination is essential.

Because federal statutes do not define what constitutes discrimination, the federal and the state courts have developed parameters for identifying three basic types of illegal discrimination.

First, an employee can demonstrate overt discrimination that the courts have labeled facial discrimination. An example of facial discrimination involves the intentional actions of an employer to pay lower pension benefits to women than they do to men[21] or to place advertising that reads "Wanted—Girl Friday."

Second, disparate treatment discrimination occurs when an employer's overt actions or policies provide for different treatment of employees based solely on race, sex, religion or national origin. Under this analysis, the employee may show discrimination from circumstantial evidence of the employer's conduct.[22] An example of disparate treatment would be the case of an employer refusing to hire women with preschool children but agreeing to hire men with preschool children.[23] Facial discrimination can also be proven under the disparate treatment analysis.

Finally, if intentional discrimination on the part of the employer cannot be shown, employees may still demonstrate that the employer's practices, while facially neutral and fair in form, are nonetheless discriminatory in operation. This disparate impact may be shown when apparently neutral policies fall harshly on women or on other groups of people protected under Title VII. Proof of discriminatory intent on the part of the employer is not a necessary element in proving illegal discrimination under disparate impact. An example of this third type of discrimination is the case of an employer unreasonably requiring a minimum height and weight for cor-

> *If intentional discrimination on the part of the employer cannot be shown, employees may still demonstrate that the employer's practices, while facially neutral and fair in form, are nonetheless discriminatory in operation.*

rectional officers that would disqualify most women, but not most men, from holding a job.[24]

Having reviewed some of the more important legal concepts, attention can now be directed to some of the philosophical, economic and social issues surrounding the comparable worth debate. A basic understanding of these concepts will strengthen the health care supervisor's ability to handle matters of pay equity.

COMPARABLE WORTH DEBATE

In the wake of the *Gunther* case, a nationwide hue and cry is emerging for widespread reform of the methods used by managers to determine pay rate decisions. A plethora of groups have taken up the cause of pay equity for women. The National Committee on Pay Equity, Nine to Five and the National Association of Working Women are among the organizations committed to direct and deliberate challenges to the systems presently used to set wages.[25] Many state and local governments have initiated such pay equity activities as data base development in order to have a sound basis for pay rate decisions, job evaluation studies to pinpoint existing inequities, pay equity policy implementation and stronger enforcement of existing laws.[26]

The personnel issue of the 1980s

The debate regarding the issue of comparable worth has surfaced regularly during the past four years. In the summer of 1980 Eleanor Holmes Norton, former chair of the Equal Employment Opportunity Commission (EEOC), stated her belief that comparable worth would be *the* personnel issue of the 1980s. Within a few months of this pronouncement, the American Compensation Association debated the issue of comparable worth at its annual convention; a national joint task force issued a report of its 18-month study of the subject; the EEOC held public hearings on the issue and the Supreme Court announced the *Gunther* decision, which was acclaimed by many as a major step forward in the campaign for comparable worth.[27]

Contrary opinions about comparable worth persist, despite the Supreme Court decision. Clarence M. Pendleton, Jr., Chair of the U.S. Commission on Civil Rights, recently expressed his views on the concept of comparable worth by stating that comparable pay for women is ". . . the looniest idea since Looney Tunes came on the screen."[28] White House economist William Niskanen referred to comparable pay as ". . . a truly crazy proposal."[29] Diann Rust-Tierney, staff lawyer at the National Women's Law Center, feels that the comparable worth debate is "one of the most important issues facing women."[30] On this point, Mr. Pendleton agrees and has been quoted as stating that "this issue is indeed becoming the focus of civil rights of the '80s."[31]

A National Committee on Pay Equity was founded in 1979 to pursue pay equity for women by directing attention to the issue of comparable worth, by providing specific assistance to other groups or individuals pursuing pay equity and by providing overall leadership for a national drive to implement the theory of comparable worth.[32]

In November 1983 a federal judge ruled that the state of Washington had discriminated against women and awarded a judgment for back pay and wages that is projected to cost the state $1 billion.[33] The court did not find that the state was guilty of discrimination in failing to hire women. Nor was the state found to have not paid women equal pay for equal work. At issue was the question of comparable worth. The judge found the state guilty of failing to provide equal pay between women and men for work considered of comparable worth.

A labor settlement reached on July 14, 1981, after a nine-day strike between Local 101 of the American Federation of State, County and Municipal Employees (AFSCME) and the city of San Jose, California, resulted in the allocation of $1.4 million over a two-year period for extra equity adjustments above general pay increases for predominantly female positions. In agreeing to this settlement, the city acknowledged the concept of comparable worth, although it did not adopt pay by comparable worth as a policy.[34]

The events cited clearly illustrate a drive toward implementing the concept of comparable worth. Is this drive justified? What are the arguments for and against this concept?

Arguments pro and con

In general, women earn about 60 percent of what men earn. This earnings gap between women and men can be explained, in part, by such background factors as race, education, age and continuity in employment. The specific employment setting, whether public or private, the existence of occupational segregation by sex and certain historical antecedents are also related to comparatively lower compensation received by women.[35] Although these factors are widely recognized, proponents of comparable worth argue that these factors only partially account for the earnings gap between women and men. They contend that the gap is largely caused by stereotyping and the resulting failure to establish pay rates on the basis of the comparable worth of jobs to the employer.

Those who advocate the concept of comparable worth for determining wage rates present a number of convincing arguments. In a nutshell, they argue that:

- Work by women is undervalued because of cultural and historical discrimination;[36]
- Wage surveys perpetuate the discrimination against women that is inherent in the marketplace; and
- Equal pay law does not correct inequities in the wages of women because so many jobs are not equal as narrowly defined by law.

Those who oppose the application of comparable worth theory in determining wage rates also present a number of cogent arguments against the concept. In essence, they argue that:

- Under the theory of comparable worth an employer might be forced to pay an employee more than the market dictates, thus disrupting the free labor forces of supply and demand;[37]
- Widespread acceptance of the concept would foster an avalanche of litigation because the underlying theory and the process for implementing the concept have not been well articulated and no practical, workable means of implementing the concept exists;
- Requiring compliance with the concept of comparable worth would be tantamount to a minimum wage level of $15 per hour, which would renew inflation and compound the balance of payments problems;[38]
- Implementing comparable worth would cost an estimated $320 billion;[39]
- Ensuring compliance with the concept would require the federal and state governments to

create a regulatory bureaucracy to establish and regulate pay rates;

- Markets should set pay rates in a free society because jobs do not have a separate and distinct intrinsic value; and
- Pay equity problems of women are largely explained by the fact that women often work part time, move into and out of the labor force and select occupations of generally lower value to employers.[40]

Implementation of the concept

Even if widespread support for the concept of comparable worth existed among the nation's employers, implementing this concept is another matter. First, a consensus on reliable means for determining how diverse, dissimilar jobs can be accurately compared with each other does not exist.[41] In addition, even if the methodology to establish the comparable worth of jobs was available, no one has yet articulated how comparable worth could be implemented among thousands of businesses, many with hundreds of occupations represented. Finally, the cost of implementation would be staggering, and the impacts on the labor market, labor agreements and inflation are unknown.

In addition to these more general reasons for difficulty in implementing the comparable worth concept, the job evaluation process that is touted for use in determining the relative value of jobs has serious short-comings. The Treiman Report, which is considered to be an authoritative work on the subject, found three features of job evaluation procedures that are likely to present major problems when used to determine comparable worth.[42] First, the relative ranking of jobs was found to be highly dependent on the initial selection of factors used in the evaluation process and on how heavily each factor is weighted. Since selection of factors and weights is a value judgment, how can diverse value systems among people, groups and industries be reconciled to yield a useful basis for a comparable worth judgment? In addition, because people make judgments about job factors, the evaluation process is inherently subjective and particularly subject to sex-role stereotyping even with the use of quantitative methods and the computer. Finally, many employers use several different job evaluation plans for different occupational groups of employees.[43]

Whether one favors implementation of comparable worth or is opposed to it, the debate is likely to continue and the massive problems of implementing the concept will remain. As long as perceived and actual pay equity problems remain, employers will be challenged and health care supervisors will find themselves involved in matters of pay equity.

ROLE OF THE SUPERVISOR

At this point, it should be easy to conclude that health care supervisors are vitally important in matters of employee pay equity. Although the governing board and executive management have ultimate responsibility for ensuring that the organization's personnel policies and practices are nondiscriminatory and for ensuring that employees are paid fairly based upon their relative worth to the organization, health care supervisors also have an important responsibility in these matters. Those who supervise health care employees have a duty to understand the issues relating to employee pay policies and practices. They also have an obligation to participate effectively in developing equitable pay policies and practices. Finally, supervisors have a responsibility to inform employees of and to obtain support for the organization's pay rate decisions.

The supervisor is critical in minimizing employee pay grievances and in avoiding lawsuits or in minimizing the costly effects of such suits.

Many newly appointed health care supervisors are amazed at the number of statutes, regulations, agency decisions and policy guidelines that directly affect their job. Virtually every personnel decision made by a supervisor is subject to some form of legal guideline. More restrictions may come if advocates of comparable worth have it their way. It is thus essential that supervisors be aware of the legal implications of their pay-related decisions.

Given a working knowledge of the issues, the legal constraints and the processes involved, supervisors can participate effectively in developing equitable pay policies and practices.

This means contributing to the success of, and actively participating in, the organization's job analysis, job description and job evaluation processes. If these processes are not already a part of the wage and salary determination process, then the supervisor has an obligation to advocate that a formal job evaluation program be initiated in support of the goal of internal pay equity.

If a new job evaluation system is to be implemented, organizations should avoid the copycat approach in which job descriptions and job evaluation factors are simply copied from historic documents, or worse yet, copied from documents of another organization. To avoid discrimination, policymakers should ensure that evaluation factors being used are relevant to the job and that they do not include traditional male requirements relating to strength, endurance, height, weight and similar factors unless those factors are clearly related to job performance requirements. Finally, supervisors should insist that only quantitative job evaluation techniques such as point, factor or point-factor methods are used to avoid much of the subjectivity inherent in nonquantitative approaches.

Ideally, a job evaluation system would be value-free. Since this is not possible and, in fact, may not be desirable, employers must strive to achieve a job evaluation system that is bias-free. The supervisor is in an ideal position to champion a bias-free system.

In addition to the usual process problems associated with implementing any program, two other potential problems crop up when a new job evaluation process is implemented. If managers and supervisors have had a free hand in making most pay decisions, they will likely resist giving up this autonomy. Ensuring that individuals affected by this change in the decision-making process fully understand the need for and rationale underlying internal pay equity will usually win their support for a job evaluation program. Employees might also behave apprehensively and feel their pay is being threatened. Educating employees and reassuring them that their jobs and pay are secure will usually minimize employee resistance. This is an important role of the supervisor.

Supervisors have a duty to advise and assist employees with pay matters. This means being able to thoroughly explain to subordinates the underlying principles of the organization's wage and salary program as well as the program's specific policies and requirements. This also means ensuring that pay policies, and especially practices in carrying out policies, do not intentionally or inadvertently discriminate against individual employees or have a discriminatory impact on protected classes of employees. Potential wage or salary inequities should be corrected or called to the attention of executive management for corrective action.

●　●　●

A thorough periodic assessment of the organization's job evaluation sys-

tem is essential to maintaining pay equity. This evaluation should ensure (1) that job factors selected for analysis are chosen without bias; (2) that weights assigned to job factors do not discriminate against women; (3) that application of the job evaluation process itself is as fair and objective as possible; (4) that resultant salary scales are equitable in differentiating the relative worth of jobs; and (5) that any exceptions resulting in pay differences for men and women doing the same job can be explained as legitimate exceptions to the Equal Pay Act or as a business necessity.

Vigorous, proactive, positive efforts by supervisors must be focused on preventing costly litigation about pay rate matters. In addition to the economic costs, the social costs associated with unfavorable publicity as a result of such suits must be avoided.

Given the recent renewed interest in the theory of comparable worth, it seems likely that organizations may eventually be required to modify their compensation policies and practices in order to achieve a more balanced emphasis on meeting competitive labor market rates and ensuring internal equity in pay. Continued active interest by civil rights groups, women's rights groups, the Equal Employment Opportunity Commission, and the American Compensation Association in job evaluation and the setting of pay rates is predictable. The stakes are high.

Employers must not let their own policies and practices be the petard that breaks through the wall of sensible compensation program design. If it is policy to use job evaluation and market surveys to determine pay rates, then executive management and supervisors must ensure that the job evaluation system being used is soundly based, valid, reliable and managed well. If exceptions must be made and some employees are to have wage rates above or below the level dictated by the job evaluation system, then employers must document these exceptions very carefully. Management must ensure that a legitimate business reason exists in support of the decision to make exceptions.

Health care supervisors at every level are frequently involved in deci-

sions relating to wage and salary matters. Some supervisors participate in setting wage policy. All are obligated to understand and carry out the institution's pay policies and practices. Regardless of the organizational level of supervisors, each has a basic duty to be generally knowledgeable about employee compensation, a basic responsibility to master the specifics of the organization's wage and salary program, and an overriding obligation to provide information, advice and assistance to subordinates on matters affecting their jobs and the pay they receive for performing these jobs.

REFERENCES

1. Fair Labor Standards Act of 1938, §6, 29 U.S.C. §206 (d) (Supp. III 1979).
2. Gluck, W.F. *Personnel: A Diagnostic Approach*. Dallas: Spectrum Publications, 1978, p. 405.
3. Metzger, N., "Job Analysis and Job Descriptions." *Handbook of Health Care Human Resources Management*. Rockville, Md.: Aspen Systems, 1981, p. 157.
4. Beach, D.S. *Personnel: The Management of People at Work*. New York: Macmillan, 1975, p. 652.
5. Pasquale, A.M. *A New Dimension to Job Evaluation*. New York: American Management Association, 1979, pp. 4–7.
6. Beach, *Personnel: The Management of People at Work*, 653
7. Risher, H. "Job Evaluation: Problems and Prospects." *Personnel* 61 (January–February 1984): 63.
8. Fair Labor Standards Act of 1938, §6, 29 U.S.C. §206 (d) (Supp. III 1979).
9. Civil Rights Act of 1964, §701, 42 U.S.C. §2000c–2(a)(1) (1976).
10. Weingard, M. "Establishing Comparable Worth Through Job Evaluation." *Nursing Outlook* 32 (March–April 1984): 110.

11. Smith, L. "The EEOC's Bold Foray Into Job Evaluation." *Fortune* 95 (September 11, 1978): 58.
12. Fair Labor Standards Act of 1938, §6, 29 U.S.C. §206 (d) (Supp. III 1979).
13. See S. 882, 88th Congress, 1st Session §4 (1963).
14. See, e.g., Molthan v. Temple University, 442 F. Supp. 448, 455 (E.D. Pa. 1977). In Molthan, plaintiffs sued the university alleging sex discrimination against women in hiring, promotion, tenure, salary and placement of women employees or applicants for faculty, administrative and professional positions within the university. The court denied relief because the plaintiffs failed to show that the jobs were equal. Also see Wetzel v. Liberty Mutual Insurance, 449 F. Supp. 397, 407 (W.D. Pa. 1978). Wetzel involved a suit by female claim representatives who alleged that they were paid less than male claim adjusters performing "essentially the same work." The court agreed that the women did perform substantially the same work as men.
15. Corning Glass Works v. Brennan, 417 U.S. 188, 201 (1974).
16. 29 U.S.C. §206(d)(1)(1976). The statute thus

permits a company to pay women doing a given job less than men doing the same job if the men and women work in different locations, regardless of whether cost of living factors justify the difference.

17. Title VII, §703(a) 42 U.S.C. §2000e–2(a)(1976).
18. 42 U.S.C. §2000e–2(h)(1976).
19. County of Washington v. Gunther, 452 U.S. 161 (1981). Justice Brennan wrote the opinion of the Court, joined by Justices White, Marshall, Blackman and Stevens. Justice Rehnquist wrote a dissenting opinion joined by Chief Justice Burger and Justices Stewart and Powell.
20. Seligman, D. "Pay Equity Is a Bad Idea." *Fortune* 109 (May 14, 1984): 138.
21. See Arizona Governing Committee v. Norris, 463 U.S. 000 (1983).
22. See generally, Cox, P. "Equal Work, Comparable Worth and Disparate Treatment: An Argument for Narrowly Construing County of Washington v. Gunther." *Duquesne Law Review* 22 (Fall 1983): 65–150.
23. Phillips v. Martin Marietta Corp., 400 U.S. 542 (1971).
24. Dothard v. Rawlinson, 433 U.S. 321, 329 (1977).
25. Grune, J.A., and Reder, N. "Pay Equity: An Innovative Public Policy Approach to Eliminating Sex-Based Wage Discrimination." *Public Personnel Management Journal* 12 (Winter 1983): 396.
26. Hartman, H.I., and Treiman, D.J. "Notes on the NAS Study of Equal Pay for Jobs of Equal Value." *Public Personnel Management Journal* 12 (Winter 1983): 406.
27. Brinks, J.T. "The Comparable Worth Issue: A

28. *Richmond Times-Dispatch*, November 17, 1984, pp. 1, 13.
29. *Richmond Times-Dispatch*, November 25, 1984, p. 1.
30. Ibid., 1.
31. Ibid., 1.
32. Grune and Reder, "Pay Equity: An Innovative Public Policy Approach to Eliminating Sex-Based Wage Discrimination," 396.
33. Cawley, G. "Comparable Worth: Another Terrible Idea." *The Washington Monthly* 15 (January 1984): 53.
34. Farnquist, R.L., Armstrong, D.R., and Strausbaugh, R.P. "Pandora's Worth: The San Jose Experience." *Public Personnel Management Journal* 12 (Winter 1983): 358.
35. Eyde, L.D. "Evaluating Job Evaluation: Emerging Research Issues for Comparable Worth Analysis." *Public Personnel Management Journal* 12 (Winter 1983): 425–428.
36. *Richmond Times-Dispatch*, November 25, 1984, p. 1.
37. Ibid., 1.
38. Ibid., 1.
39. Ibid., 1.
40. Eyde, "Evaluating Job Evaluation," 426.
41. Treiman, D.J. *Job Evaluation: An Analytic Review.* Washington: National Academy of Sciences, 1979, p. 1.
42. Hartman and Treiman, "Notes on the NAS Study of Equal Pay for Jobs of Equal Value," 410.
43. Ibid., 410–411.

Salary Administration Bombshell." *Personnel Administrator* 26 (November 1981): 37.

Bioethics committees: panacea of the 1980s?

Bowen Hosford
*Lawyer, Freedom of Information
  Officer
National Institutes of Health
Bethesda, Maryland
Member
Ethics Committee
Fairfax Hospital
Falls Church, Virginia*

THE NUMBER of bioethics committees in hospitals, hospices,
and nursing homes is increasing. As
the 1980s began, a survey indicated
that only one percent of American
hospitals had such committees,[1] but
before the decade was half over another survey revealed that 25 percent
of hospitals had established them.[2]
While part of the difference probably
results from the two surveys' differing definitions of the committees, the
growth is striking. Also, ten percent
of hospices have bioethics committees, and leaders in many nursing
homes have displayed an interest in
them. The American Medical Association, the American Hospital Association, the American Academy of Pediatrics, and the National Hospice

*This article was written by Bowen Hosford in his
private capacity. No official support or endorse-
ment by the National Institutes of Health, the Department of Health and Human Services, or Fairfax
Hospital is intended or should be inferred.*

Health Care Superv, 1986,4(4),1–11
© 1986 Aspen Publishers, Inc.

Organization have endorsed bioethics committees.

That their number is increasing does not mean that bioethics committees are fully accepted, that pitfalls are nonexistent, or that the committees will continue to be influential. A physician-bioethicist described them as the "panacea of the 1980s." In ancient medicine, panaceas were drugs that promised to cure all diseases, but the promise was always false.

PURPOSE

The committees consider ethical aspects, including legal and social facets, of medical decisions. Their members educate themselves and other health care providers about bioethics and may write guidelines for their institutions or advise on medical treatment.

Many of the dilemmas that committees examine concern withdrawal or withholding of treatment from clients who are in a vegetative state or a terminal condition. Other subjects include client confidentiality, informed consent, and clients' and families' right to choose or refuse treatment.

Any ethical subject that worries health care providers may be brought to a bioethics committee for discussion or resolution. New York City hospital committees on which philosopher-bioethicist Ruth Macklin serves have discussed whether a pregnant woman should be forced to have a Caesarean section to save the life of her fetus and have written guidelines for avoiding conflicts of

interest in talking to new mothers about giving up their babies for adoption. Members of the Ethics Committee at Fairfax Hospital in Northern Virginia have discussed informed consent and client confidentiality problems arising from blood tests for the acquired immune deficiency syndrome (AIDS) antibody.

MEMBERSHIP

A hallmark of bioethics committees is diverse membership. Members from inside the institution may include physicians, nurses, social workers, chaplains, the institution's legal counsel, administrators, and members of governing boards. Typical members from outside the institution include lawyers, philosophers, and members of the clergy.

Theoretically, such committees apply the community's values to medical dilemmas. The health care providers who ordinarily constitute the membership represent the community and through their diversity express many of the community's viewpoints. However, although committee leaders speak of the advantages of membership by lay people, few leaders have invited lay people to join; they usually say they need to protect client confidentiality. Unvoiced additional reasons may be reluctance to allow outsiders to see that health care providers experience friction among themselves that is common to other humans or reluctance to allow opinionated people to rush in and apply easy slogans to hard problems.

One method of including lay people who would respect confidentiality would be to ask them to become dollar-a-year employees of the institution and to pledge not to reveal information about clients. Another would be for the bioethics committee to accept as members more of the institution's own supervisors and workers. Granted, such employees would be vulnerable to the accusation that they are not truly independent, but, aside from that, they could as logically represent the community as outsiders could. Also, they would be protected by the institution's liability insurance, whereas outside members would be protected only if riders were written to the policies.

FUNCTIONS

Education

A primary committee function is for the members to educate themselves and others about bioethics. For example, they may examine medical decisions that have been made earlier. This task is called retrospective review and is so important that some observers consider it a separate function.[3]

The Ethics Committee at Fairfax Hospital has been primarily an example of an education committee. At monthly meetings, physicians or nurses discuss difficult cases they have had and ask members to comment. In addition, its chairman, physician Ian Shenk, initiated a series of bioethical conferences, each of which is sponsored by a hospital department. Attending physicians, house officers, medical students, nurses, and others participate. One of them tells of a current ethical problem concerning a client, and attendees examine its ethical aspects. Currently, the committee's functions are evolving. Members are moving toward a counseling role, to facilitate discussions among patients, families, and health care providers in ethical dilemmas.

Preparing guidelines

A second bioethics committee function may be writing guidelines for the institution's staff, particularly for do-not-resuscitate (DNR) orders. For example, guidelines written by members of the committee at the University of Minnesota Hospitals and Clinics state that competent clients have control over DNR decisions concerning them. When clients are incompetent, physicians are to reach such decisions with family members, in the following order: spouse, adult children, parent or parents, adult brother or sister, legally appointed guardian, or aunts, uncles, and cousins.

Counseling

Members of some committees proceed to a third function, counseling on unresolved ethical dilemmas. They make sure all the medical facts have been gathered, promote communication among members of the medical team or with the client and family, and discuss ethical principles. They usually arrive at a common viewpoint and so do not take votes. The word "counseling" is more appropriate for this function than the often used word "consulting," because the members are not consultants in the usual medical sense.

ISSUES

Prolonging life

A survey of cases heard during five years by the committee at University Hospitals, Cleveland, Ohio,[4] revealed that most of them concerned whether life-prolonging treatment should be curtailed. Usually, the clients were in a persistent vegetative state (PVS), that condition like Karen Ann Quinlan's, in which they had lost the thinking portion of their brains but retained some automatic functions. The Cleveland committee members recommended in about half of such cases that life-prolonging treatment be stopped or reduced and in approximately half that it be continued or increased.

The work of committees evolves as medical capabilities advance.

The work of committees such as the one in Cleveland evolves as medical capabilities advance. For example, until a few years ago, a person whose lungs took in and expelled air and whose heart pumped blood was considered to be alive, but then health care providers began to face the problem of explaining to relatives that some people with those attributes were dead. Such clients, of course, were those whose brains had died but who were on respirators. In the early years, the Cleveland committee members dealt with family reluctance to allow respirators to be disconnected.

Resuscitation

Another dilemma caused by increasing medical capabilities is the use of resuscitation. Throughout much of human experience a heart that fibrillated or stopped was beyond help. Less than 40 years ago Claude S. Beck and two other physicians at Lakeside Hospital in Cleveland used electric shocks to save a 14-year-old boy whose heart was fibrillating.[5] They were successful only because they had been performing chest surgery on him and he was still on the table, because they had experimented with shock treatment and had electrodes at hand, and because they could reopen the boy's chest and apply the electrodes to his bared heart.

The cardiopulmonary resuscitation (CPR) technique that thousands of people have learned is less than 30 years old. It was discovered almost by accident by a 72-year-old Johns Hopkins electrical engineer, W.B. Kouwenhoven, who with teammates was experimenting on dogs, applying electric shocks externally. The team noticed that when they placed heavy electrodes on dogs' chests, blood pressure rose in the legs. The question arose: Would merely pressing on the chest pump blood through the body?[6] The answer has saved many people from death.

But soon health care providers, and then the general public, questioned the wisdom of resuscitating some people or keeping them alive with new machinery. Prolonging life sometimes meant prolonging death.

Right to die

A right-to-die movement sprang up, illustrating another influence—an increasing demand by people to be allowed to make their own medical decisions. Today, 60 percent of Americans surveyed believe that terminally ill or permanently bedridden people have a right to die, even if physicians disagree.[7] In their 1985 sessions, lawmakers in 13 states passed natural-death acts—the most ever for a single year—and to date 35 states have laws. These give people, while competent, the right to sign living wills commanding that they not be kept alive by artificial means if they should become incompetent and be in a terminal condition.[8]

An early incident in the movement for people to be allowed to make their own decisions was the Karen Ann Quinlan case. After attending a party, she stopped breathing for a time, probably from drinking gin-and-tonics after taking tranquilizers and barbiturates. Her upper brain was damaged, so that she fell into a persistent vegetative state. Physi-cians put her on a respirator, but her father later successfully sued to have it disconnected.[9] The court's decision recognized Karen's right to decide for herself, because, though uncon-scious, she was expressing her pre-sumed wish through her father. Con-trary to expectations, she breathed on her own after doctors weaned her from the respirator. She was moved to a nursing home, where she died in 1985, ten years after attending that party as a young adult. When she died she was approaching middle age, with some gray hairs.

DEVELOPMENT OF BIOETHICS COMMITTEES

In 1976, while pondering the deci-sion that would allow Karen's respira-tor to be disconnected, the chief jus-tice of the New Jersey Supreme Court studied a Texas pediatrician's recommendation for establishing eth-ics committees as a means for physi-cians to share responsibility,[10] but the chief justice misunderstood the idea. In the decision, he wrote that such a committee should advise on whether Karen would return to a knowing state. He had in mind a prognosis committee, composed only of physi-cians. After he wrote the court's opin-ion, such committees sprang up in New Jersey hospitals, but they are not the diverse-membership commit-tees discussed here.

Other bioethics committee precur-sors include medical-moral commit-tees in Catholic hospitals. Although these committees deal with reproductive issues, they are concerned with other dilemmas that have also excited people during the rise of bioethics. For example, in 1971 the U.S. bishops listed as ethical problems client autonomy, informed consent, and consideration of the "proportionate good" of a suggested procedure. They condemned unnecessary medical procedures and ghost surgery.[11] Ghost surgery is a procedure in which a physician who is unlisted on the consent form and who is unknown to the patient performs the surgery. Today, medical-moral committees consider a wide range of subjects,[12] and some have been renamed ethics committees or bioethics committees in recognition of their broad interests. In any event, the bioethics committee movement is particularly strong in Catholic hospitals.

Thanatology committees

Another development, during the early 1970s, was the advent of thanatology committees, which existed in part because of the problems described by Elisabeth Kübler-Ross in *On Death and Dying*.[13] She recommended frankness in dealing with death, and her book led to studies by others on better ways of communicating with dying patients. Some early thanatology committees, such as the one at Hennepin County Medical Center, Minneapolis, Minnesota, evolved into bioethics committees. Neurologist Ronald E. Cranford, head of the Hennepin committee, became a national leader in the bioethics committee movement.

Government action

Patient rights

Government action also spurred the bioethics committee movement. The passage of living-will legislation by about two-thirds of the states has already been mentioned. A few states, led by California, have also passed durable power-of-attorney laws that allow people to designate representatives who can make medical decisions for them if they later become ill and incompetent. In 1979, Massachusetts legislators approved 13 rights for clients in their relations with hospitals and nursing homes and 8 in their relations with physicians. If the rights are ignored, clients can sue.

For example, Massachusetts clients are entitled to informed consent, including, in the case of breast cancer, "complete information on all alternative treatments which are medically viable."[14] In California, doctors must hand clients a pamphlet explaining the treatments for breast cancer.

Research and clinical practice

Federal lawmakers and officials have also been interested in ethical aspects of medical research and clinical practice and have required that Institutional Review Boards (IRBs) be set up at research institutions.[15] Such boards have stopped repetitions of medical-research scandals such as injecting cancer cells into clients who had not been fully informed or deliberately failing to treat syphilitics. Thus, the IRBs, which are composed of people with diverse backgrounds who consciously apply ethical principles, are models for bioethics committees.

Withholding treatment of babies

The strongest federal government move has come about in the last few years as a result of Baby Doe controversies in Bloomington, Indiana, and Long Island, New York. Fictitious names for such babies are used by lawyers and judges, who are required to protect the babies' identities.

"Infant Doe" was the fictitious name for the Bloomington baby, but people called him "Baby Doe." He was born on April 9, 1982, with Down's syndrome and an esophagus that ended in a blind pouch, which prevented his being fed by mouth. Below the pouch, the rest of his esophagus led in normal fashion to his stomach. However, a hole in the wall of his lower esophagus led to his windpipe, allowing air into his esophagus and digestive juices into his windpipe.

The dilemma was whether surgeons should be allowed to connect the two ends of the esophagus and close the hole. His parents refused to allow the surgery, Bloomington judges upheld the parents' right to forego it, and state supreme court justices voted not to interfere. Baby Doe died before the U.S. Supreme Court could be asked to act. All those events took place within six days.

The court records are sealed, but ethicists have said they learned that the parents and judges acted on the mistaken belief that all Down's syndrome babies are profoundly retarded and that the success–failure ratio in surgery to repair Baby Doe's trouble was only 50–50. Actually, Down's syndrome babies' capabilities vary widely in later life, and the surgery success rate is more like 90 or 95 percent. A bioethics committee could have helped, because its members would have made sure parents and judges had correct information.

Among those who were repulsed by the case was President Reagan. At his instructions, the Secretary of the Department of Health and Human Services (DHHS) notified health care providers that a section of the federal Rehabilitation Act applied to babies as it did to other handicapped people: Withholding treatment only because babies were handicapped would be unlawful. The Secretary followed that with an "interim final" Baby Doe Regulation, telling hospitals to post signs telling people they could call a Washington hot line to report violations.[16] But a judge threw out the regulation, saying it was too hastily drawn and too vague.[17]

Infant care review committees

DHHS responded with what might be referred to as Baby Doe Regulation II,[18] which made concessions to health care providers, many of whom had opposed the first regulation. Notices inviting people to report violations were to be small and placed only in physician and nurse areas. The government would not interfere with reasonable medical decisions, and—a significant development, sparked by many public comments— the regulation endorsed bioethics committees to consider the care of disabled babies with life-threatening conditions. In the regulation, DHHS referred to them as "infant care review committees" (ICRCs).[19]

Judges threw out that regulation also, stating it was not authorized by the Rehabilitation Act.[20] The Supreme Court has agreed to review that decision, however, and was expected to issue a ruling during its 1985–1986 term. If the Supreme Court rules in the government's favor (and the present court has done so in most of its cases), Baby Doe Regulation II could be revived. During its brief existence, it aroused intense interest among hospital leaders. They saw in it a familiar technique: The government was telling them that ICRCs were good (that was the carrot) and that, if they did not establish ICRCs, they might be visited by government Baby Doe squads when a question arose about an infant's treatment (that was the stick).

Role of states in infant care decisions

Meanwhile, as a result of a compromise among medical groups and right-to-life groups, *state* governments will be concerned with decisions for disabled infants with life-threatening conditions. In 1984, leaders of 19 organizations endorsed amendments to the federal child abuse law.[21] (This is a federal law, but the states implement it with the help of federal grant money.) The medical groups endorsing the

amendments included the American Academy of Pediatrics, American College of Obstetricians and Gynecologists, American College of Physicians, American Hospital Association, American Nurses' Association, Catholic Health Association, and National Association of Children's Hospitals and Related Institutions.

Leaders of some of those groups endorsed the amendments reluctantly, considering them to be the best obtainable compromise. Officials of the American Medical Association continued to oppose the amendments. Their opposition is misplaced, however, because the Baby Doe Protection Law (as the amendments may be called) can help health care providers convince the public that decisions for babies reflect the community's conscience.

The Baby Doe Protection Law applies to the "withholding of medically indicated treatment" from disabled babies who have life-threatening conditions.[22] It describes such withholding as child abuse and neglect and calls on state child protection agencies to deal with violations. It gives much deference to reasonable medical judgment, however. The federal government will help state officials through training, technical assistance programs, and clearinghouses that will provide information on medical treatment and community resources.

Baby Doe regulation III

The government has issued "Baby Doe Regulation III" to implement the amendments.[23] This regulation also encourages infant care committees but offers no carrots and no sticks—no federal hot line, no Baby Doe squads, no posters in hospitals inviting calls to Washington. Hospitals are to name representatives to work with state child protection agencies.

The regulation spells out suggested functions of a committee as follows:

- Educate itself and others. Act as a resource to hospital personnel and families of disabled infants; committee members are to learn about community resources.
- Recommend policies for withholding medical treatment from infants with life-threatening conditions, using definitions in the Baby Doe Protection Law. Develop guidelines for management of specific types of cases.
- Offer counseling and review, acting on requests brought by any member of the committee, the hospital staff, or parent (or guardian) of an infant.[24]

Officials in many hospitals undoubtedly will set up infant care committees to comply with the encouragement in the new law and regulation.

•   •   •

From the foregoing, one might think that everybody agrees with the need for bioethics committees, but skepticism exists, perhaps particularly among some physicians wary of having decision making wrested from them.

One might think that everybody agrees with the need for bioethics committees, but skepticism exists, perhaps particularly among some physicians wary of having decision making wrested from them.

Physicians have shown, however, that they are concerned about how their marvelous new powers should be used. A study of the medical literature reveals that physicians have been ahead of the public in recognizing dilemmas. They have started many bioethics committees and chair or cochair most of them.[25,26] Nevertheless, philosopher-bioethicist Macklin (pers. com.), who serves on three bioethics committees in the New York City area, said, "We spend a lot of time reassuring physicians that the committee is not there to tread on their turf—to intrude on their decision-making authority."

Officials of the American Medical Association and American Hospital Association have emphasized that the members are not to usurp that authority. Most committees are "optional-optional," as University of Texas law professor John A. Robertson has described them.[27] That is, a health care provider has the option of bringing a problem to the committee, and, once the committee has considered the problem, the provider has the option of accepting its advice.

However, bioethics committees, particularly those that advise on the care of disabled newborns, inevitably influence decisions. Members of an American Academy of Pediatrics task force suggested that committees review every decision involving a deliberate withholding of life-sustaining treatment from a disabled baby for whom a long life was possible. A committee might suggest that the state child abuse agency be called in or that the problem be taken to court, possibilities that would focus much attention on the committee's views.

One way to ease physician resistance is to continue to ask highly qualified and respected physicians to join or to lead the committees. Another is to demonstrate the committees' advantages. Bioethics committees decrease nurse and physician stress, reduce legal dangers, and, above all, can convince the public that the community's conscience is

reflected in medical decision making. Thus, their existence in itself can ward off further public and governmental intrusion.

Such results can be achieved if the committee members learn much about bioethics and move cautiously. A committee's first task will be self-education, and its second will be education of other health care providers. Only then can the members appropriately consider other functions. It is also desirable for the committees to have lay community representation and probably to advertise that clients and their families, as well as medical personnel, can seek their counsel. Without careful moves on everybody's part, the promise of bioethics committees, like promises of old-time panaceas, will turn out to be empty.

REFERENCES

1. President's Commission for the Study of Ethical Problems in Medicine and Biomedical and Behavioral Research. *Deciding to Forego Life-Sustaining Treatment.* Washington, D.C.: Government Printing Office, 1983, pp. 443–49.
2. "Hospital Ethics Committees Surveyed." *Hospitals* 58 (May 16, 1984): 52.
3. Services and Treatment for Disabled Infants; Model Guidelines for Health Care Providers to Establish Infant Care Review Committees, 50 Fed. Reg. 14,893 (1985).
4. Youngner, S.J. "Case Consultations." Paper presented at Conference on Institutional Ethics Committees and Healthcare Decisionmaking, sponsored by the American Society of Law and Medicine and the Sisters of Mercy Health Corporation, Detroit, Michigan, April 12–13, 1984.
5. Beck, C.S., Pritchard, W.H., and Feil, H.S. "Ventricular Fibrillation of Long Duration Abolished by Electric Shock." *Journal of the American Medical Association* 135 (1947): 985–86.
6. Kouwenhoven, W.B., Jude, R., and Knickerbocker, G.G., "Closed-chest Cardiac Massage." *Journal of the American Medical Association* 173 (1960): 1064–67.
7. Findlay, S. "60% Say the Ill Have Right to Die." *USA Today*, May 2, 1985.
8. Benedetto, R. "35 States Embrace 'Living Will' Movement." *USA Today*, July 18, 1985.
9. *In re* Quinlan, 70 N.J. 10, 355 A.2d 647 (1976).
10. Teel, K. "The Physician's Dilemma, a Doctor's View: What the Law Should Be." *Baylor Law Review* 27 (1975): 6.
11. National Conference of Catholic Bishops. *Ethical and Religious Directives for Catholic Health Facilities.* St. Louis: Catholic Health Association of the U.S., 1971.
12. Lisson, E.L. "Active Medical Morals Committee: Valuable Resource for Health Care." *Hospital Progress* 63 (October 1982): 36–68.
13. Kübler-Ross, E. *On Death and Dying.* New York: Macmillan, 1969.

14. Mass. Gen. Laws. Ann. ch 111 §70E (West 1983).
15. The National Research Act, Pub. L. No. 93–348 (1974).
16. 48 Fed. Reg. 9630 (1983).
17. American Academy of Pediatrics v. Heckler, 561 F. Supp. 395 (D.D.C. 1983).
18. 49 Fed. Reg. 1622 (1984) (to be codified at 45 C.F.R. §84.55).
19. Ibid.
20. American Hospital Ass'n. v. Heckler, 585 F. Supp. 541, *aff'd*, Nos. 84–6211, 84–6231 (2d. Cir., Dec. 27, 1984), *cert. granted*, 53 U.S.L.W. (U.S. June 17, 1985) (No. 84–1529).
21. Child Abuse Amendments of 1984, Pub. L. No. 98–457, 98 Stat. 1749 (1984).
22. Ibid.
23. Services and Treatment for Disabled Infants.
24. Ibid.
25. Williamson, W.P. "Life or Death—Whose Decision?" *Journal of the American Medical Association* 197 (1966): 793–95.
26. Caroline, N.L. "Dying in Academe." *New Physician* 21 (1972): 654–57.
27. Robertson, J.A., "Ethics Committees in Hospitals: Alternative Structure and Responsibilities." *Quality Review Bulletin* 10 (January 1984): 6, 8.

Life, death, and liability: Duties of health care providers regarding withdrawal of treatment

Ilene V. Goldberg
Assistant Professor of Business Policy and
*   Environment*

Ira Sprotzer
Associate Professor of Business Policy and
*   Environment*
Rider College
Lawrenceville, New Jersey

R APID DEVELOPMENTS in medicine's ability to prolong life-sustaining processes such as breathing, nutrition, and kidney function have forced society to redefine death and to struggle with medical, legal, and ethical questions involving the right of individuals to control their dying process.[1] Despite the controversy surrounding these issues, the law has increasingly given protection to the individual's right to medical self-determination, even when the individual's decisions regarding medical treatment result in death. Most states now explicitly recognize living wills (documents that authorize refusal or withdrawal of life prolonging medical treatment). There have also been recent efforts to decriminalize euthanasia.

An important aspect of protecting the right to medical self-determination is ensuring a relationship between patients and their health care providers (e.g., physicians, nurses, and hospital administrators)

Health Care Superv, 1990, 9(2), 33–42
©1990 Aspen Publishers, Inc.

whereby the patient's wishes can be understood and carried out. In that context, this article will consider the duties and potential liabilities of health care providers with regard to refusal and withdrawal of medical treatment.

DEVELOPING THE "RIGHT TO DIE": REDEFINING DEATH

Traditionally, death was defined as the "irreversible cessation of cardiopulmonary function."[2] This definition did not include the lack of brain activity as a criterion for death because, until recently, no method existed for determining that brain activity had ceased. Moreover, until recently no mechanical means were available to maintain heart and lung action.[3]

Advances in medical technology over the past quarter century have made the traditional definition of death obsolete, because it is now possible to maintain breathing and heartbeat in patients who have experienced irreversible loss of brain function.[4] To consider patients "alive" in such cases would place tremendous financial and emotional burdens on the patients, families, and hospitals.[5] In addition, death must now be defined in terms of lack of brain activity to maintain organ transplant programs; to preserve organs for transplant, the donor's cardiopulmonary system must continue functioning until the organs can be removed. Under the traditional definition of death, such a donor would be considered as still "alive" because the heart and lungs continue to function. Therefore, without a redefinition of death, the organ-removal process would be deemed to "kill" the donor.[6]

In response to these concerns, most states have adopted the definition of death pro-

vided by the Uniform Determination of Death Act (UDDA):

Section 1 (Determination of Death)
An individual who has sustained either (1) irreversible cessation of circulatory and respiratory functions, or (2) irreversible cessation of all functions of the entire brain, including brain stem, is dead. A determination of death must be made in accordance with accepted medical standards.[7]

While the UDDA brings the legal definition of death more in line with modern technology, it does not resolve all questions. The UDDA (and all other state laws that have been "updated" to define death in terms of "brain death") requires an irreversible cessation of *all* functions of the *entire* brain, *including the brain stem.*

It is therefore still possible for a person to have brain damage so severe that irreversible loss of consciousness and perception (sometimes referred to as a persistent vegetative state or "PVS") has been suffered; but the person will legally be considered to be alive, and "life" may be maintained indefinitely by mechanical means.[8]

Some ethicists, physicians, and attorneys argue that death should be defined to include PVS patients or anencephalic babies who are born without the portion of their brains that enables them to sustain conscious activity such as thought or emotion.[9] However, the majority view (and the minimum requirement under the law) is that unless the entire brain has ceased to function, the patient is still "alive," even if in an irreversible coma.[10] Whether the PVS patient should be forced to exist in that vegetative state is another question, however. Partially in answer to that question, courts and legislatures have developed guidelines concerning the "right to die."

Since the distinction between life and

death is blurred, it is not surprising that there is controversy regarding the appropriate medical treatment of a patient who is terminally ill and in pain, or who is in a persistent vegetative state, or who has no hope of returning to a "quality" life. Recent surveys have shown that most people fear a long, costly, painful dying process far more than death itself. Therefore, courts and legislatures have increasingly given effect to the right of persons to refuse or withdraw life-prolonging medical treatment.[11]

The right to control one's own body is a basic concept that is recognized both in common law and as part of the constitutional right to self-determination. However, this right is not absolute. Particularly difficult

---

The right to control one's own body is a basic concept that is well recognized both in common law and as part of the constitutional right to self-determination.

---

questions arise where patients are incompetent to make specific treatment decisions for themselves. These patients are unable to directly exercise their right to accept or refuse medical treatment. This does not necessarily mean, however, that the incompetent patient does not have a right to medical self-determination.[12]

Life-sustaining treatment may be withheld or withdrawn from an incompetent patient in some circumstances when it is clear that the individual patient would have refused the treatment under the circumstances involved.[13] For example, most jurisdictions have statutes that recognize the durable

power of attorney, a document that authorizes a relative, friend, or other trusted individual to act as a surrogate decision maker in making medical treatment decisions on a person's behalf if that person becomes incompetent to make such decisions. Justice O'Connor's concurring opinion in *Cruzan v. Missouri Department of Health* indicates that states may have a duty under the Constitution to give effect to the decisions of surrogates. However, it is up to the individual states to craft appropriate procedures for safeguarding incompetents' rights to medical self-determination.[14] It is therefore important to consult state law, because jurisdictions differ with respect to the circumstances under which treatment can be withdrawn from an incompetent patient.[15] However, despite variations in state law, it appears that the clearly expressed wishes of patients with regard to refusal and withdrawal of treatment are generally being given increasing respect.

Individuals who do not clearly express their intentions regarding life prolonging medical treatment increase the likelihood of family discord and confusion if such decisions need to be made in their behalf. There is also a much greater likelihood that the courts will have to be consulted in order to resolve disputes and protect health care providers from civil or criminal liability.[16] Therefore, if patients do not make their desire to refuse or withdraw treatment clear (preferably in a living will with a durable power of attorney), such treatment may be continued contrary to their wishes.

From the perspective of the health care provider, the issue of refusal or withdrawal of medical treatment potentially conflicts with professional values of preserving life and creates confusion regarding what course of action is medically or legally appropriate. Health care providers are also concerned as to potential civil or criminal liability in connection with discontinuing medical treatment. While courts have been reluctant to impose liability on health care providers who act in good faith, the law is still unsettled.[17]

CRIMINAL LIABILITY

To date, no physician, hospital, or other health care provider has been held criminally liable in connection with the withdrawal of medical treatment from a seriously ill patient.[18] Despite this fact, providers are rightfully concerned about the possibility of criminal liability in cases of refusal or withdrawal of medical treatment; health care providers have been prosecuted in at least one withdrawal of treatment case; and while no conviction resulted, the criminal trial process is one most providers would rather avoid. The possibility of criminal conviction is remote, but it does exist. Since concern about criminal liability affects the decisions of providers and, of course, the treatment (or nontreatment) of their patients, it is an important issue to consider.

Courts that have considered criminal liability of a medical professional for withdrawing treatment have noted the difficulty of applying the principles of criminal law to such situations. A striking example is the case of *Barber v. Superior Court of the State of California* wherein two physicians were charged with murder and conspiracy to commit murder when, at the request of the patient's family, the physicians ordered withdrawal of feeding tubes from a patient who was in a vegetative state that was "likely to be permanent."[19,20] The patient died

shortly thereafter. The court eloquently pointed out the inadequacy of the criminal law in this situation:

> We deal here with the physician's responsibility in a case of a patient who, though not 'brain dead,' faces an indefinite vegetative existence without any of the higher cognitive brain functions. . . .

> Because of the current gap between technology and law, physicians and families of these unfortunate victims are called upon to make intensely painful and personal decisions regarding their care without clearly defined legal guidelines.

> This case, arising as it does in the context of the criminal law, belies the belief expressed by many that such decisions would not likely be subjects of criminal prosecution. . . .

> Due to legislative inaction in this area, however, we are forced to evaluate petitioners' conduct within the woefully inadequate framework of the criminal law.[21, 488–89]

The court then held that a physician may lawfully discontinue life-sustaining treatment if, in accordance with accepted medical standards, the physician determines that the treatment is useless, meaning it does not and cannot improve the prognosis for recovery. It was further noted that the defendants acted in accordance with the family's (and, based on the evidence, the patient's) wishes, and there was no requirement to seek prior court approval before withdrawing treatment.[22]

Other courts considering the issue of provider liability have expressed a distaste for using the criminal law as a tool for disciplining physicians with regard to their withdrawal of treatment decisions.[23] The consensus has been that the criminal law should only be used in cases where the provider has acted in a manner that was "*grievously* unreasonable by medical standards or has failed to act in good faith."[24] Many of the cases dealing with the criminal liability issue involve requested withdrawal of treatment by a patient (through a living will or through the family's unanimous agreement that the patient would have requested withdrawal of treatment). Fearing civil or criminal liability, health care providers sought declaratory judgments to determine their rights and liabilities.[25] In such cases, courts have assured health care providers that they will not be subject to civil or criminal liability as long as they act in good faith, and in accordance with accepted medical practices. Moreover, if there is no evidence of dissension among family members or physicians, life-prolonging treatment may be withdrawn without court approval in some jurisdictions.[26]

It is necessary to relieve health care providers of liability in these cases in order to protect the patient's right to medical self-determination. If health care providers are not shielded from liability when carrying out patients' wishes (in good faith), there may be a conflict of interest between providers and patients.[27] Statutes that recognize living wills and durable powers of attorney also commonly provide that health care providers will be immune from liability if they comply in good faith with the terms of the living will.[28]

While health care providers can take comfort in the fact that the courts generally consider the criminal law as inappropriate to withdrawal of treatment cases, they should still consider the following:

- States vary with regard to the circumstances under which medical treatment may be legally withdrawn. Health care providers should be aware of state requirements and limitations. While there is no precedent to indicate that criminal liability would result from a good faith but unauthorized withdrawal

of treatment, health care providers can avoid becoming a "test case" by being aware of the laws in their jurisdictions.[29]

- The distinction between withdrawal of treatment and active euthanasia must be recognized. In the past, euthanasia was a settled issue: it was legally and (in the opinion of the majority) morally taboo. Active euthanasia is still a crime in the United States. However, it is gaining increasing approval by health care providers, ethicists, and citizens throughout the country.[30] There is potential criminal liability in "helping someone out of his or her pain." The increasingly blurred lines between life and death and between withdrawal of treatment and euthanasia may cause health care providers to cross the legal line.[31] To avoid potential liability, providers should consult with colleagues, the hospital ethics committee, or legal counsel.[32] It is noteworthy that *Barber* involved withdrawal of feeding tubes, which is considered in some jurisdictions to be akin to euthanasia.

- In addition to consulting with other providers, ethics committees, etc., it is important to make sure that the patient's wishes are being carried out. In a situation where there is family conflict or any question concerning the patient's intentions, court approval should be sought prior to withholding or withdrawal of treatment, even in those jurisdictions that do not ordinarily require prior court approval.[33] As stated above, there is no precedent that provides for criminal liability in such a situation. However, caution is advisable in this unsettled area.

CIVIL LIABILITY

Health care providers also face the possibility of civil tort liability in connection with initiating, maintaining, or removing life support systems. While courts have been

---

While courts have been reluctant to impose civil liability upon health care providers in withdrawal of treatment cases, there have been instances where liability has resulted.

---

reluctant to impose civil liability on health care providers in withdrawal of treatment cases, there have been instances where liability has resulted. Moreover, as society struggles to further define the right to medical self-determination, there will probably be more claims for monetary damages.

In *Strachan v. John F. Kennedy Memorial Hospital*, the Supreme Court of New Jersey sent a message to health care providers regarding their duty to honor the wishes of the families of "brain dead" patients.[34] The *Strachan* case centers around 20-year-old Jeffrey Strachan, who at approximately 4:30 P.M. on April 25, 1980, shot himself in the head in an apparent suicide attempt. He was taken to defendant John F. Kennedy Memorial Hospital (JFK Hospital) and at 5:25 P.M. was diagnosed by the emergency department physician as "brain dead." Later that evening a neurosurgeon examined Jeffrey and confirmed the diagnosis. He met with the Strachans and explained that nothing could be done to restore Jeffrey's brain function. He also asked the Strachans to consider donating their son's organs to the Delaware Valley Transplant Program, an affiliate of

the hospital. The Strachans wanted to think his request over and agreed to return the next morning with their decision.

Plaintiffs returned the next day and informed the hospital of their decision not to donate any of their son's organs. They also requested that he be taken off the respirator. Despite their request, Jeffrey was kept on the respirator and the Strachans were repeatedly asked to reconsider their decision. Finally on April 28th, at approximately 4:00 P.M., the respirator was disconnected after the plaintiffs signed a release.

Plaintiffs sued JFK Hospital, the physicians involved, the hospital administrator, and the Delaware Valley Transplant Program and its administrator. The action against all parties except the hospital and its administrator was voluntarily dismissed before trial. The Supreme Court held that the hospital and its administer breached a duty to plaintiffs "to act reasonably in honoring the family's legitimate request to turn over their son's body."[35] Their holding turned on whether the legal definition of death should include "brain death." The Court adopted the definition of death provided by the UDDA,[36] thus holding that Jeffrey died considerably earlier than April 28th at 4:00 P.M. when the death certificate was issued. The Court found that "the failure of defendants to honor the family members' request posed a plain affront to their dignity and autonomy and exposed them to unnecessary distress at a time of profound grief."[37]

The Court refused to impose a duty on hospitals to have specific procedures in place to respond to relatives' requests to disconnect life-support systems, although it did hold that health care providers have a duty to comply with a family's request to disconnect a brain dead patient. This case makes it clear to hospitals and other health care providers that a family's reasonable wishes with respect to an individual who has been determined to be "brain dead" must be honored, or the health care provider may be liable for damages.

Less clear is the responsibility of a health care provider to comply with the wishes of a family of a patient who is terminally ill or in a persistent vegetative state. In the case of *Estate of Leach v. Shapiro*, the court held that a health care provider may be civilly liable for wrongfully placing and maintaining a patient in a persistent vegetative state on life-support systems.[38]

On July 27, 1980, Mrs. Leach entered Akron General Medical Center suffering from respiratory distress. She suffered a respiratory-cardiac arrest; although her heartbeat was restored, Mrs. Leach remained in a chronic vegetative state. Mrs. Leach was then placed on life-support systems to sustain her breathing and circulation. On October 21, 1980, Mrs. Leach's husband, as her guardian, petitioned the probate court for an order to terminate the life support measures and the order was granted on December 18, 1980. On January 6, 1981, the respirator was disconnected and Mrs. Leach died.

On July 9, 1982, plaintiffs sued, claiming that defendants acted wrongfully in placing Mrs. Leach on life-support systems and in maintaining her thereon contrary to the expressed wishes of Mrs. Leach and her family. Plaintiffs claimed that Mrs. Leach expressly advised defendants that she did not wish to be kept alive by machines. The court recognized that absent an emergency, defendants had an obligation to secure either a court order or consent for Mrs. Leach's treatment from someone authorized to act in her be-

half, since Mrs. Leach was not capable of consenting.[39]

Moreover, even if an emergency existed, Mrs. Leach's clearly expressed desire to refuse treatment would have to be honored. The court noted that it would be unacceptable for health care providers to refuse to act in an emergency simply because the patient at some time voiced *vague* wishes not to be kept alive on machines; however, if providers refuse to follow the *clearly expressed* wishes of the patient and her family, they may be liable for damages.

The courts are not in agreement regarding the issue of civil tort liability for maintaining a patient in a vegetative state on life-support systems against the patient's wishes. In *McVey v. Englewood Hospital Assn.*,[40] the Superior Court, Appellate Division, of New Jersey held that the defendant hospital and physicians could not be held liable for failing to comply with a comatose patient's undocumented oral request, as expressed by family members, to terminate life support. In *McVey*, the patient, Elizabeth Palermo, suffered a severe stroke at the age of 91 and was taken to Englewood Hospital. She was in a deep coma suffering from respiratory failure and was connected to a respirator. Family members were told by defendant Dr. Rabin, a neurologist, that her brain stem activity was minimal, and she would die if taken off the respirator. Mrs. Palermo's family demanded that she be removed from the respirator, but defendants refused to comply because the patient was not brain dead. Approximately one month later, the family members obtained a court order declaring Mrs. Palermo incompetent and appointing plaintiffs as her coguardians, with authority to make decisions on her behalf. They immediately requested that the respirator be discontinued and it was, with Mrs. Palermo dying four days later.

The family members lost their suit for compensatory and punitive damages. The court noted that "hospital and medical personnel are charged with the heavy responsibility of saving lives and endeavoring to restore bodily function and that the decision to turn off a respirator is ordinarily a medical one, for which the attending physician must take responsibility.[41] Furthermore, hospital and medical professionals do not have the duty or the expertise to explore the extent of conflicting interests, views, and purposes when an incompetent's relatives want to discontinue life support because of such asserted wishes. In conclusion, the court held that *the time had not come* for health care providers to be liable for the failure to comply with undocumented requests to withdraw life support from a patient in a permanent vegetative state, absent the appointment of a guardian.[42] The unspoken implication in the court's opinion is that in the future, when the legal standard of appropriate conduct for health care providers in this type of situation is more certain, the time *may* come when health care providers might be liable for refusing to remove a patient from a life support under circumstances similar to those in the *McVey* case.

Similarly, in *Bartling v. Glendale Adventist Medical Center*,[43] the court declined to impose civil liability on health care providers due to the lack of legal standards to guide those providers' actions. In *Bartling,* the court affirmed the dismissal of a lawsuit in connection with the maintenance of a patient on a ventilator. When admitted to the defendant hospital, the patient was suffering from severe depression, emphysema, cardiovascular disease, and lung cancer. When his left lung collapsed, he was placed on a ventilator. He often tried to forcibly remove the ventilator and was restrained from doing so by wrist cuffs. He executed a living will and durable power of attorney; and in fact, he and his family released the hospital and its physicians from any civil liability for honoring his wishes. Although the court noted that it had previously held that a competent, nonterminally ill adult patient has a constitutionally based right to refuse treatment[44] and that the case law in this area was evolving toward greater recognition of patients' rights, it stated that "it could not be said that a common or comprehensive legal standard existed to guide the medical community at the time of the decedants' hospitalization—one that clearly should have compelled the hospital to 'pull the plug' on his ventilator."[45] As such, the court affirmed the dismissal of the lawsuit. The question of civil liability, therefore, remains open while the "common, comprehensive legal standard to guide the medical community" is being formed.

Therefore, health care providers reviewing the issue of civil liability in connection with initiating, maintaining, or removing life support systems should consider that

- the law with regard to civil liability varies from state to state. Providers should be aware of the law in their particular state.
- while some statutes and courts have protected providers from civil liability in these cases, the possibility of provider civil liability is more likely than criminal liability.
  - Providers *have* been found civilly liable for maintaining patients on a respirator contrary to the patient's (or family's) wishes.
  - Even in cases where health care pro-

viders were not found liable, the courts appeared to leave the question open for future consideration when legal standards become clearer.

- Civil liability is a more likely outcome than criminal liability in cases where physicians act unreasonably in treating (or failing to treat) their patients. As a result, there is a real, rather than remote, possibility that a provider may be sued civilly in connection with medical decisions with respect to life support systems. As indicated above, courts differ as to whether there will be liability; however, the potential for it is greater in civil cases than in criminal cases.

• • •

Many of the issues surrounding refusal and withdrawal of medical treatment are so new and complex that the U.S. society has not resolved the ethical or legal questions involved. Questions such as where life ends and death begins, how to determine the circumstances when withdrawal of treatment is appropriate, and who should make such decisions will have to be resolved before the law in this area can become settled. Naturally, society is a long way from resolving these issues, since they involve such fundamental social, moral, medical, and legal considerations. Nevertheless, a body of law has developed that increasingly recog-

nizes the right of an individual to direct his or her own medical care. To that end, an individual's clearly expressed intention to discontinue medical treatment will generally be honored, even if death results from the withdrawal of that treatment. Legislatures and courts have also encouraged health care providers to abide by the wishes of their patients by giving immunity to health care providers who comply in good faith with the provisions of a living will. Courts have also been reluctant to impose liability on health care providers for withdrawal of treatment absent a living will if it were done in good faith (with the consent of family or guardian) and was in accordance with accepted medical practice.

It would appear that as the law gives individuals increased control over the private matter of their own medical treatment, health care providers may face more civil suits for maintaining life support systems against the patient's (or family's) wishes. In any event, while society is in the process of catching up with medical technology, individuals can best protect their right to medical self-determination by expressing their wishes clearly in the form of a living will and durable power of attorney. Health care providers can best protect themselves by keeping abreast of medical and legal developments in connection with these issues and by communicating effectively with their patients as to their wishes regarding life-prolonging medical treatment.

REFERENCES

1. *Strachan v. John F. Kennedy Memorial Hospital*, 109 N.J. 523, 532 (1988); Comment, *Law at the Edge of Life: Issues of Death and Dying*, 7 Hamline L. Rev. 431 (1984).

2. *Strachan* supra note 1 at 532, citing *In re Quinlan*, 70 N.J. 10, 26–27 cert. den. sub nom. *Garger v. New Jersey*, 429 U.S. 922, (1976); Black's Law Dictionary at 448 (4th ed. 1968).

3. *In re the Welfare of William Matthew Bowman* (here-inafter referred to as *Bowman*) 617 P. 2d 731, 734 (Wash 1980), citing C. Wasmuth, *The Concept of Death,* 30 Ohio St. L. J. 32, 38 (1969).

4. Hamline L. Rev. supra note 1 at 435; Abraham, L. "Ethicists Try to Define Status of Vegetative Patients." *American Medical News* (Feb. 24, 1989): 3, 45.

5. *Bowman* supra note 3 at 734; *Strachan* supra note 1 at 534; Hamline L. Rev. supra note 1 at 433, citing "A Definition of Irreversible Coma." *JAMA* (August 5, 1968): 337, 339. (Report of the Ad Hoc Committee of the Harvard Medical School to Examine the Definition of Brain Death.)

6. *Strachan* supra note 1 at 532.

7. 12 U. L. A. 236 (Supp. 1983) (reprinted in President's Commission for the Study of Ethical Problems in Medicine and Biomedical and Behavioral Research, Deciding to Forego Life-Sustaining Treatment at 9 n.7 (1983)).

8. Hamline L. Rev. supra note 1 at 435; Abraham supra note 4.

9. Abraham, L. supra note 4 at p. 45; Youngner, et al. "Brain Death and Organ Retrieval." *JAMA,* 261, no. 15 (1989): 2205.

10. Abraham supra note 4 at p. 46.

11. *Matter of Conroy,* 98 N.J. 321 (1985).

12. *Cruzan v. Missouri Department of Health,* 50CCHS Ct. Bull. P. B4106 (1990).

13. *Conroy* at 360–61.

14. *Cruzan* at B4138.

15. *Conroy* supra note 11 at 360–385; Otten. "In Recent Rulings, Consensus on Right to Die Seems to Fade." *Wall Street Journal* (November 18, 1988): B1.

16. *In the Matter of Spring,* 405 N.E.2d 115, 121 (Mass. 1980); *Barber v. Superior Court of State of Cal.,* 195 Cal. Rptr. 484 (Cal. App. 2 Dist., 1983).

17. Areen, J. "The Legal Status of Consent Obtained from Families of Adult Patients to Withhold or Withdraw Treatment." *JAMA* 258, no. 2 (1987): 229–35.

18. Glantz, L.H. "Withholding and Withdrawing Treatment: the Role of the Criminal Law." *Law, Medicine and Health Care* 15, no. 4 (1987/1988): 231, 232.

19. *Barber* supra note 16.

20. Id. at 486.

21. Id. at 488–89.

22. Id. at 491–92.

23. Glantz supra note 18 at p. 231.

24. Id.; See also: *Commonwealth v. Edelin,* 359 N. E. 2d 4, 13 (Mass. 1976); *In the Matter of Spring* supra note 16 at 121; *Matter of Conroy* supra note 11.

25. *John F. Kennedy Hospital v. Bludworth,* 452 So. 2d 921, (Fla. 1984); *In Re Quinlan* supra note 2.

26. See *Bludworth* supra note 24 at 926.

27. Id at 924; *Satze v. Perlmutter,* 379 So. 2d. 359 (Fla. 1980).

28. See, e.g., Fla. Stat. § 765.01 et. seq. (1984).

29. Glantz supra note 18.

30. Fletcher, J. "The Courts and Euthanasia." *Law, Medicine and Health Care* 15, no. 4 (1987/1988): 223; Pellegrino, E. "Ethics." *JAMA* 261, no. 19 (1989): 2843, 2844.

31. Anonymous. "It's Over, Debbie." *JAMA* 259, 1988: 2094–98.

32. *In the Matter of Spring* supra note 16 at 121–22.

33. *Re W.* 424 So.2d 1015 (La. 1982); *Leach v. Akron General Medical Center* 426 N.E. 2d 809, (Crt. Com. Pleas Ohio 1980); *Barber* supra note 16; *In the Matter of Spring* supra note 16.

34. *Strachan v. John F. Kennedy Memorial Hospital,* supra note 1.

35. Id. at 529.

36. Id. at 533.

37. Id. at 534.

38. *Estate of Leach v. Shapiro,* 469 N.E. 2d 1047 (Ohio App. 1984).

39. Id. at 1053.

40. *McVey v. Englewood Hosp. Assn.* 216 N.J. Super. 502 (App. Div. 1987).

41. Id. at 506.

42. Id. at 507.

43. *Bartling v. Glendale Adventist Medical Center,* 229 Cal. Reptr. 360 (Crt. App. 2nd Dist. 1986).

44. *Bartling v. Superior Court,* 209 Cal. Reptr. 220 (Crt. App. 2nd Dist. 1984).

45. *Bartling* supra note 42 at p. 363.

Part II
Employment and the Supervisor

Surviving the employment documentation jungle

Charles R. McConnell
Vice President for Employee Affairs
The Genesee Hospital
Rochester, New York

DOCUMENTATION is the subject of an increasing amount of attention and concern among those who work in health care organizations. That is, *medical* documentation is receiving increasing attention and concern. Malpractice lawsuits and legal actions brought by regulatory agencies have made most elements of the health care industry extremely sensitive to the problems caused by medical documentation that is inaccurate, inconsistent, or nonexistent. Far more often than some health care managers would care to admit, a legal proceeding arising from some aspect of medical care hinges on a record entry that does not accurately reflect a corresponding order or that is missing, indecipherable, or in some other way lacking. Similarly, the outcome of a legal proceeding can depend on whether the appropriate consent form was executed and can be pro-

Health Care Superv, 1988, 6(2), 68–86
© 1988 Aspen Publishers, Inc.

duced. Dramatically increasing numbers of medically related legal actions, along with increasing monetary settlements and damage awards and skyrocketing insurance premiums, have created considerable sensitivity to the need for improved clarity, objectivity, and quality in medical documentation.

Medical documentation—the patient record in all of its forms, be it an inpatient chart or outpatient visit record—is generally receiving the attention it deserves. Employment documentation, however, remains in a woefully distant second place with health care management.

Employment documentation, consisting of all records generated concerning an individual employee's relationship with a health care employer, is rapidly increasing in importance to the health care supervisor. To most supervisors working in health care delivery, employment documentation is fully as important as medical documentation and is in some cases even more important. Although some supervisors are also caregivers and are thus directly involved in creating medical documentation or are responsible for its creation, a great many supervisors have no involvement with medical documentation. For example, the head nurses will bear responsibility for both employment documentation and medical documentation but the housekeeping supervisor, the business office manager, the personnel director, and the maintenance supervisor will have considerable employ-

ment documentation responsibility but will not ordinarily be concerned with medical documentation. Regardless of organizational level, every managerial person working in health care has, virtually by definition, the responsibility for employment documentation.

THE EMERGING IMPORTANCE OF EMPLOYMENT DOCUMENTATION

Medical documentation is governed almost completely by law, accreditation standards, and professional review processes. However, employment documentation is governed only partially by law and accreditation standards. A great deal of what can be described as employment documentation arises from adherence to a sense of good business practice and consideration of the possible future needs for certain information. Although there are certainly some recognizable legal requirements governing much of an organization's employment documentation, in the business of health care delivery this area of documentation is not nearly as fully dictated and monitored from without as is the medical documentation of patient care.

Although record retention requirements exist in most aspects of employment law, other than mentioning a few specific kinds of documents the law provides only limited guidance as to what the employer must generate and retain. Little or no guidance is provided regarding certain kinds of documentation problems that are likely to arise.

Kinds of employment documentation

The kinds of employment documentation found in health care organizations are: formal, informal, and initiating or supporting. Within these three general categories are documents that are thoroughly covered in employment law and documents that are not at all covered in employment law:

1. *Formal documentation* is documentation that is largely covered by the law, regulatory requirement, or other outside standard. It includes most of the items in employee personnel files and a few employee-related records that may be found in places other than the personnel file, such as separately maintained payroll records.

2. *Informal documentation* is documentation that is generally not governed by law, regulation, or standard. It may be as truly informal or unstructured as a supervisor's anecdotal notes (an extremely important area of concern to be dealt with later). It also consists of memoranda generated in the course of business operations, and internal reports such as those presenting productivity statistics or reporting on employee activities (e.g., project status reports and progress reports).

3. *Initiating or supporting docu-mentation* is source documentation used in the creation of other records that might themselves be considered formal or informal. For example, an employee time card is the source document for a payroll record; the time card must be retained for a certain length of time under law and the resulting payroll record must be retained even longer. Another example, this one lying on the informal side of initiating or supporting documentation, is a maintenance work order generated to have a desk repaired. The work order will likely be the source document for a portion of a maintenance activity report. But what becomes of the completed work order and the resulting activity report is governed solely by the business practices of the organization or of, perhaps, only the maintenance department.

All of these kinds of documentation—formal, informal, and initiating or supporting—are potential sources of problems for the health care supervisor.

Problems arising from documentation

Documentation can make considerable trouble for supervisors when

---

Documentation can make considerable trouble for supervisors when they do not have it and it appears not to exist.

---

they do not have it and it appears not to exist. Also, it can create considerable trouble for supervisors when they do have it but it is poor, weak, inconsistent, incomplete, or generally lacking in some respect. Documentation can pose problems for supervisors when there appears to be too little or too much of it.

Most difficulties that arise concerning employment documentation do not ordinarily come from running afoul of some legal documentation or record retention requirement, at least not directly. Rather, most problems with employment documentation occur when supervisors or their health care facilities are subject to legal actions, whether in the form of complaints filed with employee advocacy agencies such as the Equal Employment Opportunity Commission (EEOC), the state division of human rights, or individual lawsuits brought by attorneys on behalf of former or present employees.

LEGAL IMPLICATIONS OF EMPLOYMENT DOCUMENTATION

Every piece of paper ever generated relative to a particular employee has the potential of becoming the key that turns an employee complaint for or against the organization, and thus for or against the supervisor.

It is beyond the scope of this discussion to pursue the many possible reasons why some former or present employees (but especially present employees) take their complaints to attorneys or advocacy agencies. It

should suffice here to remind supervisors that people who feel they have not been heard within the organization will indeed be heard when they sue the employer or file a complaint with an advocacy agency. The employee who sues the employer or otherwise files a complaint is suddenly no longer talking to a deaf ear, if that indeed had been the case. Rather, the individual is now talking with attorneys who have settlement authority and enjoy ready access to top management, or with agency officials who likewise have access to management because they have the force of law behind them.

Like many other laws, those governing employment relationships are not hard, fast, inflexible rules. Rather, they are principles and guidelines that are subject to interpretation. As far as employment law is concerned, much of the time a wrong is not in fact a wrong but is merely a perception that something wrong has been done or an injustice has been committed.

Employment law and the laws governing individual lawsuits deal primarily with civil law. There are some significant differences between civil law and criminal law. For an individual or organization to be charged with wrongdoing under criminal law, there must be some legal basis for the charge. There must be evidence that a crime or misdemeanor has been committed, and there must be a demonstrable connection between the individual or organization charged and that crime or misdemeanor. There will perhaps be an arrest resulting from a direct connection with the occurrence of an incident, or there will perhaps be an indictment resulting from a grand jury proceeding. Under civil law, however, there need not be a direct and immediately demonstrable connection with a wrongdoing. There can be no arrest and charge under criminal law based on someone's notion of a perceived wrong that is generally unsubstantiated. However, under civil law it is just that—the notion of a perceived wrong—that ordinarily triggers a legal action. An individual who believes that he or she has been wronged by the work organization need only make a statement of sufficient clarity to encourage an advocacy agency to look into the matter, or need only secure an attorney who will take on the matter and file a lawsuit.

Thus a formal complaint pursued by an advocacy agency or a lawsuit brought by an attorney, either of which the organization must defend itself against, can result from an individual's perception that he or she has been done an injustice. A great many employment-related complaints and lawsuits do in fact arise from simple individual perceptions of wrongdoing. An advocacy agency such as EEOC will ordinarily pursue most of the complaints it receives; that is why the agency exists and that is why most of its employees are paid. Although such an agency will ordinarily screen out the obviously frivolous or unfounded complaints, as long as its representatives agree that there is a

chance of actual wrongdoing related to the complainant's perception of wrong, it will pursue the matter and the organization that has been charged will have to expend resources responding to the complaint. Should the individual take the matter to a private attorney, there is ordinarily a high probability of securing legal representation. Some aggrieved employees—undoubtedly a small minority—will agree to pay an attorney on a time-used basis to pursue a complaint. Understandably, most such employees who pay their attorneys as they go will be able to find representation for all but the most blatantly unfounded complaints. Most employment matters pursued by attorneys are taken on some form of contingency fee basis in which the attorney receives a predetermined portion of any resulting damage award or is paid by way of a negotiated settlement. Since a great many employment lawsuits are settled as nuisance actions to simply allow the employer to escape the time and expense of a long, drawn out legal battle, the complainant's attorney is ordinarily paid.

When work begins in earnest on attempting to resolve a formal complaint or lawsuit, the advocacy agency or the employee's attorney will seek out employment-related documentations of all kinds. An advocacy agency will use a great deal of this documentation in making its decision on the complaint. It is often extremely difficult to comply with an agency's request for documentation. It is sometimes necessary to furnish literally thousands of pages of paper that must be sifted and sorted from years and years worth of records and copied. But it is potentially even far more difficult to comply with the documentation requests arising in an individual lawsuit.

Not all employment-related lawsuits go all the way to the courtroom. A great many, perhaps the vast majority, are resolved by settlement at some point along the way to the courtroom. A few lawsuits end along the way by being thrown out by a judge as unworthy or decided on the spot on the basis of being obvious, but the majority are simply settled. Sometimes management will agree to settlement on the advice of legal counsel because pursuit of the case has revealed management to be vulnerable in some respects. However, much of the time the organization, although believing no wrong has been done and no law has been broken, will elect to cut its losses through a settlement rather than face the expense and inconvenience of a protracted battle through the court system.

A strategy frequently followed by plaintiffs' attorneys in employment-related cases involves deliberately making the process so inconvenient, frustrating, confusing, time consuming, and expensive for the organization that management will be willing to settle. And although settlement usually means that monetary damages paid to the plaintiff are considerably less than those originally sought, it also means that the plaintiff does

achieve a victory of sorts and it also means that the plaintiff's attorney gets paid. Negotiated legal fees are invariably a part of every settlement. It is within the pursuit of the legal strategy of attempting to tie up the organization's time and resources for protracted periods that employment documentation becomes so important.

Documentation thus becomes one of the opposition's major weapons in the legal process known as discovery—that is, the process of seeking out evidence and questioning involved parties in establishing a case. The trigger that brings this weapon into play is the *notice to produce,* a legal notice requiring that certain kinds of documentation be furnished. The notice to produce is usually served in conjunction with one or more notices of deposition requesting the presence of certain involved parties for questioning by the employee's attorney.

The notice to produce

The notice to produce is furnished under what is referred to as a federal rule of civil procedure. The notice indicates that under this rule the organization is "required to produce for copying and inspection" essentially anything that may be even possibly or remotely related to the charge in question. The discovery phase of a lawsuit frequently may be described as a protracted fishing expedition in which the plaintiff's attorney does just that—fish for evidence that may eventually be used to support the allegations in the lawsuit. The fishing grounds are ordinarily members of management or other employees of the organization, and the bait for the fishing expedition—furnished by the organization—is the mound of documentation secured through the notice to produce. Subject to a usually generous time limit that may be furnished by a federal judge, the fishing expedition may range over many grounds for a considerable length of time, leaving many participants who are subject to questioning—that is, subject to being deposed—lying awake at night wishing that some way to end the case would present itself so they can get back to the business of running the organization and delivering health care.

It is of course possible to file objections to the sometimes seemingly outlandish demands of the notice to produce. However, the objection process is somewhat cumbersome and time consuming. Ordinarily, the organization that is defending itself against a particular charge or set of charges

---

Ordinarily, the organization that is defending itself against a particular charge or set of charges will have to furnish a great deal of paper and put up with a great deal of questioning.

---

will have to furnish a great deal of paper and put up with a great deal of questioning. Consider some examples of documents requested in a notice to produce served in a case involving a former employee who sued an organization for denying an advancement opportunity to her on the basis of age and sex:

- the personnel file or any personnel document, in whatever form or forms ever maintained, including, but not limited to, performance appraisals, pay records, discipline records, training and experience records, job assignment records, transfer or promotion records, and all other related records for . . . (here appeared a list of the names of more than 20 people);
- the defendant institution's personnel policy manual in all of its forms and revisions as existed at any time from January 1, 1978 to date of trial;
- copies of any rules, policies, or regulations that the supervisor alleges that the plaintiff broke at any time during her employment, or that the supervisor alleges any other employees of the department broke at any time;
- all writings related to the supervisor's handling of any alleged violation of rule, policy, or regulation by the plaintiff or by any other employee;
- all job postings or advertisements or announcements made in any respect, whether internal or external, for any job opening in the department from January 1, 1978 to date of trial;
- all writings relating to the hiring

or transfer into the department of . . . (here appeared nearly four dozen names of present and former employees of the department); and

• the document or documents that the supervisor is believed to have on file concerning each employee in the department, including notes maintained by the present supervisor in addition to employee files originated by the previous supervisor, including all comments, whether positive or negative, from the beginning of keeping such notes or records to date of trial.

Although the foregoing are offered simply as examples, they were adapted from a real case in which requests such as these were but 6 of more than 40 documentation items requested. The demands ranged from a single slip of note paper to literally cartons of documents.

Again, all of this—which some might be tempted to label as legal harassment—is a sometimes necessary part of the process of resolving a lawsuit. It should be kept foremost in mind that much of this document request activity may be presented by the plaintiff's attorney in an effort to create a climate conducive to settlement while pursuing a wide-ranging fishing trip for evidence. Every piece of paper that may be even remotely connected to anything that could lead to pertinent information is susceptible in this process.

It would pay for the supervisor to be always mindful that every piece of paper generated concerning a particular employee is a potential exhibit in a legal proceeding. Of course, much employment documentation lies well beyond the control of the individual supervisor, including most of what is maintained in an individual's personnel file and how long it is maintained. It nevertheless behooves the supervisor to understand the documentation requirements of the system even though much of the operation of the system lies beyond the supervisor's control. However, there is much important documentation that the supervisor can control or greatly influence. In the area of controllable employment documentation there are a few things the supervisor can do during the day's work to ensure that life for the supervisor and organization will be easier than it might otherwise be if they are sued under employment law.

Obviously, what the documentation system requires and what the supervisor does overlap in a number of places. For example, the organization's system may require that performance appraisals and written warning notices be used in certain instances. But exactly how these are completed is left to the supervisor. And certainly it is often the supervisor's responsibility to ensure that such pieces of system documentation find their way into the appropriate personnel files.

To make the best of any opportunities to control employment documentation, it is necessary to first understand the organization's employment documentation system, and then to consider how the supervisor should work within the system to influence the quality of employment documentation.

THE EMPLOYMENT DOCUMENTATION SYSTEM

The personnel file

The supervisor generally has little control over what kinds of documents go into the personnel file. As already noted, however, the supervisor can control whether some items that should go into the personnel file do indeed get there.

Although its contents can vary slightly, the personnel file will ordinarily include: employment application; resume, if any; reference checks; letters of reference and recommendation; employee benefits enrollment forms; employee handbook receipts; personnel actions, such as grade, pay, and title changes, and departmental assignment changes; and employee status changes, such as a change in marital status or address. Also ordinarily found in the personnel file are performance appraisals, commendations or special notices, disciplinary actions, and verifications of employment and income for credit purposes. Some forms relating to an employee's use of workers' compensation or disability insurance may appear in the personnel file, but the medically related portions of these claims will ordinarily (or at least should) be held in a separate, personnel health file because they consti-

tute medical records and are thus confidential.

Concerning the maintenance and confidentiality of personnel records, the organization should have an official policy that controls access to those records. Only persons who have a legitimate business need to know should have access to personnel records. Individuals with a business need to know would ordinarily include:

- certain employees of the human resources department,
- a particular employee's immediate supervisor and that superior's supervisors,
- the organization's legal counsel, and
- interested supervisors and managers who may be considering a particular employee as a transfer candidate.

However, employee privacy is a rapidly growing concern and the access requests of even anyone included in the aforementioned categories should be carefully considered to make certain that a legitimate business need to know exists before a particular personnel file is made available.

The personnel record policy should also control the disclosure of personnel record information to outside agencies and individuals, requiring either employee consent or legal subpoena for disclosure and including language clearly intended to protect the confidentiality of such records.

The policy also should include a provision describing the circumstances under which employees may be allowed to review their personnel records. Such review will ordinarily be permitted by appointment and in the presence of a representative of the human resources department. Although an employee will not be permitted to remove anything from the personnel file—although the file contains confidential employee information, it remains the property of the organization—the employee may be permitted to enter objections, explanations, or other comments into the record should he or she desire to do so.

Significant problems in employment litigation can be created by gaps in the personnel file. In an organization that may have hundreds or even thousands of personnel files, it is not unusual for occasional performance appraisals, pension statements, disciplinary actions, employee handbook receipts, and rate change notifications and the like to be missing. When a particular item is not found in the file where it is thought to be, it is a common reaction to wonder whether the item was misplaced, or perhaps wonder if the item does not exist either because it was destroyed or never generated in the first place. A simple but important step the supervisor can take to ensure that gaps in the personnel file are kept to a minimum is to faithfully send to the human resources department the record copies of all appropriate documents as soon as they are generated.

Another problem commonly encountered in personnel files is documents that are not filed in chronological order. In many personnel record systems, documents are filed in the order in which they are received. This is not necessarily the order in which they are generated and dated. Also, when files are unbound so certain documents can be copied, the files are not always reassembled in their original order. Although not nearly as serious as missing documentation, the lack of chronological order can add to the difficulties encountered in locating all documents pertinent to an employment litigation.

The personnel health record

While in some ways considered a part of the personnel file, an employee's personnel health file is primarily a medical record. As such it should be maintained separate from the personnel file. Far stricter rules of confidentiality apply to the personnel health record. As with medical records in general, information from the personnel health record moves from and to medical personnel legitimately involved in the medical care of the individual and then only with the consent of the employee (who in this case is more properly identified as a patient than as an employee). Personnel health records maintained in the regular personnel file, as once was commonly the case in many organizations, are subject to casual scrutiny by far more persons than have a legitimate medical or legal need to know. Also, the availability of this information can lead to other problems. Consider, for example, the case of an employee who successfully pursued a claim that he was denied a transfer opportunity because of an occasionally recurring medical condition that caused the manager to decide he was an attendance risk.

Personnel record retention

A document that no longer exists cannot be called on in employment litigation, and there are indeed some documentation that can be destroyed after a specified amount of time. However, the legal guidelines for personnel record retention are a grand mixture of sometimes conflicting and frequently overlapping requirements. Because of the maze of regulations involved, it is becoming increasingly more risky to destroy any employment documentation.

In addition to a variety of laws passed by the various states, there are federal requirements governing most employment documentation. Within the federal laws, for example, one will find that:

- under the Fair Labor Standards Acts (FLSA), records concerned with wages, hours, and conditions of employment must be maintained for at least 3 years;
- records designated in the Equal Pay Act must be retained for 3 years;
- under the Age Discrimination in Employment Act (ADEA), certain information must be retained for at least one year while other documents must be kept for at least 3 years;
- the Employee Retirement Income Security Act (ERISA) requires that certain key documents be retained for at least 6 years;
- the Occupational Safety and Health Administration (OSHA) calls for some documents to be retained for as long as 20 years; newer legislation such as New York State's Right-to-Know Law dealing with exposure to toxic substances requires that certain documents be retained for as long as 40 years.

The threshold for retaining most employment documentation is six years. Since six years happens also to be the statutory limit for filing most employment-related actions, it might be concluded that a personnel file can be destroyed in its entirety six years after the particular employee leaves the organization. However, there are still the OSHA and other longer-term requirements to consider. There are also legitimate reference checks and other requests that regularly call for access to records that are more than six years old. Today it is perhaps more appropriate to retain personnel records indefinitely, although certainly records that are more than five or six years old can be committed to microfilm for ease of storage without significantly affecting ready access to the information they contain.

Other employment documentation system elements

The organization's performance appraisal form is part of the formal documentation system. Also part of the system are warning notices, suspension notices, discharge or dismissal notices, and all other paperwork related to disciplinary actions. Employee transfer requests may also be part of an organization's system. And although they do not ordinarily appear in personnel files, the organization's job descriptions are part of the formal employment documentation system.

If any of the foregoing, or other items that have not been mentioned, are generated because doing so is an organizational requirement, they are part of the documentation system and most will find their way into personnel files. Guidelines for the supervisor to keep in mind when generating much of this formal documentation are furnished in the following sections.

PAPER VOLUME

One piece of paper does not seem like much. Two, three, or four pieces of paper do not seem like much. However, when everything generated regarding employment in a work organization is considered, it amounts to quite a volume of paper. This volume should be kept in mind by all who design forms or paperwork systems or who use and contribute to these processes. These people should think again before creating a new form if an existing form can be revised to do the work of two; they also should think again if inclined to call for a three-part form when a two-part form could do the job.

Simply put, the more paperwork there is, the more difficult it is to keep track of. When an organization is involved in employment litigation, the more paper there is, the more pa-

When an organization is involved in employment litigation, the more paper there is, the more paper can be called on in the notice to produce, and the more difficult it is to locate any single document.

per can be called on in the notice to produce, and the more difficult it is to locate any single document.

THE SUPERVISOR AND EMPLOYMENT DOCUMENTATION

The remainder of this article contains guidelines to help the individual supervisor survive in the jungle of employment documentation. Coping with this documentation requires a conscientious attitude toward paperwork and a determination to keep that paperwork—at least the essential minimum of paperwork—timely, accurate, and complete. Although some managers shy away from paperwork as much as possible, they should recognize and accept this work as an essential part of the job and be determined to keep on top of it as much as possible.

Keep anecdotal note files

It is helpful for the supervisor to maintain anecdotal note files, in some instances a separate file for each employee, and many supervisors do exactly that. Anecdotal files will ordinarily contain miscellaneous information that is not sent to the central personnel file, including notes on certain discussions held or problems encountered, or notes—both positive and negative—relating to employee performance that will eventually be reflected in an employee's next performance appraisal. This anecdotal file also may hold records of disciplinary actions that do not reach the central personnel file, such as the dates and times and circumstances surrounding oral warnings that may have been given. The anecdotal note file generally will contain informally recorded information pertinent only to the supervisor and the individual employee, information that does not go to the employee's personnel file. However, the anecdotal file may also include the supervisor's copies of the employee's performance appraisals and the supervisor's copies of other personnel documents, such as warning notices that have already been placed in the main personnel file.

Not everything the supervisor needs or wishes to retain relative to his or her relationship with a particular employee must, or should, find a permanent home in the personnel file. This informal documentation, most of it temporary in nature and all of it pertinent to this particular super-visor–employee relationship, should be kept in the anecdotal file.

Follow all applicable procedures

The supervisor should not fall victim to the temptation to take shortcuts by skipping or skimping in creating the formal documentation required by the organization's system. The supervisor should complete everything that he or she is required to complete, obtain any necessary signatures, and transmit the documents to their proper destinations. If the supervisor is utilizing multipart forms for which systems changes have rendered one or two copies obsolete, extra copies should be destroyed immediately.

As far as documented disciplinary actions are concerned, the supervisor should always endeavor to obtain employee signatures as required by the organization's procedures. An employee who is subject to a written disciplinary action should be reminded that he or she has the right—and is indeed encouraged—to note any comments or objections on the document. Should an employee still refuse to sign a disciplinary notice, the supervisor should repeat the request in the presence of a colleague—preferably another supervisor or the immediate superior—and have that person witness the employee's refusal to sign. Although it may not always be possible to immediately obtain such a witness, doing so might help avoid later problems. Many an employee who refused to sign a warning notice has later claimed that he or she had never seen the warning at all.

In doing a performance appraisal, the supervisor should make certain to follow the system's requirement to conduct an appraisal interview and should see that the date of that interview, along with the earlier date on which the appraisal was actually written, appears on the form. Once again, the supervisor should endeavor to obtain the employee's signature acknowledging receipt of the appraisal. As with a disciplinary action, the employee should be encouraged to enter any objections or other comments on the appraisal and every effort should be made to ensure the employee's understanding that the signature does not necessarily mean acceptance of, or agreement with, the evaluation but rather that the evaluation has been received and discussed.

An organization's job descriptions, another common element of formal employment documentation, are rarely complete or up-to-date at all times. However, incomplete or outdated job descriptions constitute another area of potential difficulty. When the content of a job obviously changes, the job description should be updated as soon as possible. However, even lacking obvious change, the supervisor should review each job description in the department at least once each year and make appropriate changes.

Other documents, such as transfer requests, also require careful and consistent handling. Many transfer request forms require the supervisor to provide a written indication of why the particular transfer candidate was not accepted for the available position. Fully as much employment selection is based on gut feeling, the supervisor's overall reaction to a particular candidate, as occurs by objective analysis and assessment of a candidate's experience and qualifications. However, gut feelings cannot be documented in any objective manner, and the supervisor can be easily led to fabricate a rejection based on experience or qualifications that might not stand up when compared with the documented experience and qualifications of other candidates. It is certainly not wrong to allow gut feelings and subjective assessment to carry some weight in the decision process. But rather than go on record with subjective assessments, it is far better to enter something on the order of "A more suitable candidate selected." The supervisor might someday be put on the spot to define what was meant by "more suitable candidate," but the risk of this occurring is considerably less than the upfront risk created by entering something on the order of "Since this is a public contact position, I selected an individual who seemed to be more pleasant and more comfortable dealing with people."

Include dates and names

Dates are especially crucial to all employment documents. Dates are ordinarily not a problem with forms that specifically require dating, as most forms do. Although blank date spaces may occasionally be found, most people fill in the date when it is specifically requested. The major problem with dates occurs with informal documentation, especially the supervisor's anecdotal notes and informal handwritten accounts of various events.

There is a simple but important rule for any supervisor to observe in creating informal documentation: Never set pen or pencil to paper without first dating the page. In countless employment litigations, difficulties have arisen and controversies have been created because nobody was able to say with any degree of certainty when a particular document was generated.

Other problems in using informal documentation are frequently encountered due to an inability to recall who was present at a meeting, conversation, or incident that gave rise to a particular note. In employment litigation it is frequently necessary to try to piece together a complete chronology of events and identify all persons involved at every stage. Faithfully dating every note and naming those persons who were present will go a long way toward making life easier in the event that the supervisor's files are brought under legal scrutiny.

Use accurate, objective language

Subjective assessments, emotional language, or inflammatory terminology should be kept completely out of informal documentation. This advice should apply in even the most personal of documentation that a supervisor sincerely believes no other person will ever see.

The supervisor should be scrupulously careful in choice of language. If, for example, a note expresses concerns about an employee a supervisor believes may be stealing from the organization, terms such as "thief" or "theft" should not be used. Theft is a crime that is largely defined by arrest and conviction. Likewise, thief is a label that legally applies to someone who has been convicted of theft. Since the supervisor is ordinarily dealing with suspicions, supposition, or circumstantial evidence rather than factual proof at the early stages of his or her concern, it is far better to use terms such as "unauthorized possession of property" (a phrase that appears on many institutions' discharge notices as the closest indication of theft that will appear in formal employment documentation).

As a general rule, the supervisor should apply language that appears in the organization's work rules and disciplinary procedures when describing an employee's transgressions, whether suspected or proven.

The ideal approach involves a supervisor's determination to put nothing on paper that would be embarrassing or overly uncomfortable if it went public. When files are brought into the legal process in employment litigation, they are indeed public in that they are opened to far more eyes than those of the supervisor. If the files include emotional, inflammatory, or slanderous remarks or labels, or if they contain outlandish charges that cannot be substantiated, the opposition's legal counsel can make life extremely difficult for the supervisor. In a worst-case but completely realistic scenario, imagine that the institution is sued, the supervisor is called on to produce his or her anecdotal notes, the supervisor and notes go through the deposition process and wind up in court, and the case turns against the organization based in part on a note in which the supervisor jotted demeaning terms about an employee—and those words are quoted in the daily newspaper.

Check for errors

Most people do a great many things in business on a once-through basis, completing forms and generating other documents without checking what has been done. This tendency is especially true with informal documentation when thoughts and observations are simply jotted down. Most people are even more inclined toward going once-over-lightly when they are working under the constraints of time. All documentation errors cannot be avoided, but the supervisor should at least put forth nominal effort (e.g., proofreading each note or document once) into minimizing documentation errors.

In employment litigation, simple errors made in all innocence can be extremely troublesome. For example, in one particular case an employee claimed that he was a Technician II,

a grade 5 in the organization's salary system, when in fact he had been carried all along in the system as a Technician I, salary grade 4. Claiming that since a Technician II was paid at a higher rate but that he had been receiving Technician I pay for several years, he produced two job descriptions that identified his position as Technician II and three performance evaluations on which his title was entered as Technician II. He had been hired as a Technician I and according to his supervisor and the payroll system, he was indeed a Technician I. Where had the discrepancy emerged? As best determined after the fact, when the job description had undergone a major revision four years earlier, it had been erroneously labeled Technician II instead of Technician I and no one noticed the error. Later, when the job description had to be revised, the error was carried from the old document to the new without being noticed. When the institution began a new performance evaluation system, the evaluation forms for the system's first use were prepared for each employee by taking the job titles and job duties directly from the job descriptions. The technician's supervisor then admitted that he had prepared the employee's two most recent performance evaluations by simply referring to the earlier evaluation. Thus a single error was spread throughout the documentation system and finally emerged in the form of trouble.

Someone—in all probability, a plaintiff's attorney—will use errors or gaps in employment documentation, or apparently sloppy management or lax recordkeeping, to create doubt. Where there is room for doubt, there is room to instill the belief that something done in error might have

---

Where there is room for doubt, there is room to instill the belief that something done in error might have actually been done willfully or maliciously.

---

actually been done willfully or maliciously.

Strive for reasonable legibility and clarity

Much informal documentation exists in handwritten form. Even many critical parts of much formal documentation are handwritten, since many forms are completed by hand. The handwriting of various individuals within a business organization can range from textbook perfect to virtually indecipherable. Handwriting problems have always existed and will probably always remain to some extent. However, noticeable change has been occurring in documentation systems. As computerization spreads into more and more facets of business operations, more records are being completed by computer and thus fewer records are generated by hand. However, since there will always be the tendency—as well as the need—to drop brief jottings into anecdotal note files, a bit of cau-

tion is in order. It might seem that it will always be possible to ask the author of a particular note to decipher something others have not been able to agree on. However, since a given scrap of paper may be called into evidence years after its generation, it is often impractical if not impossible to call on the author. For example, a crucial part of a case hinged on a note written years earlier by a manager who had long since retired and moved a great distance away. A controversy raged over a single word in one sentence: Was the word "charge," or was it "change"? The sentence made perfect sense either way, but with dramatically different meanings.

The supervisor should be wary of faint writing that does not copy well, and ink colors, such as certain blues, that do not copy well, if at all. The world of employment litigation thrives on photocopies, and documents that cannot be clearly photocopied present problems for both sides, causing added delays and extra work. Faint copies from decent originals present problems enough; such originals can be recopied on a better machine. A supervisor's primary concern should be with the original documentation; poor originals make nothing but poor copies.

Periodically clean out the files

If anything exists in writing, even in so-designated personal files, it can be accessed by opposing legal counsel. That is, *if* it exists.

Aside from matters of producing documentation for litigation, it is simply good business to periodically rid files of excess baggage. Some anonymous wit once described a refrigerator as a place where leftovers are stored until they are old enough to qualify as garbage. Filing capacity is treated in much the same way; many things are kept that are no longer pertinent and should be discarded. It is helpful to engage in a file purge of the office once or twice a year. If a supervisor can set aside a few hours, he or she will find that it is far better to do this task personally rather than to delegate it to an assistant or secretary. First, it is the supervisor's documentation that is involved and thus the supervisor's judgment is most appropriate in deciding what to keep and what to discard. Second, by cleaning out the files, the supervisor fills a mental filing cabinet with information about what has been retained and where it is stored.

The supervisor should look with a truly critical eye at boxes and boxes of aging documentation, such as old workorder slips, that threaten to fill a warehouse. This material simply takes up space. Most of it will never again be accessed for any practical business need, but when it is requested by an attorney engaged in a fishing expedition, it can suddenly present problems of sheer bulk.

However, it is necessary to purge outdated anecdotal notes and other aging documentation before the supervisor is asked for this material in a legal notice to produce. After all, the phrasing that will appear on a notice to produce may include: "Notes in whatsoever form on (name of employee)" or "Any writings in whatsoever form concerned with. . . ." The supervisor may see in one of the legal notices served that an anecdotal file is thought to exist "on information and belief." This is essentially the opposition's way of saying, "We have reason to believe that such a file exists, so if it does in fact exist, we want it." If a supervisor destroys any documentation after having been served with a notice to produce that documentation, he or she stands in violation of the law even though those who served the notice may not be absolutely certain that the records exist and may not know exactly what form the records take.

Other factors should be considered when handling most formal documentation and probably a great deal of informal documentation. According to a policy implemented in 1986 by the EEOC, the destruction of personnel records by employers facing investigation by the EEOC may be used as evidence that illegal discrimination has occurred. The EEOC may then find discrimination based on an investigation that is less than complete when an employer withholds records from investigators. When this occurs, the EEOC can establish a case without a subpoena. If records are missing, the EEOC will take steps to determine why a respondent to a discrimination charge did not keep the records as required by regulations. Where it is found that a respondent knowingly destroyed or knowingly failed to keep certain records in anticipation of a charge of discrimination, investigators can draw what is referred to as an *adverse inference* that the information destroyed would have been unfavorable to the respondent. Once a charge is filed against an employer, the employer is required to keep all personnel records relating to the charge until final disposition is achieved.

•   •   •

Good documentation is good business. Good documentation is also one of the supervisor's best defenses in employment litigation.

Legal considerations aside, it is easier to operate effectively when all available documents say what they ought to say and are found where they ought to exist, and when those documents that have outlived their practical and legal usefulness are destroyed.

On the legal side of the documentation discussion, one primary tactic for wearing management down toward settlement is endless discovery, endless questioning, and continual chasing of an endless supply of documentation obtained in response to the burdensome notice to produce (which may lead to second, third, and fourth notices to produce).

A supervisor should control documentation. A supervisor should not let the documentation itself take control. Complete, honest, objective documentation, with every piece created as though it might someday go public or be subject to legal scrutiny, will work *for* the supervisor far more often than it can be forced to work *against* the supervisor.

Job descriptions: development and use

Joan Gratto Liebler
Associate Professor
College of Allied Health
  Professions
Temple University
Philadelphia, Pennsylvania

"LOST AGAIN! I just don't understand it; we lost the grievance hearing," lamented the supervisor at the weekly unit managers' meeting. "The third loss this month, and all because I didn't spell it out in the job description!"

"What is there to say?" asked the manager. "I simply expect the worker to come in and get to work—turn on the washing machines, check the water temperature, add the right detergents and so forth. I know it isn't elegant, but I ask you, what is there to say about that kind of job?"

"HOSPITAL FACES CHARGES OF DISCRIMINATION," the headlines of the local newspaper announce. Unrest and confusion seep into the organization. "On what basis are these charges made?" the concerned manager wonders. "Efforts have been made to match candidates

Health Care Superv, 1983,1(2),23–30
© 1983 Aspen Publishers, Inc.

for the job with the job qualifications, and we have spelled these out in the job description. What is discriminatory about that?"

"More budget bad news—partly as a result of increased costs in the administrative categories," the administrator tells the unit managers. "One major increase that has been isolated is a great increase in workers' compensation claims. With the way our job descriptions are worded, it seems that just about everything is a job-related illness or injury. This needs review."

"Oh, oh! The atmosphere here today is so sharp that it's like working in a room full of unsheathed swords! What's the matter here?" remarked the unit supervisor to colleagues. The answer: "The job ratings have been completed, and our unit workers have been ranked lower and placed in lower job categories than their buddies in the Group Practice Unit. Yet we all *know* these workers are doing the same job. How could *they* have rated our workers' jobs differently?"

The opening examples represent a variety of situations in which the job description was a pivotal element in some decision. A specific audience received and used the information communicated through the formal job description.

The job description is a major management tool for communicating the responsibilities, specific duties, organizational relationships, authority delegation and qualifications for each job. Formulating the job descriptions

The job description is a major management tool for communicating the responsibilities, specific duties, organizational relationships, authority delegations and qualifications for each job.

for the positions within each organizational unit is the responsibility of the unit manager. In carrying out this aspect of the staffing function, the manager puts in place the cornerstone for each job. It is on the basis of the formal job description that individual candidates will be selected, trained, evaluated, promoted and even separated from the organization.

The job description is also the basis for a job rating and wage and salary program for the organization. The primary purpose for formulating the job description is to communicate information about a job in such a way that it meets the needs of persons who will be involved in those processes.

Where does one begin when writing a job description? The traditional approach to developing job descriptions starts with task detailing and job analysis. These are necessary steps, steps that the manager will complete in great detail. But perhaps a better starting point is one that focuses on the broader picture: a comprehensive delineation of the uses that will be made of the job description. In developing any form of communication, one key to success is to pitch the communication toward the recipient of the information. In short, know the audience. What audiences receive the job description information? This can be answered through a review of the uses and purposes of job descriptions.

USES AND PURPOSES OF JOB DESCRIPTIONS

Compliance with legal, contractual and accrediting requirements

The following outline summarizes the relationship of the job description to the other personnel management functions.

Job analysis and job classification
- wage and salary scale
- exempt/nonexempt status under the Fair Labor Standards Act
- collective bargaining unit inclusion
- transfer and promotion pattern

Recruitment
- advertising
- preliminary screening
- testing

Selection
- information for prospective employee
- focus of interview
- determination of physical fitness for job as described

Orientation and training: tailored to job qualifications

Evaluation
- performance evaluation
- basis for error correction and retraining
- reference point in grievance hearings

Separation from organization (both temporary and permanent): basis for determining job-related illness, injury or inability to perform work.

These management functions must be carried out, in turn, in the overall context of compliance with various legal, regulatory, contractual and accrediting mandates. What are these mandates? They are the constraints that influence or limit management activities with respect to workers. Managers would do well to take inventory of the specific constraints that apply to their organizations. These vary from one organization to another. For example, not every hospital will be concerned with labor union contracts. Some health care institutions receive their accreditation from the Joint Commission on Accreditation of Hospitals; others seek approval from the American Osteopathic Association.

Constraints may vary from state to state, as in the detailed provisions of workers' compensation or unemployment compensation, which are matters of state regulation. A major purpose or use of the job description, then, is to contribute, primarily in an indirect way, to overall compliance with these legal, regulatory and accrediting requirements. This is accomplished in both a direct and indirect fashion.

Although it would be slavishly bureaucratic to develop job descriptions solely to ensure compliance with legal requirements, the fact remains that the institutional licensure regulations issued by appropriate state agencies, the federal "Conditions of Participation" (Medicare, Medicaid) and the accreditation standards of the voluntary accrediting agencies require such formal job descriptions. Their requirements rest in part on the premise that organizational accountability, the assessment of proper staffing patterns and compliance with nondiscriminatory patterns of employment all presume the existence and active use of formal job descriptions. In writing job descriptions, therefore, the manager should remain aware that these formal documents may come under review at the time of site visits made in connection with the enforcement of such regulations.

Job rating and classification

Before employees are selected and hired, the organization develops a job classification. This classification is based on the results of the job rating process. In job rating, each set of functions within each unit of the organization is analyzed using some set of common denominators. In health care, these variables include complexity of duties; error impact; contacts with patients, families and other individuals both within and outside of the organization; degree of supervision received; and nature of duties, ranging from unskilled to highly technical and professional. Mental and physical demands as well as working conditions may also be assessed because these variables may make a job different from a seemingly similar position in the organization.

When developing a job description, it is useful to compare the draft of the description with the job rating scale specific to the organization. From this "dry run," changes in actual wording may result so that the final expression of job duties and related conditions matches the categories or factors to be assessed. Without such a correlation between the job rating scale and the job description's wording, inequities could be fostered. Similar jobs could receive different ratings based on a lack of proper wording in a particular job description.

Ideally, the overall job rating process contains safeguards against discrepancies; ideally, the personnel manager makes such job rating information available to unit managers. It is still the duty and prerogative of line managers to take active steps in these matters and anticipate the job rating process.

In addition to the overall job classification, the wage and salary and fringe benefit package will be predicated on information gained in the job description or job rating process. Another key to success in developing useful job descriptions is to assess the written document for its adequacy in conveying information about the factors used in job rating and wage and salary considerations.

Two additional outcomes of the job classification that concern the manager are the determinations made for exempt and nonexempt positions under the Fair Labor Standards Act (FLSA) and the applicability of a union contract in terms of jobs included in a particular bargaining union. In both of these cases, information about supervisory activity is critical. Thus there is another benchmark against which to measure the adequacy of the job description: Does it contain sufficient information to justify inclusion—or exclusion—of a job in terms of overtime pay and related FLSA provisions? Is the nature of the job clearly delineated in terms of rating as skilled or unskilled, technical or professional, for purposes of union contract applicability?

Recruitment

Certain steps in the recruitment process involve information derived from the job description. Internal job posting may involve the placement of the complete job description in a specified location, such as on an employee bulletin board. Potential transfer employees essentially participate in a self-selection or rejection process as they read this job description. They can take the opportunity to assess such practical aspects of a job as shift work or weekend coverage requirements in terms of their availability to work such hours.

The physical, mental or technical demands of the job also may sway the potential transfer employee to reconsider applying for a position. Then, too, the job description may have the effect of encouraging applicants. Does the job description contain enough information to help prospective employees make such a preliminary determination?

Those involved in the preliminary selection interviews, usually members of the personnel department, need sufficient information about all the jobs in the institution to carry out initial screening. The unit managers must convey, through the job description, key points of information about duties, responsibilities and qualifications. It is important to note that the unit manager is the individual most familiar with the work of the unit. This information must be conveyed in a way that it can be understood by persons who are not involved in the unit or department on a daily basis.

Awareness of the wide audience who will use the job descriptions will help the manager write them in un-

Awareness of the wide audience who will use the job descriptions will help the manager write them in understandable form.

derstandable form. The unit manager may find it useful to try out the wording of a job description on another manager. Does the wording convey enough information for this person, familiar with the health care setting, but not necessarily familiar with the details of the specific department, to form a basic idea of the job?

The final selection process

A major use of the job description occurs during the selection process as the candidate is matched to the job. During the selection interview, information about the duties, responsibilities and qualifications is conveyed. One sensitive overlay to the selection process, which includes all aspects of the interview, testing and physical examination, is the strict avoidance of discriminatory practices, even inadvertent discrimination.

When the job, as summarized in the job description, is the focus of the interview, it is easier to avoid the pitfalls of interviewing that could suggest discriminatory practices. Thus with a job description that spells out such expectations as weekend coverage, shift work availability and similar requirements, the manager and prospective employee can deal with that set of expectations without the manager probing in any way into such questions as days of religious observance, arrangements for child care and other topics that are off limits for direct inquiry. The emphasis is on the job as it is described.

Job qualifications, and mental, physical and technical demands become the objective measures of candidate suitability when they are derived from job duties. These in turn foster a positive climate of compliance with nondiscriminatory practices.

For example, if the job duties include frequent routine interaction with patients in need of emergency care and the patient population involved is non–English speaking, a qualification of fluency in a specific language is not discriminatory. If the unit manager can tie each qualification to one or more job duties, the likelihood of discriminatory practices

in the employment selection process is diminished. Sometimes it may seem that one is stating the obvious, such as ability to read, write, speak English (or some other language) with ease, hear, see and lift—so why spell these out?

Another method to use in making a dry run of the job description that helps the manager determine the level of detail needed under the foregoing conditions is working with the personnel manager using a sample of applications that have been received over some period of time. How does the manager's job description hold up? On what basis would the manager hire, or not hire, a particular individual in light of the job description as it is written?

Employee development and retention

Job descriptions: Ho hum! Who needs them? The list of users turns out to be extensive. At each point of employee development, activities focus on the work to be done within each job. Orientation and training programs take on greater meaning as they are tailored to specific job duties and qualifications. Training outcomes can be stated in terms of the trainee's ability to perform the duties. This is another step toward objective evaluation of candidates.

Job descriptions also provide a focus for performance evaluations. Has the worker accomplished the duties and responsibilities made known in the job description? Error correction, retraining and, if necessary, disciplinary action are carried out in the context of the job for which the individual was hired. In cases of grievance, emphasis will be given to the worker's accomplishment of the job duties, with the presumption that these have been made known to the worker. A comprehensive, up-to-date job description is a valuable management document in such cases.

Finally, in cases of illness or injury under review by such agencies as Workers' Compensation or the Occupational Safety and Health Administration (OSHA), the basic determination of job relatedness is made using the job description. The boxed insert is a summary of uses for the job description. How would the manager's current descriptions hold up when scrutinized in relation to each of these applications?

Summary of Uses of the Job Description

- fosters or contributes to overall compliance with legal, regulatory, contractual and accrediting mandates;
- serves as a basis for job rating, job classification and wage and salary administration;
- serves as a basis for determining exemption or inclusion under provisions of the Fair Labor Standards Act and collective bargaining agreements;
- provides information to prospective employees and to employer representatives during the recruitment and selection process;
- serves as a basis for orientation and training programs at the time of initial selection, transfer or promotion;
- serves as a basis for performance evaluation, error correction, retraining requirements and grievance determinations; and
- provides information to determine eligibility for claims under Workers' Compensation, OSHA and similar programs.

CONTENT OF THE JOB DESCRIPTION

Can a single document, the job description, convey all the essential information needed for all of the foregoing uses? No, it cannot. Therefore, the manager may build into the wording specific references to related policies and documents. Internal consistency will be maintained by using the exact wording for job titles listed on the departmental organization chart. Statements of qualifications should include a reference to departmental work standards. Job duties should

---

Job duties should carry a notation that they are to be performed as outlined in the policy and procedure manuals.

---

carry a notation that they are to be performed as outlined in the policy and procedure manuals.

The following list summarizes key points contained in job descriptions. Related source documents for each key point appear in the parentheses.

Job title (departmental organization chart)

Flow of authority and degree of responsibility (departmental organization chart):

- who the employee reports to
- who the employee is supervised by
- the level of supervision received

Job classification:

- exempt/nonexempt status (Fair Labor Standards Act listing)
- bargaining unit inclusion (collective bargaining agreement)
- transfer and promotion pattern (organization-wide job classification)

Conditions of employment (employee handbook; departmental work rules; collective bargaining agreement):

- hours of work
- rules of conduct
- schedule changes for emergency coverage

Job duties (work standards; employee evaluation procedures; policy and procedure manuals for department):

- level of expected performance
- details of duties.

How can this information be conveyed succinctly in the job description? One way is to include a statement that reminds the user of interlocking administrative documents, such as the following:

This job description has been developed in connection with the overall statements contained in the employee handbook, organizational and departmental work rules and the collective bargaining agreement. Duties are carried out according to the details of the policy and procedure manual and departmental work standards.

WRITING A SUCCESSFUL JOB DESCRIPTION

In tennis and other racquet sports, conventional wisdom emphasizes the notion of keeping your eye on the ball. Managers can adopt this motto with a slight modification: Keep your eye on the goal—job descriptions that convey technical information to satisfy many uses. The content of the job description can be developed through the use of task detailing and position analysis and similar fact-gathering methods. The odds are in favor of success for the manager who combines thorough position analysis and technical writing with a sense of the overall context in which this important document will be used.

Sexual harassment: a problem for the health care supervisor

Gayle L. Goldberg
Assistant Dean of Students

Janet Thompson Reagan
*Associate Professor, Health
    Administration
California State University
Northridge, California*

WHY SHOULD a health care manager or supervisor be concerned with sexual harassment? Because sexual harassment affects the well-being of employees, patients and the organization itself. Within the past few years, personnel and management journals have begun to bring this problem to the attention of supervisors and managers in the business sector. However, treatment of this subject in the health care literature has been inadequate at best. Even within such comprehensive works as *Handbook of Health Care, Human Resources Management*, sexual harassment is accorded approximately one page in a volume of more than 850 oversized, double-columned pages.[1]

Sexual harassment is a major management problem for the 1980s. What is sexual harassment? How does sexual harassment affect employees and the organization? How should com-

Health Care Superv, 1985,3(3),55–65

plaints of sexual harassment be handled? What measures can be taken to prevent sexual harassment in the work place? Only through a thorough understanding of the problem and its implications can the health care manager protect employees and patients from potentially dehumanizing experiences, and protect the organization from legal actions that are costly in terms of both dollars and reputation.

DEFINITION OF THE PROBLEM

Sexual harassment, or the boss's "dirty fringe benefit,"[2] has been defined in the guidelines of the Equal Employment Opportunity Commission (EEOC) and through case law. The EEOC guidelines, published on April 11, 1980, define sexual harassment as follows:

Unwelcome sexual advances, requests for sexual favors, and other verbal or physical conduct of a sexual nature constitute sexual harassment when (1) submission to such conduct is made either explicitly or implicitly a term or condition of an individual's employment, (2) submission to or rejection of such conduct by an individual is used as the basis for employment decisions affecting such individuals, or (3) such conduct has the purpose or effect of substantially interfering with an individual's work performance or creating an intimidating, hostile, or offensive working environment.[3]

Although EEOC guidelines are not law, the U.S. Supreme Court, in Griggs v. Duke Power Company, has

stated that all EEOC guidelines will be accorded "great deference."[4]

Essentially, the foregoing EEOC definition distinguishes two categories of sexual harassment: tangible benefits and atmosphere of discrimination.[5] The tangible benefits category addresses the first two instances in the EEOC definition, that is, those instances of sexual harassment in which a clear relationship exists between a specific, overt, discriminatory act and an adverse employment action. The atmosphere of discrimination category addresses the third instance in the formal definition, or the employee's right to an environment "free from psychological harm flowing from an atmosphere of discrimination."[6]

SCOPE OF THE PROBLEM

Sexual harassment is a significant problem receiving insignificant attention. This absence of attention may be attributed to the fact that problems related to sexuality are sensitive by nature and receive limited discussion. It also appears that sexual harassment may not be perceived as a legitimate cause for concern. Such sentiments are reflected in the words of a 38-year-old male, a plant manager: "This entire subject is a perfect example of a minor special interest group's ability to blow up any issue to a level of importance which in no way relates to the reality of the world in which we live and work."[7] Furthermore, in testimony before a Senate committee, Phyllis Schlafly stated: "Sexual harassment on the job is not a problem for virtuous women, except in the rarest cases."[8]

These statements deny that sexual harassment exists, or at least suggest that it exists only for employees of questionable moral character. Fortunately, such opinions represent the negative extreme.

Although many managers today recognize sexual harassment as a potential problem, there appears to be a general lack of understanding of the scope of the problem. Sexual harassment appears to be one of those problems that "simply can't happen here." Yet several studies serve to illustrate how prevalent sexual harassment is in today's work place.

In one of the first surveys conducted on the prevalence of sexual harassment in the work place, Cornell University researchers surveyed female civil service employees attending a convention on sexual harassment. Of the 155 respondents, 70 percent reported that they had experienced sexual harassment.[9]

Redbook magazine's 1976 nationwide survey on sexual harassment found that 90 percent of the 9,000 readers who responded indicated a personal incident of sexual harassment.[10] However, the study's legitimacy was questioned because the target population was not selected at random. In response to this criticism, the editors of *Redbook* and the *Harvard Business Review* collaborated on a new survey, one which presented a number of scenarios and solicited views as to whether the situations contained elements of sexual harassment. This survey demonstrated that sexual harassment is clearly a problem to be addressed by management, yet also illustrated a general disagreement among men and women on the frequency of occurrence of sexually harassing behaviors.[11]

In a 1979 study of sexual harassment in the Illinois state government offices, a random sample of 4,859 female employees was drawn. Fifty-nine percent of the 1,495 respondents reportedly experienced incidences of sexual harassment.[12] The Ad Hoc Group on Equal Rights for Women found a 73 percent incidence rate for sexual harassment among United Nations workers.[13] A 1980 survey of federal employees reported 42 percent of female employees and 15 percent of male employees have experienced sexual harassment on the job.[14] Documentation from the Working Women's Institute of New York indicated that 70 percent of working women experienced harassment.[15]

Perhaps of more significance to health care managers, a survey of registered nurses attending a nursing program at Memphis State University revealed that 60 percent of the respondents had been subject to sexual harassment within the past year. Of that 60 percent, 25 percent of the respondents reported "being so upset they were unable to work normally."[16]

Although the statistics may fluctuate with each survey, the overall message is clear. Sexual harassment exists, and it is a common problem in the work place.

FACTORS AFFECTING SEXUAL HARASSMENT

Speculation abounds as to why sexual harassment exists. Certainly causation may be linked to social and psychological elements, particularly women's roles in Western culture and the changing of those roles today.

In considering female victims, the problem of sexual harassment can in part be traced to gender stereotyping in Western culture. Quite often the old roles remain. Men are viewed as dominant, aggressive and power-seeking; women are viewed as nurturing, compliant and submissive.[17] The idea that men may be aggressive sexually and expect women to comply, or at a minimum to be flattered by their attentions, is viewed as "normal." The explanation is, "that's the way men are."

Sexual harassment also revolves around the issue of power—who has it and who does not.[18,19] Victims of sexual harassment generally are those who have little power within the organization and who may be hesitant to report incidents for fear of retribution. Any employee, male or female, may be in a position where he or she depends on the positive recommendation of a supervisor for future advancement or for retaining employment. Failure to respond to

Victims of sexual harassment generally are those who have little power within the organization and who may be hesitant to report incidents for fear of retribution.

requests for sexual favors, or to submit to an objectionable work environment, may place the employee in an economic trap: Job security is jeopardized to retain personal ethics. Considering today's high unemployment rate, how many employees can risk losing their jobs and financial support for their families over a moral issue?

Sexual harassment is a sensitive topic, particularly considering that the personal implications of sexual attraction and harassment make it difficult to discuss. As Driscoll points out, employees now rely on their work environment as a source of social interaction, and the adage of not mixing business with pleasure has become more difficult to heed.[20] The issue is sensitive, too, because of the reliance on individual perception for the definition of sexual harassment. Sexual harassment is unwanted sexual behavior. But at what point is the line to be drawn between acceptable flirtation and sexually harassing behavior? Behavior with slight sexual overtones may be considered acceptable by one employee and not by another.

Some managers have avoided the topic because of a belief that sexual harassment, much like a new strain of flu, will not infect their organization, and a belief that any consciousness raising may only serve to create, rather than circumvent, a problem. The fear is that employees will listen to the symptoms of a sexually harassing incident and then perceive themselves to fall into this situation. Such a situation is certainly possible. However, by avoiding discussions of what constitutes sexual harassment, managers also eliminate the possibility of discovering very real incidents that can have a devastating effect on employee morale and productivity, as well as on the reputation and financial future of the organization.

IMPACT OF SEXUAL HARASSMENT

Individual reactions to harassment vary. In 1976 a study conducted in the Work Clinic at the University of California Hospital in San Francisco documented a number of physical and psychological symptoms experienced by harassment victims. These included: chronic fatigue; loss of strength; various aches, weaknesses and pains; depression and the symptoms of depression, such as sleeplessness and poor motivation; nervousness; hypersensitivity; hostility; memory loss; and feelings of victimization.[21] On the job, these symptoms cause employee absenteeism to increase, morale to decline and productivity and a sense of accomplishment to diminish.

The organization is also a victim of sexual harassment, facing a possible increase in various costs attributed to labor turnover, medical bills, reduction in productivity and legal fees. One government agency estimated that "sexual harassment of federal workers was responsible for costing taxpayers $189 million over a two-year period"[22] as a result of increased employee turnover, health care costs and lost productivity. In the health care setting, these losses are particularly detrimental as the industry struggles to contain costs. As Elliott and Kaiser state: "At a time when improving productivity is becoming one key to survival for health care institutions, no further justification for eliminating sexual harassment is needed."[23]

A further consideration for the health care manager is the impact of sexual harassment on patient care. As indicated in the previously cited survey of nurses attending a program at Memphis State University, a serious consequence of sexual harassment was distraction of nurses from performing their duties.[24] One student nurse reported: "Sexual harassment is upsetting, frightening and distracting. I can list instances of harassment in my two years of nursing that made it difficult for me to concentrate fully on nursing."[25] Even if sexual harassment did not result in labor and legal costs, the goal of providing quality health care would remain as an impetus for health care organizations to eliminate such behavior.

Additionally, the victim in the

health care setting may be the patient. In this instance, patient care clearly is jeopardized, and the well-being of both the patient and the facility are at risk. Surely, health care managers view quality patient care and the reputation and financial position of the facility as adequate reasons for eliminating sexual harassment.

EMPLOYER LIABILITY FOR SEXUAL HARASSMENT

The federal courts did not hear the first sexual harassment case based on Title VII of the Civil Rights Act until 1974, ten years after that law was passed. In earlier cases, sexual harassment was not viewed as discriminatory, but rather as a personal matter between employees. It was not until 1976 in Williams v. Saxbe that the court ruled that behavior need only "create 'an artificial barrier to employment that was placed before one gender and not the other, even though both genders were similarly situated.'"[26] Sexual harassment became a form of sexual discrimination and, as such, became subject to litigation under Title VII.

What liability does the employer have for the protection of workers from sexual harassment? As stipulated in subsections of the EEOC guidelines, and as established through case law, employers are responsible for the actions of supervisory employees as well as for the sexually harassing behaviors of co-workers and others outside the organization, unless the employer had no knowledge of the incident and could not be reasonably expected to have known about the incident.

The 1980 guidelines stated that an employer: "is responsible for its acts and those of its agents and supervisory employees with respect to sexual harassment regardless of whether the specific acts complained of were authorized or even forbidden by the employer and regardless of whether the employer knew or even should have known of their occurrence."[27]

Court decisions

These guidelines were reflected in a change of attitude by the courts, as earlier court decisions were overturned. For example, in Miller v. Bank of America (1979), the appeals court ruled that the employer was responsible for the sexually harassing behavior of its supervisors, just as a taxi company would be responsible for reckless driving on the part of its drivers.[28]

Subsection (d) of the guidelines stipulates that employers are also responsible for the sexual harassment of employees when the harassing behavior is conducted by nonsupervisory personnel or the public. However, liability is waived if the employer is unaware of the actions and could not be expected to have knowledge of such actions.

The principles set forth in this section of the guidelines were cited in the 1980 decision by the Minnesota Supreme Court in Continental Can v.

State of Minnesota, which held the employer liable for the sexually harassing actions of its workers.[29] The plaintiff in the case complained of co-worker harassment to her supervisor. Instead of taking corrective measures, the supervisor informed the woman that such behavior should be expected when working with men.[30]

Another important employer liability case dealt with sexual harassment by the public. In EEOC v. Sage Realty (1980), the employer required an employee to wear a provocative poncho. As a result, the employee was subjected to sexually derogatory remarks by the public. When the plaintiff refused to wear the poncho, she was fired. Because the harassment by the public resulted from a condition of employment, Sage Realty was liable for sexual harassment under Title VII.[31]

Predicted trends

What are the predicted trends for future litigation in the area of sexual harassment? As Faley has suggested, the future will certainly contain more cases focusing on atmosphere of discrimination cases, more complaints by men and more cases dealing with homosexual harassment.[32]

A new trend has already surfaced. In addition to complaints of sexual harassment under Title VII, supervisors or co-workers also may be charged with criminal offenses, including such possibilities as criminal assault and battery, self-exposure and rape. Employers normally would not

be liable for such charges. However, the *Harvard Business Review* has stated: "Under certain circumstances and in some jurisdictions, . . . employers may be subject to civil liability related to such criminal actions for failing to provide a safe and secure work environment."[33]

In the past, employers found guilty of sexual harassment involving negative employment actions could expect to reimburse the plaintiff for any back pay. In cases involving an atmosphere of discrimination, employers could expect no more than the cost of legal fees and the slap on the wrist of a court injunction. Now, with a trend toward including civil or criminal charges in complaints of sexual harassment, the employer's financial liability could increase substantially.

PREVENTION OF SEXUAL HARASSMENT

What steps can be taken to prevent sexual harassment from occurring in the work place? How should a complaint of sexual harassment be handled?

Policy statements

Certainly the cornerstones of any attempt to discourage sexually harassing behavior are the development and distribution of a policy prohibiting such action and describing concomitant sanctions.[34] Any policy statement should be strongly worded and should include a definition of sexual harassment and sanctions on such behavior. It should also consider such issues as homosexual harassment. Linenberger and Keaveny[35] suggest that the wording of this policy be drafted by a committee representing both management and staff. Addressing the health care setting, Duldt further refines this committee membership to include "administrators, personnel director, affirmative action representative, nursing representatives, and legal advisors. . . ."[36]

The policy statement should specify possible sanctions on sexually harassing behavior. Yet to move from the point of complaint to the point of sanction, a complaint of sexual harassment must follow channels through the grievance procedure. Special procedures, both formal and informal, should be developed for instances of sexual harassment. These procedures should circumvent the supervisor, if appropriate, and minimize embarrassing attention to both the complainant and the accused. Overall, the grievance procedures must ensure impartiality and a fair investigation so that the rights of all parties are protected. To further protect employee rights, grievance procedures should include steps to protect complainants from reprisals by the accused or co-workers.

Policy statements, sanctions and grievance procedures provide a start for a program of prevention. However, training of employees and increasing sensitivity to the issue are required as well.

Comprehensive training

Training for employees may be provided through orientation sessions for new employees, a series of informative workshops or, more appropriately, a combination of the two. Material could be introduced on employees' rights under Title VII, how to recognize sexual harassment, organizational and legal sanctions against such behavior, and resources available to victims of sexual harassment.

Employees should be informed of possible measures to protect themselves in instances of sexual harassment. For example, an article appearing in *The Massachusetts Nurse* suggested that because

sexual harassment is seldom witnessed, it is important that (1) personal notes be kept on each incident, (2) the employer be formally notified of the behavior, and (3) documentation of work competency be obtained so that employer or supervisory retaliation can be disputed.[37]

Special training also is required to sensitize supervisors to the issues involved in sexual harassment. The supervisor may play a pivotal role in sexual harassment complaints and, therefore, must be aware of how to recognize a potential problem and how to manage sexual harassment complaints. The attitude conveyed by the supervisor is instrumental in informing victims that their complaints will be seriously considered and advising perpetrators that their behavior will not be tolerated. If properly conducted, training of su-

The supervisor is instrumental in informing victims that their complaints will be seriously considered and advising perpetrators that their behavior will not be tolerated.

ing Women's Institute of New York; Alliance Against Sexual Coercion in Cambridge, Massachusetts; Coalition Against Sexual Harassment in Minneapolis; Women Organized Against Sexual Harassment in Berkeley; and Center Against Sexual Harassment in Los Angeles.

pervisors further increases communication at all employee levels, fostering strong peer relations and trust between supervisory and lower level employees. Trust and peer support are vital when dealing with an issue as sensitive as sexual harassment.

In educating staff about sexual harassment, several avenues are available to administrators. The use of in-house resources, such as health educators, can be employed to increase awareness and develop appropriate skills. Films, such as *Preventing Sexual Harassment*[38] and *The Workplace Hustle*,[39] are available for institutional use.

Various service organizations also offer training assistance. The U.S. Office of Personnel Management has developed training materials alerting supervisors and managers to the problem of sexual harassment and steps to take to prevent its occurrence. This program is described by Deichman and Jardine in their 1981 article in *Personnel Journal*.[40] Other service agencies provide assistance to victims of sexual harassment and serve as information centers. Examples of these agencies include Work-

HANDLING COMPLAINTS OF SEXUAL HARASSMENT

In addition to taking measures to prevent sexual harassment, supervisors and managers should be prepared to handle complaints. A supervisor who has received an allegation of sexual harassment should follow certain procedures.

First, the supervisor should listen to the complaint. He or she should be certain to obtain all relevant facts—the specific behavior and possible witnesses. This information should be written up later as part of the documentation of the incident. Because the issue to be dealt with is sensitive and may be subject to personal bias, managers must take great care that their words and actions, both at the time of the complaint and throughout the investigation, reflect an attitude of concern for the employee and a sensitivity to the issue. A decision should be made as to the appropriate channels and whether informal or formal avenues of grievance should be followed.

After the complaint is received, investigation of the incident should be timely, tactful and thorough. Any corroborating evidence should be solicited from witnesses. Furthermore, steps should be taken to assure that the complainant and the accused are protected from retaliatory actions of supervisory staff or co-workers. Once the outcome of the investigation is determined, disciplinary actions, if appropriate, must be prompt and should be tailored to the situation. The manager may choose to provide assistance to the victim in the form of counseling.

This procedure may be applicable in the typical work situation, but what happens in the health care setting, where the harasser may be a physician and the victim a powerless staff nurse or a patient? Physicians have their own self-policing procedures that, in the face of continuing sexual harassment in the health care setting, do not appear to be effective. Elliott and Kaiser[41] contend that the only viable solution to such a situation is for the board chair and several trustees, rather than the administrator, to confront the accused physician. Considering that sexually harassing behaviors on the part of the physician can jeopardize patient care and the reputation and financial viability of the facility, such action cannot be construed as an overreaction to a minor incident.

Sensitive handling of sexual harassment complaints and providing a program of prevention are not easy tasks, but they are essential ones. Such a program can possibly prevent sexual harassment. Also, if an incident does occur and escalates to the point of litigation, the courts may deal less severely with employers who have an active program of sexual harassment prevention.[42] However, such policies are not a guarantee of employer protection from liability. As stated in the 1979 ruling in Miller v. Bank of America:

It would be shocking to most of us if a court should hold, for example, that a taxi company is not liable for injuries to a pedestrian caused by the negligence of one of its drivers because the company has a safety training program and strictly forbids negligent drivers.[43]

• • •

Again, the question is asked. Why should health care managers and supervisors be concerned with sexual harassment? They should be concerned because sexual harassment potentially exists in all organizations; because it can cause major organizational and legal problems; and because it can be prevented. In the health care industry, where top level management and physicians are usually male and the support staff in both administration and patient care are usually female, the likelihood of perceived and actual sexual harassment is increased. Managers must begin to devote resources to the prevention of sexual harassment now, or lose resources to its consequences later.

REFERENCES

1. Metzger, N., ed. *Handbook of Health Care. Human Resources Management.* Rockville, Md.: Aspen Systems Corporation, 1981.
2. Hubbartt, W.S. "Sexual Harassment: Coping with the Controversy." *Administrative Management* 41 (August 1980): 34.
3. Equal Employment Opportunity Commission. "Discrimination Because of Sex Under Title VII of the Civil Rights Act of 1964, as Amended. Adoption of Interim Interpretive Guidelines." *Federal Register* 45, no. 72 (April 11, 1980): 25025.
4. *Griggs v. Duke Power Company.* 401 U.S. 424 (1971).
5. Faley, R.H. "Sexual Harassment: Critical Review of Legal Cases With General Principles and Preventive Measures." *Personnel Psychology* 35 (Autumn 1982): 586–87.
6. Ibid., 587.
7. Collins, E.G.C., and Blodgett, T.B. "Sexual Harassment . . . Some See It . . . Some Won't." *Harvard Business Review* 59 (March–April 1981): 77.
8. Linenberger, P., and Keaveny, T.J. "Sexual Harassment: The Employer's Legal Obligations." *Personnel* 58 (November–December 1981): 62.
9. Hoyman, M., and Robinson, R. "Interpreting the New Sexual Harassment Guidelines." *Personnel Journal* 59 (December 1980): 996.
10. Faley, "Sexual Harassment," 584.
11. Collins and Blodgett, "Sexual Harassment . . . Some See It . . . Some Won't," 78.
12. Hoyman and Robinson, "Interpreting the New Sexual Harassment Guidelines," 996.
13. Ibid.
14. Collins and Blodgett, "Sexual Harassment . . . Some See It . . . Some Won't," 79.
15. Riddle, P., and Johnson, G.A. "Sexual Harassment: What Role Should Health Educators Play?" *Health Education* 14 (January–February 1983): 20.
16. Duldt, B.W. "Sexual Harassment in Nursing." *Nursing Outlook* 30 (June 1982): 336.
17. Biles, G.E. "A Program Guide for Preventing Sexual Harassment in the Workplace." *Personnel Administrator* 26 (June 1981): 49.
18. Collins and Blodgett, "Sexual Harassment . . . Some See It . . . Some Won't," 80.
19. Renick, J.C. "Sexual Harassment at Work: Why It Happens, What to Do About It." *Personnel Journal* 59 (August 1980): 658–62.
20. Driscoll, J.B. "Sexual Attraction and Harassment: Management's New Problems." *Personnel Journal* 60 (January 1981): 34.
21. Renick, "Sexual Harassment at Work," 660.
22. "Sexual Harassment at Work." *The Massachusetts Nurse* 52 (March 1983): 4.
23. Elliott, C., and Kaiser, G. "Sexual Harassment Hurts Productivity." *Modern Healthcare* 12 (September 1982): 106.
24. Duldt, "Sexual Harassment in Nursing," 337.
25. Watson, C. "Ordeal by Harassment." *Nursing Mirror* 155 (18 August 1982): 38.
26. Faley, "Sexual Harassment," 586.
27. Equal Employment Opportunity Commission, "Discrimination Because of Sex Under Title VII of the Civil Rights Act of 1964, as Amended," 25025.
28. Biles, "A Program Guide For Preventing Sexual Harassment in the Workplace," 51.
29. Ledgerwood, D.E., and Johnson-Dietz, S. "The EEOC's Foray into Sexual Harassment: Interpreting the New Guidelines for Employer Liability." *Labor Law Journal* 31 (December 1980): 742.
30. Biles, "A Program Guide for Preventing Sexual Harassment in the Workplace," 52.
31. Ibid.
32. Faley, "Sexual Harassment," 595.
33. Mastelli, G.L. "Appendix: The Legal Context." *Harvard Business Review* 59 (March–April 1981): 95.
34. Hirsh, H.L. "Sexual Harassment in the Health Care Workplace." *Nursing Homes* 30 (May–June 1981): 47.
35. Linenberger and Keaveny, "Sexual Harassment: The Employer's Legal Obligations," 66–67.
36. Duldt, "Sexual Harassment in Nursing," 342.
37. "Sexual Harassment at Work," 14.
38. *Preventing Sexual Harassment.* Rockville, Md.: BNA Communications, Inc., 1980. Film.
39. *The Workplace Hustle.* San Francisco: Clark Communication, Inc., 1980. Film.
40. Deichman, D.C., and Jardine, A.F. "Preventing Sexual Harassment." *Personnel Journal* 60 (May 1981): 343.
41. Elliott and Kaiser, "Sexual Harassment Hurts Productivity," 106.
42. Faley, "Sexual Harassment," 597.
43. Ibid., 590.

Wrongful discharge and discipline

George D. Pozgar
Vice President, Corporate Affairs
Episcopal Health Services
Smithtown, New York

DISCIPLINE AND discharge action are two of the most unpleasant management tasks supervisors can confront in their careers; this article will be helpful to supervisors who face these tasks. The ability to fairly balance the rights of the employee and the needs of the organization is an extremely complex objective, much like walking a tightrope: If you lean too far either way, you will fall off.

WRONGFUL DISCHARGE

"Wrongful discharge claims are difficult, time consuming and expensive lawsuits to defend and, when they reach the jury, employers are losing about 75% of the time."[1] The liability of employers for wrongful discharge is a serious concern for many hospitals. From a historical perspective, employees were often discharged from employment at the will of the employer. The

Health Care Superv 1989, 8(1), 57–67
©1989 Aspen Publishers, Inc.

employment at will doctrine provides, in general terms, that employment is at the will of either employer or employee, and employment may be terminated by the employer or employee at any time, for any or no reason, unless there is a contract in place that specifies the terms and duration of employment. This doctrine provided employees with few employment rights.

In recent years, legislation has been adopted that prohibits discharge of employees on the basis of handicap, age, race, creed, color, religion, sex, national origin, pregnancy, filing of safety violation complaints with various agencies (e.g., the Occupational Safety and Health Administration), or union membership. A recent case illustrates the importance of considering these factors before taking action.

The Civil Service Commission in *Theodore v. Department of Health and Human Services*[2] was found to have acted improperly in suspending a black licensed practical nurse as a result of a physical altercation with a white coworker. The white nurse had been accidentally struck by a crib being pushed by the black nurse. Evidence at trial supported the black nurse's contentions that she had apologized for the accident. The white nurse struck the first blow and spoke inflammatory slurs. The black nurse's reaction had been defensive. The facts revealed no grounds for suspension or disciplinary action against the black nurse.

In addition to race, gender is an important factor in employment decisions. Although it is unlawful to lay off employees on the basis of sex discrimination, there are circumstances under which the courts will permit the use of gender as one of several factors to consider in laying off employees. A prima facie case of sex discrimination in *Jones v.*

Hinds General Hospital[3] was established by evidence showing that a hospital laid off female nursing assistants while retaining male orderlies who performed the same functions. The court held that Title VII of the Civil Rights Act was not violated by the hospital's use of gender as a basis for laying off its employees. General was a bona fide occupational qualification for orderlies since a substantial number of male patients objected to the performance of catheterizations and surgical prepping by female assistants.

It is worthy to note that discrimination is not limited strictly to employer–employee relationships but can be applied in situations in which a hospital's discriminatory practices can affect the ability of a nonemployee to obtain a job with a third party. This occurred in *Pardazi v. Cullman Medical Center*,[4] in which the United States Court of Appeals held that a physician's claim for relief under Title VII of the Civil Rights Act of 1964 was valid based on the allegation that the hospital's denial of staff privileges interfered with his employment relationship with a third party. Dr. Pardazi, an Iran-educated medical practitioner, had entered into an employment contract with an Alabama corporation that required Dr. Pardazi to become a staff member of the defendant hospital. Dr. Pardazi argued that the hospital's discriminatory practices denied his appointment; denied him the right of an attorney at rehearing; extended his observation period from four months to one year, a deviation from the medical staff bylaws; and interfered with his employment opportunities. The United States District Court's summary judgment for the hospital was reversed and the case remanded.

Procedural issues are as important as personal issues such as discrimination. For example, the Supreme Court of Michigan in *Renny v. Port Huron Hospital*[5] found, as did the jury that previously heard the case, that the employee's discharge hearing was not final and binding because it did not comport with the legal standard of elementary fairness. The central elements necessary to fair adjudication in administrative arbitration proceedings are: adequate notice to persons who are to be bound by adjudication; right to present evidence in arguments, and opportunity to rebut opposing evidence and argument; formulation of issues of law and fact, in terms of application of rules with respect to the parties concerning a specific transaction, situation, or status rule specifying point in proceeding when final decision is rendered, and other procedural elements, as may be necessary to ensure means to determine the matter in question. The supreme court found that there was sufficient evidence for the jury to find that the employee had not been discharged for just cause.

The existence of a just-cause contract is a question of fact for the jury when the employer establishes written policies and procedures and does not expressly retain the right to terminate an employee at will. The fact that the hospital followed the grievance procedure with the plaintiff is evidence that a just-cause contract existed on which the plaintiff relied. The employee handbook provided for a grievance board as a fair way to resolve work-related complaints and problems, but this was not a mandatory procedure to which the hospital's employees had to submit.

The employee was not bound by the grievance board determination that her discharge was proper, because evidence supported a finding that she was not given adequate notice of who the witnesses against her would be. In addition, she was not permitted to be present when the witnesses testified, and she was not given the right to present certain evidence. The evidence that was presented indicated that her earnings from her subsequent professional employment did not equal her earnings prior to discharge, and that she had experienced increased expenses due to the loss of her health insurance and to other financial losses that she suffered resulting from her discharge. Therefore, the jury awarded the plaintiff damages of $100,000.

PUBLISHED POLICIES AND PROCEDURES

The rights of the employee have been expanded through the judicial system. They now include employee rights as described in employee handbooks as well as personnel policy and procedure manuals.

The provisions of a hospital employee handbook were held to be binding in *Duldulao v. St. Mary of Nazareth Hospital Center*.[6] The Appellate Court of Illinois held that the employee handbook imposed obligations on both the hospital and employee. The hospital was wrong in not permitting a nurse her rights to follow the hospital's progressive disciplinary policy prior to termination. The plaintiff had argued in this case that the defendant had breached the employment relationship by not affording her the benefit of the progressive disciplinary policy established for nonprobationary employees and described in the employee handbook.

A nurse's aide was awarded $20,000 in *Watson v. Idaho Falls Consolidated Hospi-*

tal, Inc.,[7] when the hospital, as employer, violated the provisions of its employee handbook in terminating her employment. Evidence that the employee was making $1,000 a month at the time of her discharge and was not able to find suitable employment following her discharge supported the award of $20,000. Although the nurse's aide had no formal written contract, the employee handbook and the hospital policies and procedures manual constituted a contract in view of evidence to the effect that these documents had been intended to be enforced and complied with by both employees and management. Employees read and relied on the handbook as creating terms of an employment contract and were required to sign for the handbook to establish receipt of a revised handbook explaining hospital policy, discipline, counseling, and termination. A policy and procedures manual placed on each floor of the hospital also outlined termination procedures.

Given the severe consequences of misinterpretation, it is wise to word manuals carefully.

No cognizable claim for damages was stated in *Hinson v. Cameron*[8] by a nurse's aide whose at-will employment was terminated by a hospital on the basis of a supervisor's charge that the aide failed to administer an enema to a patient. The nurse's aide had not been ordered to perform an illegal act; thus, the tort of wrongful discharge could not be made. In this case, the hospital's employee manual could not be read as conferring tenured employment or job security.

The Supreme Court of Oklahoma held that although the employee manual listed examples of some grounds for termination, it was not an exclusive listing of all grounds for termination. Even if there might be an implied covenant of good faith and fair dealing in every at-will employment relation, that covenant does not forbid employment severance in cases other than good cause.

Similarly, in a New York case, *Battaglia v. Sisters of Charity Hospital*,[9] the Appellate Division of the Supreme Court held that the hospital's personnel manual could not be interpreted to limit the hospital's power to terminate an at-will employee. Language in the manual indicated that the personnel manual is not a contract, that it may be modified, amended, or supplemented, and that the hospital retains the right to make all necessary management decisions for the delivery of patient care services and the selection, direction, compensation, and retention of employees.

Given the severe consequences of misinterpretation, it is wise to word manuals carefully. Weiner, Bompey, and Brittain explain the importance of employment manuals:

Employment guidelines and manuals are very helpful in obtaining employee goodwill and maintaining good employee relations. They can also be excellent tools in maintaining a union-free environment. Therefore, the use, drafting, and implementation of an employment manual should be taken seriously. When drafting such manuals, employers should keep in mind the legal consequences of each provision and take care to avoid restrictive or tightly worded language. An employee handbook can be both written in accordance with the stated guidelines and help to maintain good employee communication and effective employee relations."[10]

Hospitals can help prevent successful lawsuits for wrongful discharge that are based on the premise that an employee handbook or departmental policy and procedure manual is an implied contract by incorporating disclaimers in published manuals, such as that described in the *Battaglia* case. In general terms, a disclaimer is the denial of a right imputed to a person or that is alleged to belong to him or her. Although a disclaimer is often a successful defense for employers in wrongful discharge cases, it should not be considered a license to discharge at the whim of the supervisor in an arbitrary and capricious manner.

DEFAMATION ACTIONS

In addition to wrongful discharge suits, employers may now face defamation claims brought by current and former workers, "apparently because of a greater awareness by those employees—and a growing recognition by the courts—of new protections available to them."[11] The defamation actions are being attached to or are taking the place of wrongful discharge suits,[12] and "making the employer look like the bad guy has become routine in defamation cases, since plaintiffs must overcome an employer's qualified privilege and show malice in order to recover."[13]

The nurse's aide in *Watson* claimed that the head nurse intentionally interfered with her employment relationship with the hospital, that both the head nurse and hospital had intentionally inflicted emotional distress, and that accusations prior to discharge constituted slander. The defendants made motion for summary judgment that was granted in part, as to the slander claim. Although the

nurse's aide did not appeal the issue of slander, it seems clear that charges of defamation of character will appear in an increasing number of cases.

CREATIVE DISCIPLINE

Before discharge comes discipline. Oral counseling, written counseling, written counseling with suspension, and written counseling with termination are the textbook responses to disciplinary action and discharge. Textbook theories such as these are fine in a black and white world, but few people live in such a world. Therefore, creative thinking as to what will effectively rehabilitate an employee is critical.

The following list presents some ideas for creative discipline and can easily be expanded by the supervisor. It should be noted that creativity may be limited to some extent by labor contracts.

- Use interdepartmental transfers when indicated and appropriate in the disciplinary process. Transfers are generally more effective in larger organizations, where relocation is geographically possible, such as in multisite health care systems.
- Substitute suspension for termination when possible. Do not allow the courts to do it for you. An emergency department technician's termination was properly reduced to a suspension in *Ellins v. Department of Health*.[14] The technician was discharged for failure to comply with emergency department procedures that required patient evaluation by a triage nurse. The Civil Service Commission reduced the discharge to a 60-day suspension, since the tech-

nician had bypassed the hospital's triage process because of the patient's critical condition. Under the circumstances, the city department of health failed to show that the conduct of the technician was improper, had impaired the efficiency of the hospital, or bore real and substantial relationship thereto.

- Offer the employee an opportunity to take a course in an area that will be helpful to the employee (e.g., human relations skills and communications). Depending on the seriousness of the offense, the employer may require the employee to contribute to the course fee or to pay it in full.
- Agree to purge an employee's file if there are no further disciplinary problems for six months to a year. Procedures for this action should be reviewed with counsel.
- Provide an opportunity for early retirement, when possible. When facing the need for work force reductions, instead of discharge for miscount, companies offer voluntary early retirement as an option. However, it is to be considered an option only after other strategies, such as a hiring freeze, redeployment of surplus personnel, and reduction of overtime, have been considered."[15]
- Be flexible, and allow a reasonable amount of time for employees to air their frustrations.
- Attempt to resolve disputes between employees. Look for compromise, suggest that formal complaints between employees be withdrawn, and attempt to resolve disputes over a period of two or more informal meetings. The first meeting will most likely be one of venting. Time and talk should help heal wounded egos.
- Be forceful when appropriate. A time will come in some situations when two disgruntled employees must be told that their clashes with one another are disrupting the work environment, that both are at fault, and that if their disputes between one another cannot be resolved, disciplinary action will be necessary.
- Offer the employee an opportunity to take a leave of absence. A long-term employee often suffers from burnout syndrome. A sabbatical will often restore the employee to both good physical health and a positive mental attitude. This is a benefit often provided for teachers, and it should be carried over into the health care industry. The sabbatical should be a planned event with specific objectives to be achieved during the leave.
- Develop peer counseling teams. Employees would often prefer to be counseled by their supervisors as opposed to their peers. However, peer counseling has been used successfully in some schools. Counseling programs of this nature should be coordinated with the personnel or human resources department.
- Have the employee identify the wrongdoing and provide an opportunity for suggestions for corrective action. Ask the employee what he or she would do if in your position. (Have him or her walk a mile in your shoes. You might even try walking a mile in the employee's shoes.)

Whatever approach is taken in creative discipline, the employee should not be forced to accept your suggestions for creative discipline. More traditional methods of discipline can always be followed if the employee is not receptive to the less traditional approaches. There is no magic formula that will be effective for all disciplinary cases; many cases are unique and should be treated as such. Whenever possible, whatever form of discipline you decide to use should be designed to produce a more effective and productive employee.

Too little or too much but never right is often the motto of those who criticize your disciplinary actions. When is too little too little and too much too much? This is a rhetorical question whenever sentencing is handed down for wrongdoing. Some supervisors will argue that all discipline should be punishment, and no allowances should be made for rehabilitative actions. Do not get caught in this trap. You can be fair, firm, consistent, caring, and creative all at the same time.

LIMITING LIABILITY FOR WRONGFUL DISCHARGE

Based on the issues presented, it is possible to develop guidelines for employers to reduce their exposure to liability for wrongful discharge. They can decrease their liability by

- developing an appropriate application that realistically determines an applicant's qualifications prior to hiring;
- developing a two-tiered interview system for screening applicants (the interviews should be conducted first by an appropriately trained member of the personnel department and then by the

department head of the service to which the applicant is applying);
- soliciting appropriate references and following up with a telephone call for further information;
- developing constructive performance evaluations that reinforce good behavior as well as instruct in those areas needing improvement;
- developing a progressive disciplinary action policy for those times the employee fails at job performance;
- providing inservice education programs for supervisors on subjects such as employee interviews, evaluations, and discipline (various colleges, universities, and consultants provide inservice educational programs for employers at reasonable costs);
- avoiding the creation of vindictive-sounding files on employees (beware of comments such as, "You are treading on thin ice"); and
- being careful of employment contract language. Contracts that provide a "termination for cause only" clause are binding on the employer.

An employment contract in *Eales v. Tanana*[16] that provided that an employee hired up to retirement age could be terminated only for cause was upheld by the court. Therefore, remember the following:

Employers must clearly communicate to employees during recruitment that their employment is at-will and can be terminated at any time by the employer. During the course of employment, handbooks and personnel manuals must provide a fair and unambiguous standard for employee discipline and termination....At the termination of employment, the discharge decision should be carefully reviewed by a member of the management familiar with the issues of wrongful discharge. At this point the employer may seek from the employee a release from all legal claims for additional consideration.[17]

SOME HELPFUL ADVICE

In disciplining employees, avoid excessive criticism, because there is nothing more discouraging than constant criticism. Criticism does not have much value because it offers no solutions; it is important to suggest a better way of doing things. "To reduce the sting of criticism, try sprinkling a little praise with it."[18] More important, encourage self-discipline. Mature people have power over their emotions. They discipline themselves so that they do not have to follow the crowd but can think, act, and make decisions independently.[19] When self-discipline fails, remember that sometimes punishment is necessary. People learn through the penalties of their mistakes.[20]

In disciplining employees, avoid excessive criticism, because there is nothing more discouraging than constant criticism.

Beyond taking appropriate disciplinary action, you should take the time to listen and show that you care. A good supervisor gets things done by working with other people. However, do not avoid discipline, because fair discipline will increase productivity and improve employer–employee relationships, as well as reducing absenteeism, grievances, tardiness, and turnover.

Even though you are acting constructively, remember that uncertainty is an absolute. The consequences of a particular disciplinary action are unknown, and with every management decision there is risk of making a wrong one. You cannot please everyone. In fact, disciplinary actions will always set off a chain of events. The one disciplined will seek sympathy from peers and will place blame on another. Before taking action, think about the consequences.

When considering your options, be careful of bias. Avoid adding weight to facts because they support your opinion. Consider all the factors, and be confident of your decision. There is generally more than one solution to a problem, and knowing that you made your best choice at the time is what really counts. If we always knew what the outcome of an action would be, we would all be at the racetracks. Many generals have said after the battle was over, "If I had only known, I would have fought differently and won the battle if not the war."

Consider the facts before instituting disciplinary action. Beware of hearsay and personal vendettas. Be sure to define your problem and investigate it thoroughly before making conclusions. Let reason rule, because emotions change with the weather, and be careful not to assume that because two events occur together, one is the cause of the other.

You can limit the need for discipline with regular employee evaluations that build characters rather than destroy ego. But if counseling becomes necessary, follow an effective and creative system of progressive employee discipline. Avoid the beat-them-over-the-head mentality at all costs.

When inappropriate behavior occurs, take action in a timely fashion. Otherwise, the behavior will be reinforced and repeated. If you do eventually take action, you will most likely hit a brick wall and find that the employee is confused and considers you unreasonable. Therefore, do not vacillate. Otherwise, you will lose control of the situation as well as respect from your employees and peers.

NO ALTERNATIVE BUT TERMINATION

When the supervisor has reached a point in the disciplinary process where there is no alternative but to discharge an employee for misconduct, the supervisor should ask himself or herself the following questions prior to discharging an employee:

- Have I violated any policies and procedures outlined in the hospital's administrative manual?
- Have I been arbitrary and capricious?
- Have I discriminated against the employee on the basis of race, creed, color, gender, national origin, or marital status?
- Have I violated the provisions of any contract?
- Have I discriminated on the basis of a disability?
- Have I violated any policy or procedure contained in the employee handbook?
- Have I discriminated against the employee because he or she filed a worker's compensation claim?
- Have I violated any hospital bylaws, rules, or regulations?
- Have my reasons for discharge been consistent with hospital practice?
- Have I discriminated against the employee because he or she has filed a lawsuit?
- Is there opportunity for the employee to appeal the discharge? (Appeals procedures encourage employees to challenge supervisors' decisions and are often used as a gripe mechanism. Be creative and fair, and you will have few appeals.)
- Have there been any oral promises made between the employer and employee?
- Has the employee been asked to perform an unsafe work assignment?
- Have I violated any local, state, or federal regulations?
- Has the employee been terminated because he or she refused to perform an illegal act?
- Have I discriminated against the employee because he or she has children?
- Have I discriminated on the basis of pregnancy?
- Have I discriminated on the basis of union activity?
- Have I discriminated on the basis of religion?
- Have I discriminated against the employee for reporting violations to regulatory agencies?

IS IT FAIR?

"Is it fair?" is the ultimate question that a supervisor must ask when deciding if termination is proper. Consider the following examples. A former nurse's assistant brought an action against a nursing home on the basis of retaliatory discharge in *Shores v. Senior Manor Nursing Center*.[21] The circuit court dismissed the complaint for failure to state a cause of action. The former employee appealed the decision. The Appellate Court of Illinois held that the former nursing home employee had a cause of action for retaliatory discharge. She alleged that she was discharged in retaliation for reporting to the nursing home administrator that the charge nurse was improperly performing her functions in a way that violated the Nursing Home Care Reform Act. The circuit court was reversed, and the case was remanded for further proceedings.

Pugh v. See's Candies, Inc. is another example.[22] In this case, the Court of Appeals held that the employee demonstrated a prima facie case of wrongful termination in violation of an implied promise that the employer would not act arbitrarily in dealing with the employee.

Remember that the employer's right to terminate an employee is not absolute. It is limited by fundamental principles of public policy and by expressed or implied terms of agreement between the employer and employee. When considering termination, keep the following in mind:

Formulating a standard for substantive fairness in employee dismissal law requires accommodating a number of different interests already afforded legal recognition. The interests of employees to be protected against certain types of unfair and injurious employer action...are at the core of any employee dismissal proposal. Arrayed against these interests are employer and societal interests in effective management of organizations, which require that employees not be shielded from the consequences of their poor performance or misconduct, and that supervisors not be deterred from exercising their managerial responsibilities by the inconvenience of litigating employees' claims."[23]

• • •

Discipline is an art yet to be perfected. Our criminal system advocates that the punishment should fit the crime. From a societal standpoint, we are in continual disagreement as to whether our system of punishment is a deterrent and whether it truly rehabilitates and always fits the crime. The same holds true in organizational discipline and discharge. We must constantly be innovative in our thinking as to how we can develop a more productive and motivated staff. Just as criticism can be constructive, so can disciplinary action.

REFERENCES

1. Office of General Counsel. *The Wrongful Discharge of Employees in the Health Care Industry.* Legal Memorandum No. 10. Chicago: American Hospital Association, 1987, p. 1.
2. *Theodore v. Department of Health and Human Services,* 515 So.2d 454 (La. App. 1987).
3. *Jones v. Hinds General Hospital,* 666 F. Supp. 933 (SD Miss. 1987).
4. *Pardazi v. Cullman Medical Center,* 838 F.2d 1155 (11th Cir. 1988).
5. *Renny v. Port Huron Hospital,* 398 N.W.2d 327 (Mich. 1986).
6. *Duldulao v. St. Mary of Nazareth Hospital Center,* 483 N.E.2d 956 (Ill. App. 1985).
7. *Watson v. Idaho Falls Consolidated Hospitals, Inc.,* 720 P.2d 632 (Idaho 1986).
8. *Hinson v. Cameron,* 742 P.2d 549 (Okla. 1987).
9. *Battaglia v. Sisters of Charity Hospital,* 508 N.Y.S.2d 802 (N.Y. 1986).
10. Weiner, P.I., Bompey, S.H., and Brittain, M.G., Jr. *Wrongful Discharge Claims.* New York: Practicing Law Institute, 1986, p. 98.
11. "Employers Face Upsurge in Suits over Defamation." *National Law Journal,* 4 May 1987, p. 1.

8. *Hinson v. Cameron*, 742 P.2d 549 (Okla. 1987).

9. *Battaglia v. Sisters of Charity Hospital*, 508 N.Y.S.2d 802 (N.Y. 1986).

10. Weiner, P.I., Bompey, S.H., and Brittain, M.G., Jr. *Wrongful Discharge Claims*. New York: Practicing Law Institute, 1986, p. 98.

11. "Employers Face Upsurge in Suits over Defamation." *National Law Journal*, 4 May 1987, p. 1.

12. Ibid.

13. Ibid, p. 31.

14. *Ellins v. Department of Health*, 519 So.2d 850 (La. App. 1988).

15. Gutchess, J.F. *Employment Security in Action*. New York: Pergamon Press, 1985, p. 76.

16. *Eales v. Tanana*, 663 P.2d 958 (Alaska 1983).

17. Hill, D. *Wrongful Discharge and the Derogation of the At-Will Employment Doctrine*. Philadelphia: The Wharton School, Industrial Research Unit, 1987, p. 176.

18. Narramore, C.M. *Discipline*. Grand Rapids, Mich.: Zondervan Publishing House, 1961, p. 13.

19. Ibid.

20. Ibid.

21. *Shores v. Senior Manor Nursing Center*, 518 N.E.2d 471 (Ill. App. 5 Dist. 1988).

22. *Pugh v. See's Candies, Inc.*, 116 Cal. App. 3d 311, 171 Cal. Rptr. 917 (Cal App. 1981).

23. Perritt, H.H. *Employee Dismissal Law and Practice*. New York: Wiley, 1984, p. 354.

Managing a discrimination case

Charles R. McConnell
Vice President for Employee Affairs
The Genesee Hospital
Rochester, New York

Marion Blankopf
Attorney
Nixon, Hargrave, Devans & Doyle
Rochester, New York

FEW MANAGERS need to be reminded that legal actions related to employment are increasing. This increase seems to stem from two general causes, or, perhaps more appropriately, two forces in modern American society. These forces, each adding to the strength of the other, are (1) the population's rising consciousness of individual rights, and (2) legislation regulating terms and conditions of employment to legally ensure equal treatment for all persons.

People—and this applies to everyone, since anyone can become a victim of some kind of discrimination—are becoming more aware of their rights as individuals. These rights may be viewed as common-sense rights, such as the basic right to equality in a humane society, or they may be viewed as legal rights. Either way, the public consciousness has risen dramatically over the past two to three decades, and many people who would once have remained silent will no longer tolerate actions they perceive as

Health Care Superv 1989, 8(1), 1–14
©1989 Aspen Publishers, Inc.

infringing on their rights. For years, many people accepted the treatment they received in their employment, whether they perceived this treatment as right or wrong. More employees now tend to speak up when they believe they have been wronged, and they know resources are available to provide them with advocacy and assistance.

Prior to 1964, the only major areas of employment addressed by legislation were wages and hours and relationships with collective bargaining organizations (unions). Discrimination in employment first came under serious regulatory consideration with passage of the Civil Rights Act of 1964.[1] Several subsequent expansions and refinements of the Civil Rights Act, along with numerous other laws dealing with aspects of employment, have led the United States to the point where most forms of discrimination—whether based on sex, age, marital status, race or color, national origin, religion, qualifying handicap, or other conditions—are illegal. Since many employment practices that were once legal are now against the law, it stands to reason that many perceived acts of discrimination will become formal charges of discrimination.

Any manager at any level in the organization can be drawn into a discrimination case. Once named and involved, he or she will have no choice but to participate. A complaint charging an organization with discrimination will ordinarily name one or more agents—in this case, managers—of the organization who participated in the alleged discriminatory acts. Thus any manager can become involved in a discrimination case at any time. For this reason, it is useful to keep in mind some typical problems and decisions that may arise at various stages of a discrimination case.

THE PRECOMPLAINT STAGE

Since you usually do not know a complaint is going to arrive until it does indeed arrive, you might think of the precomplaint stage as the consideration of everything you should have been doing all along, including those critical elements you may not have thought of at all until after a complaint actually arrived. Therefore, it would be appropriate for this article to outline a complete education in employee relations for consideration. After all, effective employee relations and strict observance of all applicable laws minimize the chances of being named in a discrimination case and make those few cases that may actually come your way easier to defend against. However, such a discussion would take more space than is available in this entire issue. Without going to extremes about the importance of effective employee relations, here are a few of the key elements:

- Keep the lines of employee communication open, taking deliberate steps to be sure that your availability and attitude truly support the open-door policy that your organization probably espouses. Doing so takes conscientious effort. Do not fall victim to the most common unconscious assumption made about communication: We, as individuals and as organizations, behave as though we believe we are all better communicators than we are.

- In dealing with matters of employee conduct such as breaches of policy or violations of work rules, be sure that you use a progressive approach to disciplinary action that deals fairly, justly, and consistently with all affected employees. Use the system thoroughly but humanely, ensuring that the proper documents are created along the way. A document trail is a vital part of pursuing a discrimination case: Regarding disciplinary action, it is often necessary to prove, through progressive warning notices or other documentation, that the employee was given the opportunity to correct the offending behavior.

- In dealing with problems of employee performance, document your efforts at working with those employees who are falling short of meeting the normal requirements of the job. If you ever need to terminate an employee for failure to meet requirements, you may later have to demonstrate that you gave the employee all reasonable opportunities and assistance to attain standard performance.

- Examine every significant personnel action—warning, suspension, demotion, termination, or change of shift or job assignment—for its legal implications before it is implemented. This is best done in concert with others, especially the human resource department and often with your immediate superior as well. Occasionally, if the risk of legal action seems significant, you may wish to temper your proposed action while strengthening the document trail and illustrating that you have extended every reasonable consideration. This is not to say that you should let the fear of legal action make you back away from appropriate personnel action, but as you consider each proposed action on its own merits, you need to do whatever is reasonable and consistent while minimizing your risk.

- If you maintain anecdotal note files on your employees, do so with great care. Anecdotal note files are extremely helpful and often necessary, but they can be extremely troublesome in a discrimination case, so control them carefully. If, for example, you wisely maintain notes indicating the pluses and minuses of an employee's performance for the purpose of a later performance evaluation, get rid of the notes once the evaluation is written. All documents, even your most private and informal of notes, can be called forth in a discrimination case. Therefore, make all your anecdotal notes as objective as possible and keep them completely free from labeling and name calling. Put nothing on paper that you would be ashamed to see made public. Since anecdotal notes cannot hurt you if they do not exist, periodically purge your anecdotal files of outdated or irrelevant material. However, never destroy or discard a document once legal action has been instituted (more will be said about this later).

- Thoroughly observe the documentation requirements of your job. Use the forms that are supposed to be used in the way they are supposed to be used. File items that are supposed to be filed. Sign things you are supposed to sign, and obtain other necessary signatures. Regularly discard forms that can or should be discarded after they have served their purpose. A discrimination case involves paper, often in massive amounts, and added problems and extra expense arise because of documents that are incomplete, undated, unsigned, illegible, or missing.

You can, of course, do everything absolutely correctly and still receive a discrimination complaint. The most effective employee relations program in the world cannot prevent the occasional employee's perception of having been wronged, and it is primarily the perception that leads to the complaint. Still, it is far better to cover all bases at all times. As noted earlier, this is the way to minimize your chances of receiving a complaint, and having all the proper moves documented can only assist you in your defense against charges that might arise.

Regardless of the state of your employee relations program, a complaint can arrive at any time.

Regardless of the state of your employee relations program, a complaint can arrive at any time. As one who receives a complaint will quickly discover, there is no good time to receive a discrimination complaint.

THE COMPLAINT

Involving an attorney

One of the first decisions to be faced when you receive a complaint is whether to handle it entirely in-house or to involve an attorney. Your response depends on the type of complaint you have received. If the complaint launches a formal lawsuit in a state or federal court, then the decision is easy—an attorney is needed. Most discrimination cases, however, begin when an employee files a charge with an administrative agency.

The administrative charge will most likely provide your first formal notification that an employee has decided to pursue a discrimination case against your organization.

An employee can typically file a charge with one of two agencies: The federal Equal Employment Opportunity Commission (EEOC) or the state agency, if any, that handles employment discrimination complaints. In New York, for example, the state agency is the State Division of Human Rights. These agencies are intended to provide a less formal, and in some cases less expensive and quicker, forum than a court for resolving an employment discrimination claim.

Federal and state discrimination laws may impose differing procedural requirements on the employee. Under the New York Human Rights Law, for example, an employee must choose between filing an administrative complaint or directly filing a lawsuit in state supreme court. Once the employee chooses one avenue, he or she is generally barred from resorting to the other alternative. However, Title VII of the federal Civil Rights Act of 1964, which prohibits discrimination on the basis of race, color, religion, sex, and national origin, and the federal Age Discrimination in Employment Act (ADEA) do not contain such an "election-of-remedies" provision.[2,3] Employees must simply file their charges with the EEOC as a prerequisite to filing a federal lawsuit.

Once the employee receives a notice of the right to sue or waits the requisite amount of time, he or she can bring a lawsuit in federal court. When a complainant files a complaint with a state agency, the agency automatically sends the state complaint to the EEOC for filing there, and vice versa.

The fact that the complaint is before an administrative agency rather than a federal judge does not make the charge any less serious. The documents, findings, and testimony given before the state agency or the EEOC may show up later in a federal court action brought under Title VII or the ADEA. Because of these circumstances, your responses to the EEOC or to the state agency must accurately represent your position.

Administrative charges filed with a state agency can also be significant to an employer because the state agency typically has full remedial powers. In New York, for example, the State Division of Human Rights can order that reinstatement, back pay for lost wages, and compensatory and other damages be given to any claimant who obtains a favorable ruling after a hearing before an administrative law judge. This can be as costly as any remedy ordered under Title VII or the ADEA.

In deciding whether to handle an administrative charge internally, consider whether the complainant has an attorney. If the complainant does have an attorney, it is an indication that he or she is serious about diligently pursuing the charge, so at least one attorney may believe the employee has a fair chance to win some relief. In that situation, your organization should not proceed without an attorney.

Another important consideration is whether your organization has prior experience in handling similar charges. If you are part of a large organization, you and some of your colleagues may well have been through these procedures several times previously, either with or without an attorney. Your human resource department may be fully able to efficiently present your organization's position regarding the particular personnel action without the assistance or expense of an attorney.

On the other hand, if the charge is particularly complex or appears to involve some legal arguments, it would probably be better not to handle the complaint in-house. Whatever the choice, it is always useful to consider whether you would feel comfortable having your notes, memos, and other work products appear in court.

The initial investigation

Along with determining whether to involve an attorney, your organization, usually through the human resource department, should conduct a preliminary investigation of the charge in order to obtain a sense of the issues involved. In many situations, human resources may already be familiar with the personnel action taken or may have participated in recommending the action. In those instances, it may not be necessary to do much more than review some files and update a few facts.

If you are not fully familiar with the particular instance giving rise to the complaint, a good preliminary investigation would include separately interviewing each of the involved parties (not including the complaining parties, of course) and reviewing all pertinent personnel files and other documentation. As a guideline, do not avoid digging into or recognizing certain genuine problems involved in the situation. We all have an instinct to justify our actions and place them in the most favorable light, especially when we know, or at least firmly believe, that the employee in question was not discriminated against in any manner, whether intentional or otherwise. Yet one of the most helpful things human resources can do for its organization and attorneys is to explain at the very beginning of a case the problems and concerns that are visible. This will save both time and legal fees and help everyone make informed judgments regarding case strategy.

The internal case coordinator

Once an attorney is engaged, if necessary, and an investigation has begun, the next step is to identify one specific person in the organization to be the contact with the attorney. This will ensure that all legitimate concerns are communicated to the attorney quickly and efficiently and that the attorney will know with whom he or she should work to communicate procedural developments and other updates, discuss case strategy, and arrange employee interviews.

Depending on the size and structure of the organization, the internal coordinator for a discrimination case may be a human resource professional, an administrator, or perhaps a corporate legal counsel. A larger organization that has in-house legal counsel will ordinarily use that person as the contact who relates directly with the attorney engaged to conduct the defense. Rarely will in-house counsel serve as the attorney directly conducting the defense; corporate counsels tend to be legal generalists, and defenses in discrimination cases are usually conducted by attorneys who specialize in labor law.

In a small institution, one without a comprehensive human resource department, the case coordinator will often be the administrator or assistant administrator. In most instances, the case coordinator will be a human resource professional. Usually this person will be the chief human resource officer, although in a very large institution the coordinator may be a second-level human resource person who specializes in such matters.

Throughout the case, the case coordinator will work with the organization's attorney to plan strategy. The coordinator can generally count on active involvement in nearly all aspects of the case; the coordinator is, to the attorney, the client representative who provides the common thread of knowledge and participation that runs through the entire case from start to finish.

The case coordinator plays an extremely important role in ensuring that top management is regularly advised of what is going on at all times.

The case coordinator plays an extremely important role in ensuring that top management is regularly advised of what is going on at all times. Top management may well have valid input to offer regarding case strategy. Also, top management may have numerous questions borne of frustration with legal processes, such as the following: "Why is this costing so much? What is the total bill going to be?"; "More delays? How long is this going to last?"; "Why weren't you people able to avoid this in the first place?"; "How can they keep making all these new demands? Isn't there some way to legally shorten the process?" The case coordinator transmits those questions and concerns to the institution's attorney.

The coordinator's task is made all the more difficult and thankless in those organizations where there may be a tendency to shoot the messenger—that is, to lay the blame on the bearer of bad news. Nevertheless, this dimension of the coordinator's role is critical in that top management—especially those who approve the expenses and pay the bills—must support the manner in which the case is being pursued. As unpleasant as doing so may seem at times, the coordinator must do everything possible to keep top management current on case matters and supportive of case strategies. Bearing the bad news may be difficult, but incremental bad news is not nearly as potentially damaging to the messenger as months of silence followed by a large, costly surprise.

The coordinator may also bear considerable responsibility for ensuring the proper timing of a number of activities. Document production deadlines must be met, and meeting them often involves location, retrieval, and copying of large amounts of paper in a very short time. Also, since the scheduling of most case activities necessarily depends on the schedules of attorneys, the court calendars, or the availability of key parties, it is up to the coordinator to ensure that schedule accommodations by the organization's personnel are made whenever possible.

The coordinator will have to marshal internal resources to meet various demands and deadlines and do so in the most cost-effective manner possible. For example, the organization may be called on to produce copies of large numbers of records when there seem to be too few hands and too little time available, but turning these records over to the organization's attorney for copying can add a significant amount of expense to an already escalating bill. The coordinator will frequently find it necessary to bal-

ance matters of cost against disruptions in the organization's routines.

ONGOING ISSUES

Deciding whether to settle

Another decision is whether to consider settling the case. This decision is not an easy one, nor can the decision made in one case be generalized to other cases. The decision is ultimately in your organization's hands, but the attorney must ensure that the organization has the right information about the factors that should be considered.

When many lawsuits are first filed, many employers' initial reaction is that the suits are frivolous and there is no way they will consider paying a penny to a person who has not been discriminated against or treated unfairly in any manner. This is a valid position for your organization to maintain, but you need to know what your organization is getting into before resolving to avoid settlement at all costs.

Many readers may not need to be reminded that litigation is extremely costly. Defending a federal lawsuit involving a single plaintiff typically costs $50,000 to $150,000; an administrative law judge hearing may cost $30,000 to $50,000. The more complex the issues and the greater the number of plaintiffs, the more money will be involved. It is necessary to consider whether top management would prefer to pay legal fees to contest the case with no guarantee of a positive outcome or to pay a similar amount of money in settlement and be rid of the case.

Employers should also consider the problems of legal proof involved in a particular case. Although the employer may be wholly innocent of any unlawful act, it is one thing to know that and another to be able to prove it in court. Some situations are of more concern than others. For example, there may be no documentation of an employee's known history of poor performance or unsuitable behavior, or the decision in question may be completely subjective. Perhaps the employee has been passed over for promotion because his or her supervisor simply felt that another employee was a better choice or had greater leadership potential.

Decision criteria are hard to categorize and quantify, and if the employee can get over the first hurdle of having his or her complaint dismissed on its face, then the employer may be hard pressed to set forth a defensible justification for its actions. Also, if the case is going to be tried before a jury, the employer should consider that a jury will sometimes ignore the fine points of legal reasoning out of sympathy for a plaintiff employee who is out of a job or having problems at work.

Your organization must also decide whether publicity from the case is likely to be a major concern. Publicity can work against you in unexpected ways. There is always the potential that settling one lawsuit can encourage other employees to bring lawsuits of their own, particularly if other disgruntled employees are following the course of the case. Employees talk with each other, and employees frequently encourage each other to pursue their grievances. When an employee is perceived as having gained a victory, either by way of an actual court decision or a settlement, you can often expect to see charges filed by others who regard themselves as having legitimate grievances. You can almost hear the suppos-

edly "victorious" employee saying to another, "I won and got my settlement, and there's no reason you can't do the same. Now, I know this lawyer. . . ."

Publicity about a case is also a potential problem with regard to personnel actions such as layoffs that affected other employees and that may well be repeated in the future.

The timing of a settlement offer is also a factor to consider. Early settlement could save litigation costs and could be factually and publicly justified by the organization's unwillingness to spend its resources litigating frivolous cases. In the early stage, the plaintiff who has invested little time and put little money into attorneys' fees may be willing to go away for a small amount.

Another potentially good time for settlement is after the making of a summary judgment motion to dismiss the case, but before the trial itself. If the court dismisses part of the case or indicates that the claims must go to trial but are nonetheless not very strong, then the plaintiff may be more willing to accept a smaller settlement than he or she would have if all original claims remain intact.

Retaliation charges

As the case progresses, there are some pitfalls that your organization should try to avoid. Many discrimination charges include, or have added along the way, retaliation charges. In a retaliation charge, the employee alleges not only that the employer discriminated, but also that after the objection was made or the charge filed, the employer took adverse action because of the employee's opposition. This is a problem particularly when the subject of the complaint was not terminated, and is still working in the organization.

To minimize the chance of retaliation charges, only those with a need to know should be made aware of the filing of the original charge. If a supervisor does not know that an employee has filed a charge or otherwise opposed alleged discrimination, then that supervisor cannot be said to have retaliated against the employee. If the employee's supervisor is involved in the case or already knows about the case, then that supervisor should be made aware of the impropriety of taking any adverse action against the employee because of the charge. Further disciplinary action involving the employee should be reviewed with your attorney, if at all possible, before it is finalized.

Dealing with discovery

Document creation and destruction

Another area requiring careful thought is that of further document creation. It is possible that every document ever created concerning the employee will have to be turned over to the plaintiff's attorney. The same guideline that applied before the complaint entered applies now: Do not create any document that you would not want to see as evidence in a public trial of the case. Except for the routine documents needed to conduct day-to-day business, documents should be reviewed by the organization's attorneys before they are finalized. Information gathered at the direction of your attorneys should always be identified as such in writing. Such writings can often be protected from discov-

ery by the attorney–client privilege or another privilege.

The rules about document management during a case differ in one important aspect from the precomplaint stage: Once the complaint is received, documents should not be destroyed, for several reasons. First, an employer may be sanctioned if documents are destroyed after the plaintiff requests them during discovery. Second, it creates unfavorable impressions. Even if the documents contained harmless material, the plaintiff can use the fact that you destroyed documents after the case began to make it seem as if your organization was covering up damaging material.

Giving depositions

The other major aspect of discovery that every employer can expect to go through is the deposition, the interview of involved supervisors and other agents of the organization. For court cases, depositions typically make place in attorneys' offices. A witness is sworn and gives testimony while a court reporter prepares a transcript of the testimony. For administrative charges, the state agency or EEOC will either interview people at the workplace or call them to the agency's offices for a conference with the plaintiff present.

In conjunction with the attorney, human resource personnel should expect to spend a substantial amount of time preparing supervisors for the specific questions that will probably be asked of them. This is another time to be sure not to avoid the hard questions.

If you are subject to deposition, in addition to reviewing specific information that you might be asked about, you will also be briefed on how to conduct yourself during the deposition. Reinforced if possible with some independent study (for example, there are useful videotaped lessons available that help you prepare for a deposition), preparation should include the following:

- Listen carefully to each question. Be sure you understand the question before you attempt to respond. If you do not understand the question, or if the question is confusing, seems tricky, or seems potentially misleading, ask for clarification.
- Do not volunteer information. Answer only the specific question you have been asked, and avoid the temptation to offer seemingly related information that the question has brought to mind.
- Be wary of compound questions, those that seem to be dealing with two or more items of information within the context of a single question. Ask for clarification, or ask to have such questions broken down into simpler questions so that you can deal with the parts individually.
- Be wary of lengthy and seemingly complex questions that call for a simple yes or no response. Frequently these are not questions but statements—or even accusations—that call for your agreement or disagreement. As with questions you do not understand, ask for clarification.
- Do not guess at answers. You need not believe that you must have an answer for every question you are asked. If you do not know the answer, say so. Often the most accurate and therefore the best answer you can give to many questions, especially those concerning

events that may have happened years in the past, is "I don't know" or "I don't recall."

- Take as much time as you need to thoughtfully consider each question. Do not be intimidated by the silence following a question or by the occasional proddings, both verbal and nonverbal, that might occur. You are entitled to the time you require to give each question thoughtful consideration, and you need not worry about being labeled slow, because your pauses will not be reflected in the record.
- Do not "confess." Even if you believe that some of your past behavior or involvement might not have been fully appropriate, offer no conjecture on such matters and give no opinions concerning what you now believe you would or could have done differently. Chances are that plaintiff's counsel is hard at work attempting to attach guilt to your behavior, and you do not need to assist in the process.
- Do not be flippant or sarcastic in your responses, and do not try to be funny. If you do so, your own words will not serve you well in the eyes of the uninvolved third parties (judges and jurors) who must eventually consider your testimony.

Disruption of business

As the case continues, those who are involved on the organization's behalf, primarily the case coordinator and any other agents of the organization who have been named in the charges, will find themselves trying to

> *Although there may be prolonged periods during which circumstances seem to permit business as usual, there can also be concentrated periods of intense demands that are highly disruptive.*

conduct business as usual with minimum possible disruption by the case. Although there may be prolonged periods during which circumstances seem to permit business as usual, there can also be concentrated periods of intense demands that are highly disruptive. A number of such disruptive periods can center around depositions.

The deposition process

Depositions require that certain employees—primarily the case coordinator, named defendants, and other employees who have been called to give testimony—be off the job for blocks of time that can range from a few hours to a number of days. Equal to and often greater than the amount of time employees must spend in deposition is the amount of time they must spend working with the institution's attorney to prepare to be deposed.

It is also common for depositions to lead to more depositions. For example, mention in a deposition of certain documents that have not yet been examined may lead to an additional document request. These documents, once produced, can raise more questions that lengthen the deposition process. It is largely in the areas of document production and deposition that the discovery process seems at times to feed on itself. The process

may frequently appear as a protracted fishing expedition on the part of plaintiff's legal counsel in which more and more information is unearthed in the hope that something of substance will be revealed. Protracted discovery may often also seem to be a deliberate tactic of plaintiff's counsel applied to wear down the opposition. Surely many defendant organizations have been nudged into premature settlement when faced with costly, frustrating, time-consuming, confusing, and stressful discovery.

Changes in working relationships

As the case continues, you may also have to develop a sensitivity to new kinds of problems that may arise. If you have been charged with discrimination by an employee who remains working in the organization, you will find that working relationships have been altered in a number of ways. You may find yourself functioning with a certain amount of understandable resentment for what this employee is putting you through, and it may be difficult to keep this resentment completely out of your dealings with the employee. The employee may behave as though he or she has gained some measure of power—or at least perceived power—over you, in that you are now susceptible to charges of retaliation.

In the majority of cases where the employee remains in the work group, at some point during pursuit of the case you can expect a less-than-excellent performance evaluation, criticism of work output, reprimand, warning, or just about any action the individual does not like to be described as retaliation for having filed a discrimination charge. As long as the threat of charges of retaliation or continuing discrimination is present, there will be a certain amount of related tension in working relationships.

It is also necessary to be extra sensitive to problems that might arise with employees other than those whose charges are the subject of the case. When you are being sued by someone, other employees who have grievances of their own are invariably watching. Many an organization that has settled a case at a supposed nuisance-value level to avoid an expensive, lengthy legal battle has subsequently discovered that the perception of an employee victory has spawned legal actions by other employees.

Management morale

As the case continues, if it happens to be a legal action that drags on for several years (a common circumstance), it is important to monitor the morale of those caught up in the process. Supportive higher management is important, as is a supportive case coordinator who does everything possible to minimize the burden on individual managers who have been charged. As the months drag on, weariness and discouragement can gradually take hold, especially in those who may be subject to extended deposition demands, who may have to continue working in tension-laden relationships with an employee–plaintiff, and who may even know (or at least guess correctly) that they are the subjects of derisive commentary spread by the plaintiff and the plaintiff's allies. Top management should appreciate the fact that the manager working under such circumstances is in effect carrying a double load, performing a regular managerial job while coping with the considerable pressures of the case.

Communications

It is recommended that the organization maintain a complete chronological file of the case, adding to this file as the case progresses. In addition to being good business, this progress file is important for at least two other reasons. First, as the months turn into years and the number of documents flowing back and forth grows, it becomes increasingly necessary to refer to specific documents generated earlier in the process. Since the paper generated in the course of one protracted case could conceivably fill several file drawers, it is necessary to know where to find any particular document without an extended file search. Second, when case activity has swelled to include multiple and sometimes overlapping document requests, supplemental and expanded document requests, and requests to update previous document production, it is not uncommon to find that later requests call for duplicates of documents that have already been requested and produced. A plaintiff's attorney, who must cope with as much paper as your organization and your attorney, will sometimes misplace or forget an already produced document and ask for it again. Your organization's accessible chronological case file will help keep duplicate requests to a minimum and save on the effort required to produce additional documents.

All internal and external communications concerning an ongoing case should be carefully monitored. If you are one of the agents of the organization charged with discrimination, your role in case communication is simply stated: Speak with no one within the organization about aspects of the case except for your attorney, the case coordinator, and top management as necessary. Discussions concerning the case should be on a strict need-to-know basis, and the aforementioned are the only ones who fit the strict need-to-know criteria. Your simple, polite response to friends and colleagues who ask about the case should be that, according to the attorneys, you can talk about an active case with no one except those involved in managing the case. The need-to-know rule should be strictly applied to all intraorganizational case communication.

Inquiries from outside the organization—from the print or broadcast media, for example—should all be referred to a common point, usually the case coordinator or the organization's public relations director. In turn, the organization's spokesperson should respond to news media requests only with clear, concise statements that meet with the advance approval of legal counsel and top management.

As long as case communication with top management and the organization's attorney is thorough and complete, the less said about the case within the work environment, the better off all involved parties will be. Questions, opinions, and general discussion about the case by anyone in the work environment, whether defendant, plaintiff, or others, will serve only to add to the tensions in the environment. The less said, the better the chance of maintaining a more nearly normal work environment.

TIME FACTORS

Discrimination cases, administrative charges as well as lawsuits, ordinarily seem to last longer than they ought to last. Even a relatively simple administrative charge filed with the State Division of Human Rights can drag on for months. For the most part, the administrative agencies have a backlog of cases to be investigated, and this process simply takes time. The EEOC has its own significant backlog in most of its regional offices. After waiting the mandated time and, if applicable, requesting a notice of right to sue, an individual has the right to bring his or her own lawsuit. It is in this manner that federal discrimination cases come into being; they are first filed as administrative complaints but are then filed as lawsuits after time has passed without EEOC resolution. Thus an EEOC complaint that would seem to have started with the original filing of the administrative charge may actually start all over again several months after the original filing.

Although administrative charges can drag on for many months, it is not unusual for lawsuits to last for years. Scheduled dates and deadlines, difficult enough to establish because of the varied parties and resources concerned, frequently get postponed and rearranged because of congested court calendars, attorneys' schedules, and demands on the client organization. As disagreements and other difficulties arise in pursuit of the case, various court motions that might not have been anticipated disrupt schedules further still. Every disruption means additional delay, and every added step means a prolonging of the tensions and uncertainties created by the still-unresolved charges and additional expense for the organization.

As the case wears on, it is necessary to periodically review the organization's position concerning potential settlement. Case strategy should be continually reassessed in light of continuing legal expenses, new information that is revealed or that develops as the case progresses, and employee relations and public relations effects of the case on the organization. Even though a settlement or a loss might leave the organization open to further difficulties, a hard-won victory can have negative public relations impact as well as being financially devastating.

•   •   •

All discrimination cases, even those that drag on for years, are eventually settled in one fashion or another. It is important to remember this when you are caught up in a case that seems to show no sign of ever approaching resolution. Along the path toward resolution, be aware that what you are learning can help you better cope with—or better still, avoid—the next discrimination case that demands your involvement.

REFERENCES

1. Title VII of the Civil Rights Act of 1964, as amended, 42 U.S.C. §2000E *et seq.* (1989).
2. Ibid.
3. Age Discrimination in Employment Act of 1967, as amended, 29 U.S.C. §621 *et seq.* (1989).

Part III
AIDS, Drugs, and Employee Rights

The AIDS epidemic: Implications for health care employers

Karen H. Henry
Managing Partner
Labor and Employment Law
  Department
Weissburg and Aronson, Inc.
San Francisco, California

IN THE JUNE 5, 1981, issue of *Morbidity and Mortality Weekly Report*, it was reported that five young men, all homosexuals, had been treated in Los Angeles for a rare infection known as pneumocystis carinii pneumonia (PCP).[1] All five individuals had evidence of other infections and a defective immune system. At the same time, on the other side of the continent in New York City, physicians diagnosed Kaposi's sarcoma in 20 gay men, ranging in age from 26 to 51. The discovery of Kaposi's sarcoma, a malignancy endemic to Africa but uncommon in the United States, was cause for concern.[2] Thus, in mid-1981, the beginning of the epidemic now known as Acquired Immune Deficiency Syndrome (AIDS) was first seen.

Audrey L. Covner, a former associate with Weissburg and Aronson, Inc., participated in the preparation of this article.

Health Care Superv, 1987, 6(1), 1–12
© 1987 Aspen Publishers, Inc.

In the few short years since these initial discoveries, AIDS has sparked incredible fear in the public. The general population fears the possibility of contracting the disease. Those who have AIDS fear ostracism, loss of employment, and imminent death.

Caught in the middle are health care employers. As health care providers, they must ensure the highest quality of care, both physically and emotionally, for patients who have AIDS. As employers, they must handle issues that arise due to employees who have AIDS. Thus, unlike other employers, health care employers must have an awareness and understanding of the issues facing the patient who has AIDS, the employee who has AIDS, and the employee who, while free of the disease, may be reluctant to care for patients with AIDS or to work with other employees who have the disease. To assist health care supervisors in dealing with these various issues, this article gives an overview of the legal issues presented and provides brief answers to commonly asked questions.

LEGAL IMPLICATIONS

While many of the legal issues surrounding AIDS still require clarification, some guidance is now being provided to employers by the courts, legislatures, and administrative agencies. In general, these rulings and interpretations are in conformance with existing laws and regulations affecting health care employers.

The employee who has AIDS

A variety of legal implications are presented by employment decisions affecting employees with AIDS and the following discussion is limited to identifying the most common issues that may arise.

Handicap discrimination laws

State and federal laws banning discrimination against the handicapped will affect the hiring and continued employment of individuals with AIDS. Given the potentially expansive definition of "handicap," the term could be construed as including AIDS, and some jurisdictions have adopted such an interpretation. The significance of handicap status is that persons with AIDS who are otherwise qualified must be afforded all protections and opportunities provided by statute that would include, for purposes of federal law, the obligation to provide reasonable accommodation.

Section 503 of the federal Rehabilitation Act requires affirmative action by government contractors, while under Section 504, employers receiving federal financial assistance are prohibited from discriminating against the handicapped and must provide reasonable accommodation to such individuals.[3] Under the government view of what constitutes federal financial assistance, which includes Medicare, Section 504 would cover the vast majority of the nation's health care employers. The specific issue of whether the handicap protections in Section 504 extend to AIDS, however, has been discussed on two occasions with two conflicting results.

In June 1986, the U.S. Department of Justice (DOJ) issued a memorandum containing its interpretation of the status of AIDS under federal handicap statutes.[4] Essentially, in the DOJ's opinion, the *disabling effects* of AIDS constitute a handicap, but the *ability to spread* the disease does not. In practical terms, the DOJ determined that an employer cannot take adverse action against individuals with AIDS simply because they

---

The Department of Justice determined that an employer cannot take adverse action against individuals with AIDS simply because they have the disease, but the employer can take such action due to a fear, whether reasonable or not, that AIDS can be transmitted.

---

have the disease, but the employer can take such action due to a fear, whether reasonable or not, that AIDS can be transmitted. The DOJ's opinion was summarily dismissed, however, by the first federal court addressing the question of AIDS as a handicap.[5]

In *Tomas v. Atascadero Unified School District*, the plaintiff, a child with AIDS, was barred from his kindergarten classroom after he bit a classmate. The child's parents sought

an injunction entitling him to return to school and in granting their request, the court ruled that AIDS does fall within the federal definition of a handicap. As a result, the school district was required to reasonably accommodate the plaintiff's disability by allowing him to return to school.

States with statutes prohibiting handicap discrimination also have evaluated whether their own laws encompass AIDS. As a result, 20 states and the District of Columbia now recognize AIDS as a handicap for the purpose of their state laws. These states are California, Colorado, Connecticut, Florida, Illinois, Maine, Massachusetts, Michigan, Minnesota, Missouri, New Jersey, New Mexico, New York, Oregon, Pennsylvania, Rhode Island, Texas, Washington, West Virginia, and Wisconsin.

A case recently decided by the U.S. Supreme Court, however, may significantly affect the debate as to whether AIDS is a handicap under both federal and state laws.[6] In *School Board of Nassau County, Florida v. Arlene*, the issue was whether tuberculosis qualified as a handicap under federal discrimination law. A lower court ruling held that tuberculosis is a protected handicap, and that the Florida school district was found to have violated the provisions of Section 504 when it fired an elementary school teacher suffering from the disease. In affirming the lower court's decision, the U.S. Supreme Court stated that employer decisions as to whether employees with contagious diseases are qualified for a particular job should be based upon the following four factors, in light of reasonable medical evidence:

1. the nature of the risk of transmitting the disease;
2. the duration of the risk;
3. the severity of the risk; and
4. the probability the disease will be transmitted and will cause varying degrees of harm.

While the Court's finding in *Arlene* may be extended to other contagious diseases such as AIDS, the Court expressly noted that "whether a *carrier* of a contagious disease such as AIDS could be considered to have a physical impairment, or whether such a person could be considered, solely on the basis of contagiousness, a handicapped person"[7] is left unresolved. What the Court appears to be saying, therefore, is that persons physically impaired by a contagious disease must be reasonably accommodated if medical evidence indicates that they are qualified to perform the job without an unacceptable degree of risk to themselves or to others. Still unresolved, however, is the question of whether employees are protected when they have a contagious disease without any physical impairment.

Laws specifically addressing AIDS

In addition to laws prohibiting discrimination on the basis of handicap, employers must be alert to any state or local laws that specifically address AIDS. For example, while no state has enacted an antidiscrimination law on AIDS, some local governments have done so. Both San Francisco[8] and Los Angeles[9] have passed ordinances that flatly prohibit employment discrimination against individuals who have, or are perceived as having, AIDS, and an employer violating these ordinances is subject to criminal and civil penalties.

State and local governments also may enact other laws or ordinances regulating a variety of AIDS-related issues. For example, in both Wisconsin[10] and California,[11] state statutes prohibit the use of an AIDS blood test to determine insurability and employability. Furthermore, the California Health and Safety Code provides that the results of an AIDS blood test cannot be divulged to a third party without the patient's voluntary written authorization.[12]

Sexual preference discrimination

Several local governments have enacted statutes that prohibit discrimination against an individual on the basis of sexual preference (e.g., San Francisco Police Code Chapter 8, Article 33). These laws could serve as the basis for discrimination lawsuits, particularly because a neutral employer policy governing AIDS-related conduct could have a disproportionate impact on the gay employees of an employer's work force. For example, if a gay individual with AIDS is denied a position or suffers some other adverse employment consequences, a lawsuit may conceivably be brought alleging sexual preference discrimination.

Hospital licensing regulations

Health care providers are regulated by a variety of state and local licensing laws, and specific requirements for employees working in the facility may be included. In most states, the regulations require that employees with direct patient contact be free from infectious diseases (e.g., Cal. Admin. Code t. 22, § 70723(a)). To comply with these rules, it is common practice throughout the country to routinely test health care employees for tuberculosis, an infectious disease that is often asymptomatic.

Similar to tuberculosis, AIDS is an infectious virus that individuals may carry and even pass to others without knowing that they have the disease. Whether AIDS is an "infectious disease" for purposes of hospital licensure statutes remains unclear, but a number of considerations may affect the ultimate conclusion. First, according to present medical knowledge, AIDS cannot be easily transmitted and a person with AIDS would not present a significant risk to patients if certain guidelines and precautions are observed. Second, many state statutes specify the circumstances under which an individual can be tested for the AIDS antibody, including prohibitions upon releasing the results to a third party. These state statutes may take precedence over administrative interpretations finding that AIDS is an infectious disease for the purpose of state licensing laws. Third, a majority of states have statutes protecting the confidentiality of medical information and the hospi-

tal, as the employer, might be barred from requiring the test or obtaining the test results under such laws. Finally, a hospital's obligations under licensing laws may be affected by future developments, such as medical research regarding the transmissibility of the disease and the possibility of new AIDS legislation.

Union contracts

Many union contracts currently have antidiscrimination clauses, and an express prohibition against discrimination on the basis of sexual preference may be included. As discussed previously, such a clause could be used as a springboard for an AIDS discrimination claim. Moreover, provisions that are neutral on their face can be discriminatory if they are applied in a nonneutral fashion, or if they have disproportionate impact on certain employee groups. This means, for example, that contract provisions regulating an employee's entitlement to a disability leave of absence must be applied in a nondiscriminatory fashion to all disability leave requests, including requests from employees with AIDS. And finally, the termination of employees with AIDS generally would be subject to the contract's grievance and arbitration procedures and to any just-cause standard established for employee terminations.

Wrongful discharge liability

Although employment in the absence of a written agreement traditionally has been considered "at will," many states have developed new legal theories and causes of action that have carved out exceptions to this doctrine. The three most widely recognized exceptions restricting an employer's right to terminate an employee at will are:

1. The employee's termination violates a statute or overriding public policy.
2. The termination violates the covenant of good faith and fair dealing implied into the contract of employment.
3. The termination violates an implied-in-fact or implied-in-law employment contract that requires cause for terminations.[13]

While not all states recognize all of the above exceptions to "at will" employment, and while there are no known wrongful discharge cases arising from the termination of an employee with AIDS, a definite risk exists that such a termination could trigger a wrongful termination lawsuit. For example, an employer's termination of an employee due to a fear of AIDS may support a cause of action for violating the implied covenant of good faith and fair dealing. Without medical evidence to support the fear of the transmission of the disease, the employee may be able to show that his or her termination was done in bad faith. In jurisdictions prohibiting discrimination on the basis of AIDS or in states where AIDS is held to be a protected handicap, a termination may also support a public policy wrongful termination claim.

Employees treating AIDS patients

A somewhat different set of legal issues exists with respect to employees who care for AIDS patients. These issues, in turn, are affected by the standard of care owed to patients and the institution's obligation to exercise due care to avoid transmission of the virus to employees.

Standards of care owed to the patient

An AIDS patient should be afforded the same excellence of care provided to other patients within the facility. Indeed, other than following the precautionary measures advocated by the Centers for Disease Control (CDC) for preventing the spread of the disease, AIDS patients should be treated the same as any other patient. Moreover, if AIDS is considered to be a handicap, federal handicap law would prohibit the denial of health care treatment, or the provision of substandard treatment, to patient beneficiaries because of their status as an AIDS patient.

Other than following the precautionary measures advocated by the Centers for Disease Control (CDC) for preventing the spread of the disease, AIDS patients should be treated the same as any other patient.

Employee precautions

Current scientific knowledge indicates that the AIDS virus is transmitted through sexual intercourse, blood transfusions, or the exchange of blood or other bodily fluids such as that resulting from the use of a needle previously used by a carrier of the virus. At this time, there is no evidence that it can be passed through casual contact.

On the basis of this knowledge, the CDC has published guidelines outlining the appropriate precautionary measures that should be taken by employees treating AIDS patients.[14] Key points of these guidelines are that:

- AIDS is spread much like Hepatitis B. Therefore, the precautionary measures used to prevent the spread of Hepatitis B should be sufficient to prevent the transmission of AIDS.
- Employment restrictions on employees who have AIDS generally are unnecessary; however, further precautionary measures may be necessary for employees who participate in invasive procedures.
- General screening of employees for the AIDS virus is inadvisable.

If an employer utilizes the full CDC guidelines and initiates and monitors the use of appropriate precautionary measures, the risk of employees contracting the disease or transmitting it to other employees or patients appears to be minimal.

Workers' compensation liability

Health care employees who develop AIDS may be entitled to workers' compensation benefits even if they cannot point to a particular instance of exposure to the virus. In many states, when a health care employee catches a communicable disease and a potential exists that the disease was acquired on the job, it may be presumed to be a job-related injury. In part, this result occurs because state workers' compensation boards as well as the reviewing courts generally apply a liberal construction in favor of awarding benefits to employees.

COMMON QUESTIONS

The following are some common questions asked by health care supervisors.

What can be done if an employee refuses to treat an AIDS patient?

First and foremost, employees should be educated, individually and collectively, about the AIDS virus and how it is transmitted, to dispel fears or myths regarding the disease. This action should be taken even before an employee refuses to treat AIDS patients so that the issue may hopefully be averted. However, if education is insufficient to dispel an employee's concerns, the refusal to treat an AIDS patient should be handled in the same way as a refusal to treat any other patient. Employees should be counseled about their behavior, and if it reoccurs, appropriate disciplinary action should be taken.

In refusing to treat an AIDS patient, an employee may point to an employer's common law obligation to provide a safe working environment, or to state and federal occupational health and safety laws mandating a safe working environment. If disciplinary or other adverse action is taken subsequently, the employee may contend that such employer action constitutes unlawful retaliation for the employee's insistence on these rights. If a health care provider can establish that it is in full compliance with the appropriate CDC precautions, it may be possible to defend against any such employee's argument because current medical evidence views the CDC guidelines as the mechanism for establishing a safe environment.

Finally, the actions of employees who refuse to care for AIDS patients may constitute protected "concerted activity." Under the National Labor Relations Act (NLRA) covering private employers (and perhaps under similar state legislation governing public employer labor relations), a nonsupervisory employee has the right to "engage in concerted activities for the purpose of collective bargaining or other mutal aid or protection."[15] This right is offered both to employees covered by a union contract and to those who act collectively without union representation. Because a collective work stoppage by employees due to AIDS-related working conditions concerns could fall within the NLRA's definition of a protected concerted activity, an employer may be prohibited from terminating or otherwise discriminating or retaliating against employees on the basis of this activity. If employees only refuse to care for AIDS patients and such functions are only part of their job, however, then this selective refusal may not be protected. In any event, an employer would retain the right to temporarily or permanently replace the refusing employees.

Should employees be required to wear protective clothing, such as gloves, mask, and gown, when treating AIDS patients? What if the employee insists on protective wear?

As a general rule, employees should not be required to wear special protective gear unless such measures are appropriate under the CDC guidelines. For example, when blood or waste products are handled, the procedure recommended by the CDC does require the use of protective gloves. An employer's insistence on protective paraphernalia when it is not necessary may inhibit an employee's ability to provide proper patient care and may add to the anxiety of a patient who is already and understandably anxious about having a life-threatening disease.

Conversely, however, if employees insist on wearing protective gear in the belief that the treatment of AIDS patients without such protection would endanger their own life, then it may be questionable whether the employee can be prohibited from doing so. In some states, such as California, an employer is prohibited by statute from discriminating against an employee who complains about a potential health and safety hazard.[16] In

1984, on the basis of this statute, several nurses assigned to treat AIDS patients filed a complaint with the California Labor Commissioner contending they were unlawfully transferred from their positions because they insisted on wearing masks and other protective gear against the wishes of their hospital employer.[17] Although the hearing officer decided that the nurses' transfer was not discriminatory, he did indicate that the nurses' concern was "understandable" in view of the differing opinions in the medical community and that, as a result, their insistence on wearing the gear was protected under California labor laws. Although the subsequently-issued CDC guidelines and the current state of medical knowledge would argue against the hearing officer's conclusion, his viewpoint may have been reinforced by the recent discovery of three health care workers who contracted the AIDS virus from a single mucous membrane or broken skin exposure to blood products. In any event, employers should verify their own state law before taking action against an employee who insists on additional precautionary measures.

Should all employees having direct patient contact be tested for the AIDS virus?

The CDC guidelines recommend against mandatory testing of employees for the AIDS virus. To do so may have a variety of serious consequences. For example, as mentioned

As a general rule, employees should not be tested mandatorily for the AIDS virus. To do so may have a variety of serious consequences.

previously, several states have laws that expressly prohibit testing employees for the AIDS virus and/or using test results to make employment decisions and several prohibit the release of test results. Furthermore, many states have statutes governing the confidentiality of medical information. These statutes generally provide that medical information cannot be released without the authorization of the patient except for very limited circumstances. Again, even if the employee were required to submit to the test, the employer would be prohibited by these statutes from obtaining the results of the test.

If a health care provider develops AIDS-related policies covering its employees, must the policies be discussed, prior to implementation, with labor organizations representing the employees?

Under the terms of the National Labor Relations Act, an employer has an obligation to discuss with a labor organization representing its employees those subjects that affect the employees' "terms and conditions of employment."[18] While the list of subjects affected by the mandatory obligation is quite expansive, it is quite likely that the employer would have a bargaining obligation towards a union if an AIDS policy governing employment was developed. As with any other mandatory subject for bargaining, unilateral implementation during the term of a contract can occur only if an impasse is reached after the employer has met its bargaining obligation and the policy does not conflict with the provisions of the existing collective bargaining agreement.

If an employee sustains a stick from a needle used on a patient who has AIDS, can the employee be forced to submit to an AIDS antibody test?

As discussed above, in some states an employer cannot force an employee to submit to an AIDS antibody test, and even if the employee takes the test voluntarily, the employer may be precluded from gaining access to the results. However, if the employee subsequently develops the disease and submits a claims for workers' compensation benefits, the employee's medical records may be open to the employer, including the results of any AIDS antibody test. By requesting workers' compensation benefits, the employee arguably places his or her disease "at issue," allowing employer access to relevant medical information.

Should employees with AIDS have their duties or patient contact restricted?

As a general rule, and as long as employees are able to perform their jobs, they should be allowed to continue with their normal duties. Some special precautions should be taken under the CDC guidelines, however, if the employee performs invasive procedures, has an open wound, or has an associated opportunist infection that can be easily transmitted. Under those circumstances, or if the employee's own medical condition warrants restrictions, the employer's duty to protect both the employee and the patient may require that the employee be restricted temporarily from direct patient care or from particular job duties. These decisions should be made on a case-by-case basis and after consultation with the employee's physician as well as other medical professionals.

What steps can health care employers take to reduce employee fears in treating AIDS patients?

First and foremost, the best weapon against fear is educating both patients and staff. Employees, patients, and family members should all be educated about the transmission of the disease, the risks, and the precautionary measures that should be taken.

An approach used by some hospitals is the development of an AIDS consulting team. This team is generally composed of a variety of health care professionals, such as a physician, a registered nurse, a social worker, an infectious disease consultant, and a discharge planner. The team takes responsibility for following AIDS patients within the hospital and for assisting in the development of appropriate treatment modalities. Often, this includes educating personnel about the risks and problems associated with each individual patient.

Second, health care employers must demonstrate that their concern extends to employees as well as to patients. This can be done by developing formal policies and procedures that conform to CDC guidelines, by updating those policies as appropriate, and by monitoring actual observance of the policy.

CHECKLIST FOR SUPERVISORS

Although the law in this area is still developing and circumstances may vary at individual health care facilities, health care employers should, at a minimum, consider the following in dealing with AIDS issues:

- Supervisors should periodically review the most recent medical information concerning the transmission of the AIDS virus and its prevention.
- Based on current medical evidence, supervisors and health care employers should develop, periodically revise, and monitor their procedures for treating patients with AIDS and for handling issues arising with AIDS-infected employees.
- Health care facilities should develop and implement a detailed employee and patient education program for communicating the latest medical information on the spread of AIDS and recommending preventive measures, and the facility and its supervisors should monitor employee observance of all adopted preventive measures.
- The health care employer should develop, distribute, or otherwise communicate its procedures for handling AIDS-related disciplinary problems, such as employees who refuse to treat AIDS patients.
- Finally, before taking any employment-related actions against employees who have AIDS or who treat patients with AIDS, the health care supervisor should consider the various applicable federal, state, and local laws and their implications, the policies of his or her facility, the medical data that may be needed, and whether legal or other consultation is required.

REFERENCES

1. "Pneumocystis Pneumonia." *Morbidity and Mortality Weekly Report* 30 (June 5, 1981).
2. Cahill, K. *The AIDS Epidemic.* New York, St. Martin's Press, 1983.
3. 29 U.S.C. § 794.
4. Department of Justice. Memorandum. June 20, 1986. Charles J. Cooper. Application of Section 504 of the Rehabilitation Act to Persons With AIDS, AIDS-Related Complex, or Infection With the AIDS Virus.
5. *Tomas v. Atascadero Unified School District,* 886-609 AHS (BY) (USDC, Calif. 1986).
6. *School Board of Nassau County, Florida v. Arlene,* 106 S.Ct. 1833 (1986).

7. Ibid.

8. San Francisco, Cal., Police Code Section 3301 (1985).

9. Los Angeles, Cal., Municipal Code, Chapter III, Article 5.8 (1985).

10. Cal. Health & Safety Code § 199.21(f) (West Supp. 1986).

11. W.S.A. 103.15 (West Suppl. 1986).

12. Cal. Health & Safety Code § 199.21 (West Supp. 1986).

13. See, e.g., *Tameny v. Atlantic Richfield Co.*, 27 Cal.3d 167 (1980); Koehrer v. Superior Court, 181 Cal.App.3d 1155 (1986); Harless v. First National Bank of Fairmont, 246 S.E.2d 270 (W.Va. 1980); Trombetta v. Detroit, Toledo and Ironton Railroad Co., 265 N.E.2d 385 (1978); Touissant v. Blue Cross and Blue Shield, 292 N.W.2d 880 (Mich. 1980); Clearly v. American Airlines, 111 Cal.App.3d 443 (1980); Pugh v. See's Candies Inc., 116 Cal.App.3d 311 (1981).

14. *Morbidity and Mortality Weekly Report* 34 (November 15, 1985): 45.

15. 29 U.S.C. § 157. (Emphasis added.)

16. Cal. Labor Code §§ 6310, 6311 (West Supp. 1987); *Hentzel v. Singer*, 138 Cal.App.3d 290 (1982).

17. Decisions of the Labor Commission, No. 11-17001-1, 11-17001-2, 11-17001-3, 11-17001-4.

18. 29 USCA § 158(d) (1974).

Privacy rights and HIV testing in the hospital setting: A medicolegal quagmire for administrators

Lee S. Mann
Lecturer in Psychiatry
Department of Psychiatry
Georgetown University School of
*   Medicine*
Washington, D.C.

Thomas N. Wise
Professor of Psychiatry
Department of Psychiatry
Georgetown University School of
*   Medicine*
Washington, D.C.
The Fairfax Hospital
Falls Church, Virginia

THE ACQUIRED immunodeficiency syndrome epidemic dramatically forces hospital administrators to address the dialectic between the individual's right to privacy and the community's right to safety from contagion.

With more frequency, health care professionals are asking when should they order human immunodeficiency virus (HIV) antibody testing and whether special consent is required. What is the scope and content of the disclosure necessary to inform the patient of the need to order the test, and how should the test results be managed? Does a positive test demand a stricter level of confidentiality? Finally, are unique methodologies necessary to protect confidentiality where release is not appropriate?

PATHOGENESIS OF HIV

HIV, the etiologic agent for AIDS, is a retrovirus capable of replicating in a certain number of cells within the human body.[1]

Health Care Superv, 1990, 8(2), 57–63

The pathogenesis of HIV is related to the destruction of the helper (T4) subset of T lymphocytes, which are essential in maintaining immunologic competence.[2] The HIV has been isolated from a variety of bodily fluids: blood, semen, vaginal fluid, tears, and saliva.[3-5] Epidemiologic studies have established that fluids that provide a sufficient amount of virus for transmission are limited to blood, semen, and vaginal secretions.[2] As of 31 July 1988, the World Health Organization had registered 108,176 cases of AIDS worldwide, with the vast majority of cases, 70,208 (personal communication, Centers for Disease Control [CDC] 8 August 1988), occurring in the United States.

Thus, HIV appears to be transmitted by sexual contact between men, from men to women, and from women to men.[6,7] Large inocula given in the form of transfused blood nearly universally result in infection. Infected mothers may transmit HIV to their infants in utero, during parturition, or during breast-feeding.[8,9] Detailed serologic studies of close contacts of infected individuals show no evidence of any other form of transmission. The few documented reports of transmission to hospital workers can be attributed to contact or inoculation with infected blood.

The low incidence of transmission in hospitals—even taking into consideration accidental needle sticks from infected patients—is striking and in direct contrast to the high infection rate seen with the hepatitis B virus.[2]

The HIV agent causes the body to produce antibodies that can be detected in the blood serum. HIV antibody testing became available for clinical use in April 1985.[10] Production of antibodies to the HIV virus usually occurs within 6 to 12 weeks after exposure. Therefore, results of HIV antibody testing may be negative if a person's blood is drawn soon after exposure, even if the person does have the virus. Recently, macrophages have been found to harbor HIV, producing falsely negative test results. False positives may also occur. The window period, the period before antibody production begins, may be as long as six months.[11] The determination with a high degree of certainty that a patient has antibodies for HIV is made using a sequence of consistently reactive tests, beginning with a reactive enzyme immunoassay and including a western blot, a more specific assay.

The window inherent in the antibody testing may be significantly shortened by an alternative procedure. Reports indicate that a new test is being devised that confirms the presence of the HIV virus itself by radioactive gene probes and makes diagnosis of the HIV virus possible within days of exposure. Thus, given the serious nature of the disease and the presence of a test to detect infection, the question of suggested or required screening arises.

TESTING POLICIES—EMPIRICAL DATA

A recent study reviewed how HIV testing is performed in U.S. teaching facilities. Henry, Willenbring, and Crossley examined testing practices and policies at U.S. infectious disease (ID) teaching hospitals and at ID teaching hospitals located in Minnesota.[12] The authors felt that choosing hospitals involved in ID training would provide an accurate portrayal of HIV test–ordering policy practices at institutions with experience and knowledge in handling issues related to AIDS. Only 49% of the U.S. hospitals and 37% of the Minnesota hospitals had an HIV antibody test–ordering policy. Forty-seven percent of the U.S. hospitals and 39% of the Minnesota hospitals had a specific educational program for physicians about the HIV antibody test.

The authors then investigated how the results of the tests were managed. Restrictions included coding the blood specimen so that the patient's name was not listed and counseling the patient on HIV transmission, risk reduction, and the nature of the HIV antibody test.

The following lists the handling of HIV antibody test results for the 188 U.S. ID teaching hospitals: 46.8% entered results in the patient record, 40.4% gave results only to the physician, 6.4% entered results in the patient record but not in the computer system, and 6.4% indicated other handling procedures of test results.

Yet how do such hospitals utilize HIV testing? In essence, the study reviewed the state-of-the-art facilities. The diversity of approaches toward regulation of HIV antibody testing among hospitals is disturbing.

On the advent of any challenge, individual providers will have the burden of justifying routine screening programs on an institution-specific basis.

Specific HIV antibody test consent forms were used by 27.5% of the U.S. hospitals surveyed, while only 4% of the Minnesota hospitals used them. Also, HIV testing of persons with high-risk behaviors affords an opportunity to provide risk-reduction coun-

seling. The data suggest that there is marked variation in provision of counseling among the hospitals surveyed: Only 58.4% of the U.S. hospitals and 32.1% of the Minnesota hospitals usually provided risk-reduction information. The authors conclude that significant differences exist between all the hospitals studied.[12]

ORGANIZED MEDICINE'S RESPONSE

Health care professionals are advocating mandatory screening of patients for the protection of professionals in the workplace. In an attempt to develop a general policy, the American Medical Association (AMA) House of Delegates accepted an interim report in June 1987 to recommend that physicians should encourage voluntary testing for any individual whose history or clinical status warrants this measure. The AMA also recommended that voluntary testing should be available to patients at sexually transmissible disease and drug abuse clinics, pregnant women (first trimester) in high-risk areas, and individuals who are from areas with a high incidence of AIDS, engage in high-risk behavior and are seeking family planning services, or require surgical or other invasive procedures.[13]

The AMA report includes a statement that hospitals and medical staffs should consider mandatory testing programs for patients in high-risk areas who require surgical or other invasive procedures, if responses to voluntary testing are not satisfactory. Neither the AMA nor the CDC expressly approve the practice, and on the advent of any challenge, individual providers will have the burden of justifying routine screening programs on an institution-specific basis.

THE HOSPITAL INDUSTRY'S RESPONSE

Justification of a mandatory screening program may be difficult in light of the position of the American Hospital Association (AHA).[14] Consistent with the current CDC position, the AHA recommendation is that universal precautions be taken by all hospital employees whenever the chance of exposure to blood or other bodily fluids exists, regardless of whether the fluids are known to be infected with the AIDS virus. At minimum, these precautions require the use of gloves for any risk of exposure and the use of gowns, masks, and eye coverings for certain kinds of exposure. Furthermore, the AHA said that hospitals may wish to discontinue labeling specimens and identifying certain patients as requiring the use of infection control procedures, since the new recommendations say that all such precautions should be applied universally. The AHA concurs with the CDC's position that the use of infection control procedures for all patients would be more effective in preventing HIV transmission to health care workers than routine HIV testing of all hospital patients.[14] Furthermore, reliance on negative HIV test results to determine when to apply specific precautions may lead to a false sense of security and taking of unreasonable risks.

THE LEGAL DILEMMA

Yet what are the legal issues involved in HIV testing? Once a doctor determines that HIV antibody testing is indicated, the provider must consider the patient's right to consent to testing and the scope of disclosure required to obtain informed consent. The industry guidelines are uniform in rec-ognizing that the patient's consent must be obtained before testing. The CDC report of April 1987 states that obtaining specific consent is part of the process of pretest counseling.[15] The statutory and decisional law support this approach and allow testing without informed consent only in very limited circumstances.

One exception is a factual determination that a reasonable patient would have consented had he or she been informed. Statutes such as this one generally provide that no recovery will be allowed against a practitioner in an action brought for treating, examining, or operating on a patient without informed consent, if the action falls within an accepted standard of medical practice and the patient would reasonably have undergone such treatment had he or she been so advised.[16]

The decisional law recognized limited circumstances that justify the failure to obtain informed consent. Under what is known as the emergency exception, a provider may test without consent if the patient is unable to consent, an authorized representative is not available, and delay in testing will endanger the patient. Only medical professionals are qualified to determine whether the facts justify application of this exception. If the test results are alleged to be necessary to subsequent treatment, then the health care provider would have to show why testing could not be delayed until consent could be obtained. If the provider orders testing to protect health care workers, the rationale might include reasons that support the AHA position that universal precautions are sufficient.[16]

Current authorities indicate that consent is a prerequisite to HIV antibody testing in most circumstances; therefore, the medical profession should determine what factors

Constitutional law interpretation of pertinent cases regarding a patient's right to privacy weighed against public health concerns has been a focus of the U.S. Supreme Court.

ensure that the patient is sufficiently informed to give consent. The April 1987 CDC report states

Ideally, a person who requests testing or for whom testing is recommended should have a reasonable understanding of the medical and social aspects of HIV infection and the process of post-test counseling before giving his/her verbal or written consent to be tested. The person also should understand his/her right to choose not to be tested.[15(p.4)]

After the test is ordered, health care providers must know what they should and should not do regarding the confidentiality of the record. A positive HIV antigen test could have a devastating impact on a person's life. Disclosure of the results to third parties could have serious ramifications—discrimination in employment, housing, and health insurance, to name a few. If the regulation requires the disclosure of identity, then it also threatens the individual's privacy as well as his or her liberty, good name, and reputation. Although the precise nature and scope of any special duty to maintain the confidentiality of AIDS information is far from defined, statutes, cases, and industry standards appear to recognize the confidentiality of AIDS information. The Surgeon General's Report of August 21, 1987 clearly states that the "current public health practice is to protect the privacy of the individual infected

with the AIDS virus and to maintain the strictest confidentiality concerning his/her health records.[17(p.15S)]

The practice of notifying authorities regarding cases of patients with communicable diseases has been upheld since 1887. Clearly there are statutes and regulations that require health care professionals to report the diagnosis of defined infectious diseases to public health officials to protect the public from communicable diseases. Health care providers may also be required to take reasonable steps to avoid transmission of a contagious disease and to protect third parties exposed to the disease. In *Davis v. Rodman*, a 1921 Arkansas case, a physician treating a patient with typhoid fever was found to have a duty to notify attendants of the nature of the disease, warn them of the danger of infection, and instruct them about the usual methods approved by the profession for preventing the spread of the disease.[18] Since the AHA's position is that health care workers are best protected by the adoption of universal precautions, the use of HIV antibody serologic tests is limited, and providers may be hard pressed to justify release of testing information based on a duty to protect the workers from infectious persons within the confines of the hospital. However, the courts have recognized liability to other third parties.

Constitutional law interpretation of pertinent cases regarding a patient's right to privacy weighed against public health concerns has been a focus of the U.S. Supreme Court. In the landmark case of *Jacobson v. Massachusetts*, the Supreme Court clearly holds that states have the authority to exercise their police power to protect public health.[19] In *Zucht v. King*, the Supreme Court upheld an ordinance that set vaccination as a prerequisite for school enrollment without regard to an actual or imminent danger of an epidemic.[20]

Beginning in the 1960s, equal protection cases established that laws that infringed on fundamental rights would be held by the courts to a more demanding standard of review—strict scrutiny. The Supreme Court also introduced a middle tier with regard to equal protection analysis—intermediate scrutiny. This requires that legislation burdening certain quasi-suspect classes or impairing important, but not necessarily fundamental, rights must be substantially related to an important state interest.[21]

In *Whalen v. Roe*, the Supreme Court held that the privacy right encompasses both a general individual interest in avoiding disclosure of personal matters and an interest in independence in making certain kinds of important decisions.[22] Hence, a regulation designed to control AIDS affects both of these interests when its purpose is to identify AIDS carriers. Therefore, courts would probably utilize a strict scrutiny or intermediate scrutiny analysis when reviewing mandatory testing cases.

Clearly, the right of the individual to privacy can be affected by governmental responses that fall on a continuum. Testing could be voluntary or mandatory; it could be required in certain contexts (e.g., blood donations); but not in others (e.g., health insurance applications). Government laws that infringe on fundamental rights are unconstitutional unless they further a compelling state interest. Courts frequently apply a rational relationship test to decide whether a statute that affects the public good and also affects individual rights is unconstitutional on due process or equal protection grounds. But if a fundamental right or suspect class is involved, the court uses a strict scrutiny test.

Under this test, the government must show that a compelling state interest is served and that the statute has been narrowly drafted to accomplish the compelling end.

In addition, the primary purpose of the health law is to protect public health; concurrently, the health law is structured to protect individual rights. Therefore, it requires all actions to meet a test of medical necessity.[23] Courts have held that states may not infringe on individual rights citing health reasons unless there is a valid medical necessity for doing so, however well intentioned or sensible the action might be. State health action is legitimate even if it infringes on individual rights if a medical risk assessment has defined the health threat and its ramifications. The chosen solution to the situation must be the least restrictive medically appropriate means of dealing with the risk.

AIDS may be one of the most serious diseases of the 20th century, yet physicians lack important epidemiologic data such as the morbidity and mortality of AIDS, seroconversion rates, and the efficacy of prevention programs. Considering these facts, the authors suggest that it may be constitutional for states to require mandatory testing and follow-up reporting, as long as patient confidentiality is ensured. This could be accomplished by using no name or social security number at the time of testing; an arbitrary code could be assigned to the individual being tested so that he or she could obtain the test results. If individuals cannot be ensured anonymity, then massive testing programs would be of little value, since high-risk individuals would avoid testing for fear of discrimination and ridicule. Hence, mandatory testing in hospital settings would have little medical efficacy, since it would not provide anonymity to the patient. Therefore, if states require mandatory testing without guaranteeing anonymity, the requirement probably would not stand up to constitutional muster.

•   •   •

The results of HIV testing must protect public health while preserving individual rights against unnecessary intrusions. To determine whether actual risks justify mandatory testing and reporting, the best possible objective medical information must be considered. Legislators and courts must not cave in to public sentiment and fears. Courts must scrutinize HIV testing legislation carefully to ensure that the legislative history is accurate and the primary goal is concern for public health, not for discriminating or creating scapegoats.

REFERENCES

1. Coolfont Report. "A PHS Plan for Prevention and Control of AIDS and the AIDS Virus." *Public Health Report* 101 (1986): 341–48.
2. Francis, D.P., and Chin, J. "The Prevention of Acquired Immunodeficiency Syndrome in the United States." *Journal of the American Medical Association* 257 (1987): 1357–66.
3. Levy, J.A., et al. "Isolation of Lymphocytopathic Retroviruses from San Francisco Patients with AIDS." *Science* 225 (1984): 840–42.
4. Ho, D.D., et al. "HTLV-III in Semen and Blood of a Healthy Homosexual Man." *Science* 226 (1984): 451–52.
5. Wofsy, C.B., et al. "Isolation of AIDS Associated Retrovirus from Genital Secretions of Women with Antibodies to the Virus." *Lancet* 1 (1986): 527–29.
6. Jaffe, H.W., et al. "National Case-Control Study of Kaposi's Sarcoma and Pneumocystes carinii Pneumonia in Homosexual Men: I. Epidemiologic Results." *Annals of Internal Medicine* 99 (1983): 145–51.
7. Redfield, R.R., et al. "Frequent Transmission of HTLV-III among Spouses of Patients with AIDS-Related Complex and AIDS." *Journal of the American Medical Association* 253 (1985): 1571–73.
8. Jovaisas, E., et al. "LAV/HTLV-III in 20 Week Fetus. *Lancet* 2 (1985): 1129.
9. Scott, G.B., et al. "Mothers of Infants with the Acquired Immunodeficiency Syndrome: Evidence for Both Symptomatic and Asymptomatic Carriers." *Journal of the American Medical Association* 253 (1985):363–66.
10. Weiss, S.H., et al. "Screening Test for HTLV-III (AIDS Agent) Antibodies Specificity, Sensitivity and Applications." *Journal of the American Medical Association* 253 (1985): 221–25.
11. Groopman, J.E., et al. "Antibody Sero-Negative Human T-Lymphocytes Virus Type III (9HTLV-III) Infected Patients with Acquired Immunodeficiency Syndrome or Related Disorders." *Blood* 66 (1985): 742–44.
12. Henry, K., Willenbring, K., and Crossley, K. "Human Immunodeficiency Virus Antibody Testing." *Journal of the American Medical Association* 259 (1988): 1819–22.
13. "AMA House of Delegates Adopts Comprehensive Measures on AIDS." *Journal of the American Medical Association* 258 (1987): 425.
14. "New AHA Guidelines Urge Universal AIDS Precautions." *Medical Staff News* 16 (1987): 2.
15. Centers for Disease Control. *Recommended Additional Guidelines for HIV Antibody Counseling and Testing in the Prevention of HIV Infection and AIDS.* Atlanta, Ga., CDC, 1987.
16. Pankau, B.R. "Responding to the Issues." *The Health Lawyer* 31 (1987): 10–20.
17. Centers for Disease Control. *Recommendations for Prevention of HIV Transmission in Health-Care Settings.* Atlanta, Ga., CDC, 1987.
18. *Davis v. Rodman* 227 S.W. 612 (Ark. 1921).
19. *Jacobson v. Massachusetts* 197 U.S. 11 (1905).
20. *Zucht v. King* 260 U.S. 174 (1922).
21. Note, The Constitutional Rights of AIDS Carriers, 99 *Howard Law Review* 1274 (1986).
22. *Whalen v. Roe* 429 U.S. 589 (1977).
23. Note, Current topics in law and policy, 3 *Yale Law and Policy Review* 479, 494 (1985).

The right to know and the right to privacy: HIV testing and health care management

David C. Wyld
Assistant Professor of Management
Midwestern State University
Wichita Falls, Texas

Sam D. Cappel
Assistant Professor of Management
Southeastern Louisiana University
Hammond, Louisiana

Daniel E. Hallock
Assistant Professor of Management
Southwest Texas State University
San Marcos, Texas

AIDS IN THE WORKPLACE. Hundreds of articles have been written on this subject for various audiences over the past few years. However, the health care industry stands alone in actually having a setting in which the human immunodeficiency virus (HIV) can, under proper conditions, actually be transmitted. Medical professionals stand alone as the only workers for whom the acquired immunodeficiency syndrome (AIDS) epidemic actually poses a threat, however slight, of presenting the means and circumstances for HIV transmission to occur. Health care management must therefore focus its attention on the AIDS epidemic from a number of vantage points. The legal issues involving the health care workplace require a delicate balance between the rights of AIDS-affected individuals and those of health care workers. There must be a consideration of often conflicting, yet complementary and reciprocal, rights and responsibilities. The duty to provide medical services

Health Care Superv, 1992, 10(3), 56–66
©1992 Aspen Publishers, Inc.

must be weighed in light of not only professional and ethical standards, but also practical, personal, and personnel concerns. The privacy interests of individuals, both patients and providers alike, must be weighed by management in light of the possibility for HIV transmission.

Harrison Rogers asserts that both health care patients and providers have a right to know the serological status of each other in the modern health care provision relationship.[1] As will be demonstrated in the analysis presented in this paper, this is a highly controversial position, both legally and ethically.

THE NATURE OF THE RISK

HIV infection presents a paradox to the health care profession. On one hand, AIDS is 100 percent fatal. However, the causative agent, the HIV virus, is very fragile and very difficult to transmit. While there is a great threat from the end result of contracting AIDS, the means of transmission, which are quite clear today, are inefficient in almost all situations except sexual relations and the sharing of intravenous drugs. Also, the epidemic is largely invisible, as the majority of those who are HIV positive exhibit no symptoms.[2]

John Burnside, writing as a physician, notes that members of the medical profession are not only immune from being affected by the ostensible dangers posed by AIDS, but also by the stigma attached to the epidemic as a whole and affected individuals in isolation.[3] There are personal fears that can be understood, like concern for family, concern for the ability to continue to practice, and fear of death—very real influences in the minds of health care professionals.[4] Consider the

fact that in a 1988 survey, 25 percent of those physicians asked responded that, given the choice to not treat AIDS patients, they would elect not to do so.[5] Consider also that in a survey of nursing professionals, fully 27 percent of those responding felt that "frightened" best characterized their attitude of dealing with AIDS patients, while 19 percent answered "angry."[6]

What about an individual's refusal to work due to an irrational fear of contracting AIDS in the workplace? The most notable precedent in this area is the high standard set in the case of *Stepp v. Indiana Employment Security Division*.[7] In this case, Dorothe Stepp was a laboratory technician in Indianapolis charged with conducting blood tests. The laboratory had thoroughly discharged its duty to properly educate and protect its testing employees, providing protective gear and safety manuals. When her employer ordered her to conduct HIV tests on blood samples, Stepp refused, stating that "AIDS is God's plague on man and performing the tests would go against God will."[7(p.133)] The lab followed its formal disciplinary procedure and terminated Stepp for insubordination after a second refusal to conduct HIV testing on blood samples. Later, after her termination, Stepp claimed that the laboratory failed to provide a safe workplace, justifying her refusal. The court upheld the Indiana Employment Security Commission Review Board's denial of her claim that the discharge was unjust, finding both that the employer had acted properly in following its safety and disciplinary policy and that she had not contacted OSHA (Occupational Safety and Health Administration) to file a complaint against the employer.[7] Since Stepp did not base her legal claim on her First Amendment rights even though her action was based on a religious conviction, the court did not address the issue of whether this would be a legitimate defense for a refusal to work in an AIDS-related case. However, in the opinion, the court stated that this was an issue that would likely have to be seriously considered in future cases.

What is the actual risk of HIV transmission in the health care setting? Certainly this is dependent upon the type of procedure being performed and its potential for direct exposure to blood and other bodily fluids. There have been several dozen documented cases of health care workers seroconverting due to exposure to HIV-infected blood or bodily fluids in the work setting. The Centers for Disease Control (CDC) has conducted several studies of health care workers' accidental exposures to HIV, and as Allen observes, in agreement with most authorities on the subject, the risk of a health care worker becoming HIV positive from any single parenteral injury is roughly 1 in 200.[8] A recent study of over 1,300 dentists, of which 94 percent reported one or more accidental parenteral injuries in the past five years, revealed only one dentist who had seroconverted and who had no other risk factors for AIDS.[9] There may be other extenuating factors that may increase the odds of seroconversion in any incident, including the amount of blood involved in a needlestick or cut injury and whether contaminated blood was actually injected into the health care worker.[8] Rare cases have been reported where health care workers have become infected after exposure to contaminated blood or bodily fluids through uncovered skin lesions or cuts. However, as Allen points out, the danger of hepatitis-B infection in the health care setting is far greater than that of HIV conversion.[8]

The CDC has issued two sets of regulations for health care workers and hospitals to follow for preventing the transmission of HIV through the use of specific protocols and the wearing of protective clothing and gear.[10,11] These have been adopted by OSHA, and therefore, health care providers are subject to OSHA's enforcement program, with liability, fines, and citations for noncompliance.[12] However, one of the fears expressed by health care providers and management is that, because the protocols call for all patients to be treated as if they were HIV positive and the necessary precautions taken, there are often problems with provider complacency and sometimes disregard for the use of the precautions, despite the possible consequences.[13]

HIV TESTING

The question of HIV testing is perhaps as perplexing as any posed in the context of the AIDS epidemic. It is a misnomer to speak in terms of AIDS testing. No test has been developed that can show if a person has AIDS or AIDS-related complex (ARC) as these conditions are diagnosed based on manifestations of these latter stages of AIDS development. No test has been developed that shows positively whether or not a person has the HIV virus. Today's tests merely determine whether the person has been exposed to HIV. The tests employed only show the presence of antibodies to the HIV virus. HIV testing should consist of an initial screening

The question of HIV testing is perhaps as perplexing as any posed in the context of the AIDS epidemic.

test, the ELISA (Enzyme Linked Immuno-absorbent Assay) followed by the more sophisticated (and thus more costly and time-consuming) Western Blot, due to the small, but yet significant number of false positives produced by the ELISA test.[14] There is, however, a window period during which HIV-infected individuals do not produce antibodies, allowing for detection of HIV. While formerly this period was estimated as being between three months and a year, recent studies place the window during which individuals can be silent carriers of HIV as between three and four years.[15,16] Much of the debate over HIV testing must, of necessity, focus on the medical benefits of performing the tests versus the legal, social, ethical, and personal costs incurred by those subjected to the testing. First, the news of a positive HIV test often has a devastating psychological impact on the individual, even if the test was voluntary. The stigmatization that is likely to occur as the result of a positive HIV test is also great, with the individual facing possible loss of employment, insurance, housing, friends, and family. Various authors have offered their opinions on this subject, invigorating a legal and ethical debate on the propriety of mandatory HIV testing; a complete discussion of these opinions is beyond the scope of this paper.[17-21] However, perhaps the most powerful opinion was that offered by Barry, Cleary, and Fineberg, who said:

The medical and epidemiological facts concerning the transmission of HIV are too salient and the consequences of misinformation too profound to allow inaccurate perceptions to guide public policy ... The burden of proof for the necessity of HIV screening should rest with those proposing the tests, and the criteria for evaluating these proposals should be rigorous.[22(p.265)]

These same authors went on to state, "HIV screening can be compared to an experimental drug about which we know relatively little, that may have devastating consequences, and that is only one of many possible approaches to the problem."[22(p.265)]

There are a number of legal issues surrounding HIV testing in health care. The central issue involves the balancing of patient and employee legal rights and the danger posed by HIV-infected patients and health care workers. The common law aspects of both an individual's right to privacy and the health care provider's duty to treat are dealt with extensively elsewhere by the authors.[23] In the remainder of this paper, we will explore the legal framework governing HIV testing under federal statutory protection, dealing with the most recent decisions in this area.

HIV TESTING OF HEALTH CARE WORKERS AND FEDERAL LAW

The primary federal statutory protection for assuring nondiscriminatory treatment of the handicapped in employment, housing, and access to facilities is the Rehabilitation Act of 1973. Recent decisions regarding the Rehabilitation Act (*Frazier v. Board of Trustees of Northwest Mississippi*[24] and *United States v. Baylor University Medical Center*[25]) interpret the Section 504 provisions regarding recipients of federal assistance to include hospitals and doctors receiving Medicare and Medicaid reimbursements. Thus, most physicians and many hospitals would be liable, subject to the discrimination provisions of Section 504, for refusing to treat patients due to a fear of AIDS and for discriminatory actions against employees because of unwarranted actions based on the HIV status of patients or providers.[26]

A handicap?

The case of *Arline v. School Board of Nassau County*[27] was the first to address the issue of whether contagious diseases were to be covered under the Rehabilitation Act. The Supreme Court decided in March 1987 that Ms. Arline, a schoolteacher with a susceptibility to tuberculosis, was a handicapped individual under Section 504 of the act, which applies to all recipients of federal financial assistance.[28,29] While this case did not directly involve AIDS or HIV infection, it was an important test case for whether a carrier of a contagious disease would be protected under the Rehabilitation Act.[30,31]

AIDS has been found to be a protected handicap under the Rehabilitation Act in the cases of *Thomas v. Atascadero Unified School District*,[32] *Doe v. Dolton Elementary School District No. 148*[33] and *Recanzone v. Washoe County School District*[34] (all dealing with school children) and in the cases of *Chalk v. U.S. District Court Central District of California*[35] and *Raytheon Company v. FEHC (California Fair Employment and Housing Commission and Estate of John E. Chadbourne)*[36] (both dealing with employment). HIV infection has been ruled as a handicapping condition in access to health care in the case of *Doe v. Centinela Hospital.*[37] In this case, the plaintiff had been discharged from the hospital's drug and alcohol rehabilitation program after testing positive for HIV. Relying on the framework set forth in the *Arline* case, the judge ruled that the plaintiff's seropositivity limited his access to aid in dealing with his chemical dependency and that the hospital had wrongly asserted that fear of contagion was an adequate reason to discriminate against him due to his HIV positive status.[37,38] According to leading legal experts, the 1988 Civil Rights Restoration Act codified the *Arline* decision, amending the critical definition of a handicapped individual to include individuals with contagious diseases, but excluding those whose condition would either endanger themselves or others or would be unable to perform their job duties.[30] Gostin states that the record of the legislative debate over this definition asserts that the threat posed by the contagious disease must be a significant risk of transmission or harm, as the Supreme Court ruled in the *Arline* case, to allow for discrimination based on a person having AIDS or seropositive status.[39]

What about patient contact?

Should hospitals and other health care facilities prevent health care providers who have AIDS, ARC, or who are HIV positive from having patient contact? It appears that the Rehabilitation Act and the amendments made through the Civil Rights Restoration Act provide some protection for these categories of AIDS-affected individuals, again so long as their condition does not pose a direct threat to patients. However, while past court decisions provide guidance as to the legal aspects of this question, important ethical questions also arise.

Based on the relatively low risk of transmission found in the health care setting, are restrictions on the type of procedures which HIV-positive doctors, nurses, dentists, and other health care workers may participate in warranted or sustainable under federal law? This question is dealt with at length by Gostin, who asserts that restrictions, if any, should be based on whether the individual is a principal in invasive procedures and should be voluntarily assumed, given the professionalism of health care practitioners.[39]

Past court cases provide some guidance in terms of how federal antidiscrimination law will be interpreted in this special case of employment. In the case of *Doe v. New York University*,[40] the Second Circuit court ruled that the institution was justified in denying admission to its medical school of an applicant with a history of mental illness, based on the potential threat posed to patients, faculty, and fellow students. Likewise, in the case of *Doe v. Region 13 Mental Health Mental Retardation Commission*,[41] the Fifth Circuit court decided that the institution was within its rights to dismiss a therapist with suicidal tendencies based on the dangers posed to both herself and her patients. Thus, courts have been willing to uphold the dismissal of individuals deemed to pose a significant risk to others through their continued ability to provide medical care under the model of the Rehabilitation Act.

The case of *Doe v. Cook County Hospital*[42] is useful in seeing what form future guidelines for AIDS and health care providers may take, whether implemented by congressional action, judicial conduct, or professional association review. In this case, involving an HIV positive neurologist, the judge required the parties to sign a consent decree based upon the language of the *Arline* decision. The physician agreed to some limitations on his privileges to perform certain invasive procedures and to some additional barrier precautions he would take in order to continue performing others. He also agreed to surveillance of his condition, with the stipulation that restrictions on his practice could be increased if his condition progressed to ARC or AIDS or if future epidemiological evidence warranted such alterations.[42] This decision reemphasizes the need for professional standards, not courts, to determine whether an HIV-infected health care worker should continue to practice and in what ways.[39] This is because of the difficult question of what is "significant risk" when the chances of transmission are rather remote, but the consequences of actual transmission are fatal.[39] Lonnie Bristow agrees with this situational perspective, for it is clear that if a judged significant risk exists for the provider to engage in an activity, it should not be performed; however, if no risk to the patient exists, the knowledge that the provider is HIV positive serves no rational purpose, for it merely encourages unwarranted and baseless fears to develop.[43]

Professionals standards are necessary because of the difficult question of what is "significant risk" when the chances of transmission are rather remote, but the consequences of actual transmission are fatal.

Several decisions have been rendered in the area of HIV testing specifically. In the case of *Local 1812, American Federation of Government Employees v. United States Department of State*,[44] the federal court upheld an HIV testing program implemented by the U.S. State Department for its foreign service employees. The State Department asserted that because of the often lowered sanitary conditions and health care availability encountered in foreign service, an HIV-positive individual would be susceptible to infections due to lowered immunity. Thus, the individual would not be "otherwise qualified" for worldwide foreign service under Section 504 of the Rehabilitation Act. The court concurred in this case, allowing HIV testing to be part of the routine, extensive physical examinations required of foreign service employees.[44] In part, the court's ruling was due to the fact that a positive HIV test would only disqualify new applicants from foreign service, while present employees would still be allowed to serve in 19 countries deemed to have adequate health care systems.[45] However, the ruling leaves open the possibility that HIV testing would be allowable where there is a clear threat to the health and safety of the employee.[46]

What about the health care worker?

What about the other perspective, in which HIV testing would be conducted of health care workers in order to protect the health and safety of patients? Two past cases provide some constructive, but not conclusive, arguments of how the Rehabilitation Act will deal with this in the area of health care provision. In a case involving the much more highly contagious Hepatitis B virus, *Kohl v. Woodhaven Learning Center*,[47] the court found that the contagious disease carrier would be "otherwise qualified" and thus protected under the Rehabilitation Act. In the case of *Doe v. Coughlin*,[48] the court found the New York State Corrections System's policy of HIV testing of inmates and subsequent segregation of seropositive prisoners as violative of both the Fourth Amendment and the Rehabilitation Act.

Two 1989 decisions are illustrative of a still evolving legal doctrine in terms of the use of HIV testing in health care. The next section of this paper will look in depth at these influential, but not definitive, decisions and how they are likely to influence the situational nature by which HIV testing of health care workers may be allowed.

LECKELT, GLOVER, AND THEIR INFLUENCE

In *Leckelt v. Board of Commissioners of Hospital District No. 1*,[49] the plaintiff, Kevin Leckelt, was employed for almost eight years as a licensed practical nurse at Terrebonne General Medical Center in Houma, Louisiana. As part of the hospital's infection control policy, employees who had reason to suspect they had a communicable disease were expected to submit to testing for that condition. If the test was positive, the individual in question would be required to receive clearance before returning to work. The hospital administration learned that Mr. Leckelt's roomate and lover (Marvin Potter) had been admitted to the hospital as an AIDS patient and subsequently died. The hospital desired to have Leckelt tested for the HIV virus as part of its infection control policy (which complied with both OSHA and American Hospital Association [AHA] standards). The plaintiff refused to submit to the test, and after the hospital learned that Leckelt had previously undergone HIV testing in nearby New Orleans at his own behest, the administration requested Leckelt to turn over these results. After learning of his refusal to submit these results, and in the context of learning both that the plaintiff had not reported previous noncompliance with the infectious disease policy (upon contracting hepatitis B) and that Marvin Potter had died, Leckelt was terminated on 1 May 1986.[49]

Leckelt charged that his termination violated both the federal and Louisiana rehabilitation acts and also his expectations to privacy and to equal protection under both constitutions. The court ruled for the defendant hospital in regard to all of these claims, upholding the termination.[49] The court reasoned that the hospital's interest in learning of the defendant's HIV test results outweighed the privacy and equal protection interests of Mr. Leckelt. Furthermore, because the employer did not know the results of the testing to determine if the nurse was HIV positive, Leckelt's handicap status, which would have been supported under the *Arline* and *Chalk* decisions, was unknown. Therefore, the Rehabilitation Act Claims failed, and the defendant's refusal to comply with the order to turn over the test results constituted insubordination and just grounds for his dismissal.[49]

The implications of *Leckelt* are both significant and limited for the use of HIV testing in health care. First, the employer has a right to know test results in order to determine an individual's HIV status upon reasonable suspicion of exposure to HIV (apparently either on the job or outside of employment). However, this right is limited to those providers who play a direct delivery role in services that present the opportunity for exchange of bodily fluids (primarily invasive procedures). Also, *Leckelt* would seem to support a ban on testing programs across health care institutions. This is a position reinforced by the facts and the findings of the other major recent decision in this vein.

In the case of *Glover v. ENCOR (Eastern Nebraska Community Office of Retardation)*,[50] the Eighth Circuit Court upheld a lower court's decision that disallowed a mandatory HIV testing program by a county agency that provided services for the mentally retarded. As a sub-unit of the Eastern Nebraska Human Services Agency (ENHSA), the agency attempted to implement an ENHSA-wide program of mandatory blood testing for both HIV and the hepatitis B viruses. This policy was based on

evidence that its employees were susceptible to being bitten, scratched, or otherwise physically harmed by its clients in the context of the normal duties of employment, allowing for the possibility of infected blood to be encountered by the workers.

However, the case was, like *Leckelt*, not decided on the grounds of the Rehabilitation Act. The decision was based on the balancing of an individual's Fourth Amendment right to privacy versus the benefit of intrusion. The court agreed with the plaintiff that mandatory blood testing constituted a search and seizure.[51] Fourth Amendment questions in regard to what constitutes a reasonable search turn on a balancing of the individual's expectation of privacy versus the significance of the government's interests.[52] The defendant agency believed, as stated previously, that its workers and its clients were susceptible to transmission of both viruses in their work setting. ENCOR thus asked that a lower-than-normal standard review of the Fourth Amendment question be applied in light of the dangerousness they believed was inherent and inalterable in the health care delivery setting. The *Glover* court asserted that "individuals have a reasonable expectation of privacy in the personal information their bodily fluids contain."[50(p.140)] The court also ruled that the policy was developed disregarding the medical facts of the situation, finding that the risk to either the workers or the client in ENCOR's work setting was "trivial to the point of non-existence."[50(p.141)]

The significance of *Glover* is limited in isolation, but illustrative, when considered in the wake of the contemporaneous *Leckelt* decision, of an evolving framework in regard to federal law on HIV testing of health care workers. To date there has still been no direct ruling on the applicability of the Rehabilitation Act to HIV testing based on the danger of transmission in the workplace. It would appear from both *Leckelt* and *Glover*, supported by the decisions discussed previously in regard to the treatment of AIDS and HIV infection under the Rehabilitation Act framework, that courts will favor the rights of employees objecting to mandatory HIV testing programs, unless there is a significant demonstrable risk of transmission in the workplace and/or a reasonable suspicion of exposure to HIV.

•   •   •

Balancing the rights of suspected or actual HIV-infected individuals versus the preferences of patients, customers, coworkers, and others requires a delicate balancing of individual rights and responsibilities in light of medical and epidemiological facts. It is undoubtedly the quintessential ethical and legal problem of our time for health care management to confront. The dilemmas and the ensuing debate will be intensifying in the nineties as the number of diagnosed AIDS cases and of HIV-positive individuals rapidly expands.

Much of the literature in the management field, and unfortunately some in the area of AIDS, consists of writing that ends with such concepts as prescriptions, guidelines, battleplans, etc. for dealing with the problem being discussed.[53–55] Certainly, excellent articles[56,57] and books[58,59] abound in this vein. There is an ever present desire, however, for deductive reasoning whereby, because the topic is management, the problem, whatever it may be, can be managed in the classical scientific method, with one best way to handle the situation. The typical conclusion to an article such as this would be a section subtitled the antithesis of reality, that is, something like "AIDS Made Easy" or "Ten Steps to Effectively Deal with AIDS For Health Care Providers."

The foregoing review presents issues that are too complex to be reduced to simplistic action plans for health care management and providers. The legal and ethical problems of the use of HIV testing of health care providers are but one part of the myriad of difficulties brought on by the epidemic—among these being the complex social issues brought on by AIDS and the ramifications in the areas of hospital and health care service reimbursement, cost, capacity, and adequacy. The legal status and propriety of HIV testing will continue to be under debate and in flux for some time, as all available precedent and guidelines in this area are based on current epidemiological and medical knowledge. This is, of course, subject to change and reinterpretation as more is learned about AIDS and as the prevalence of HIV infection, ARC, and AIDS increases. Certainly, it is not an issue that has been resolved by *Leckelt* and *Glover*, but these cases have brought more insight into the proper role of HIV testing of health care workers in light of current medical and legal knowledge. However, as a society and in health care management, the picture regarding AIDS is still developing, and as such, what are hard and fast rules today may be arcane in six months. Continuing attention on the medical, legal, and social fronts for the decade of the nineties is the prescription offered by both the *Leckelt* and *Glover* decisions and by the authors.

REFERENCES

1. Rogers, H.L. Jr. "The Medical Profession and AIDS." *The Journal of Legal Medicine* 10 (1989): 1–10.
2. May, R.M., Anderson, R.M., and Blower, S.M. "The Epidemiology and Transmission of HIV-AIDS." *Daedalus* 118, (1989): 163–201.
3. Burnside, J.W. "AIDS and Medical Education." *The Journal of Legal Medicine* 10 (1989): 19–27.
4. Friedland, G.H. "Clinical Care in the AIDS Epidemic." *Daedalus* 118 (1989): 59–83.
5. Rogers, H.L., Jr., "Caring for the Patient with AIDS: Negative Feelings and Impact on Care." *Journal of the American Medical Association* 259 (1988): 1368–1371.
6. Brennan, L. et al. "The Battle Against AIDS: A Report from the Nursing Front." *Nursing88* 18 (1988): 60–64.
7. *Stepp v. Indiana Employment Security Division*, 17 IER Cases 133, (C.A. Ind. 1988).
8. Allen, J.R. "Health Care Workers and the Risk of HIV Transmission." *Hastings Center Report* 18 (1988): 2–5.
9. Klein, N. et al. "Low Occupational Risk of Human Immunodeficiency Virus Infection among Dental Professionals." *New England Journal of Medicine* 318 (1988): 1686–88.
10. Centers for Disease Control (1987). "Recommendation for Prevention of HIV Transmission in Health-Care Settings." *Morbidity and Mortality Weekly Report* 36 (1987): 1S–18S.
11. Orthmann, R. "The Latest News on AIDS as a Workplace Issue." *Employment Testing* 3 (1989): BWR:415–BWR:422.
12. Department of Labor, U.S. *HIV/HBV Infection-Control Measures for Health Care Workers (October 30, 1987)*. Washington, D.C.: Government Printing Office, 1987.
13. Orthmann, R. and Hurd, S. "Treating AIDS Patients: Three Different Perspectives." *Employment Testing* 3 (1989): BWR:381–BWR:387.
14. Cleary, P.D., "Compulsory Premarital Screening for the Human Immunodeficiency Virus." *Journal of the American Medical Association* 258 (1987): 1757–62.
15. Imagawa, D.T., et al. "Human Immunodeficiency Virus Type 1 Infection in Homosexual Men Who Remain Seronegative for Prolonged Periods." *New England Journal of Medicine* 320 (1989): 1458–62.
16. Bishop, J.E. "AIDS Virus Can Go Undetected for Years: Study Finds Some Gay Men, Infected for Four Years, Who Still Test Negative." *The Wall Street Journal*, 98:105 (June 1), B2.
17. Batchelor, W.F. "Real Fears, False Hopes: The Human Costs of AIDS Antibody Testing." *AIDS & Public Policy Journal* 2 (1987): 25–30.
18. Bauer, G.L. "AIDS Testing," *AIDS & Public Policy Journal* 2 (1987): 1–2.
19. Collins, C. "The Case Against AIDS Testing," *AIDS & Public Policy Journal* 2 (1987): 8–11.
20. Gebbie, K.M. "HIV Testing Issues: The Context for Public Health Decision Making." *AIDS & Public Policy Journal* 2 (1987): 31–34.
21. Osborn, J.E. "Widespread Testing for AIDS: What Is the Question," *AIDS & Public Policy Journal* 2 (1987): 3–4.
22. Barry, M.J., Cleary, P.E., and Fineberg, H.V. "Screening for HIV Infection: Risks, Benefits, and the Burden of Proof." *Law, Medicine, & Health Care* 14 (1986): 5–6, 259–267.
23. Wyld, D.C. and Cappel, S.D. "The Big Easy?: Legal and Ethical Perspectives for Health Care Management for Dealing with the AIDS Epidemic in the Nineties." *AIDS & Public Policy Journal* (in press, 1990).
24. *Frazier v. Board of Trustees of Northwest Mississippi*, 765 F.2d. 1278 (5th Cir. 1985), *modified* 777 F.2d. 329 (5th Cir. 1985).
25. *United States v. Baylor University Medical Center*, 736 F.2d. 1039 (5th Cir. 1984), *cert. denied*, 469 U.S. 1189 (1985).
26. Geraghty, D. "AIDS and the Physician's Duty to Treat." *The Journal of Legal Medicine* 10 (1989): 47–58.
27. *Arline v. School Board of Nassau County*, 772 F.2d. 759 (S.D.Fla. 1985), 107 S. Ct. 1123 (1987), 47 FEP Cases 530 (1988).
28. Broadus, J. "*Arline*: The Application of the Rehabilitation Act of 1973 to Communicable Diseases." *Labor Law Journal* 39 (1988): 273–285.
29. Goldberg, S.B. "The Meaning of 'Handicapped.'" *ABA Journal* 73 (1987): 56–61.
30. Turner, R. "*Arline, Chalk*, The Civil Rights Restoration Act, and the AIDS Handicap." *AIDS & Public Policy Journal* 3 (1988): 23–30..
31. Brooks, T.L. "*School Board v. Arline*: Will AIDS Fit the Mold?" *Arkansas Law Review* 41 (1988): 639–56.
32. *Thomas v. Atascadero Unified School District*, 662 F. Supp. 376 (C.D.Cal. 1986).
33. *Doe v. Dolton Elementary School District No. 148*, 694 F.Supp. 440 (N.D.Ill. 1988).
34. *Recanzone v. Washoe County School District*, 48 FEP Cases 299 (1988).
35. *Chalk v. U.S. District Court Central District of California*, 840 F.2d. 701 (9th Cir. 1988).
36. *Raytheon Company v. FEHC (California Fair Employment and Housing Commission and Estate of*

Jmohn E. Chadbourne), 46 FEP Cases 1089 (N.D. Cal. 1988).

37. *Doe v. Centinela Hospital*, 57 U.S.L.W. (July 19) 1009, 2034–2035, (D.C. C.Cal. 1988).

38. "Judge Rules HIV Infection Constitutes a Handicap (*Doe v. Centinela Hospital*)." *Employment Testing* 2 (1988): BWR: 278.

39. Gostin, L. "HIV-Infected Physicians and the Practice of Seriously Invasive Procedures." *Hastings Center Report* 19 (1989): 32–9.

40. *Doe v. New York University*, 666 F.2d. 761 (2d. Cir. 1981).

41. *Doe v. Region 13 Mental Health Mental Retardation Commission*, 704 F.2d. 1402 (5th Cir. 1983).

42. *Doe v. Cook County Hospital*, No. 87 C 6888, Consent Decree Filed February 21, 1988 (N.D. Ill.).

43. Bristow, L.R. "AIDS and the Response of Organized Medicine." *The Journal of Legal Medicine* 10 (1989): 11–17.

44. *Local 1812, American Federation of Government Employees v. United States Department of State*, 662 F.Supp. 1221 (D.D.C. 1987).

45. Leonard, A. "The Legal Issues: What Every Manager Should Know." In *AIDS-The New Workplace Issues*. New York, N.Y.: American Management Association, 1988.

46. Cone, L.A. "Testing for HIV Infection in the Workplace." *Employment Testing* 3 (1989): BWR:347–BWR:350.

47. *Kohl v. Woodhaven Learning Center*, 672 F.Supp. 1221 (W.D. Mo. 1987).

48. *Doe v. Coughlin*, 697 F.Supp. 1234 (N.D.N.Y. 1988).

49. *Leckelt v. Board of Commissioners of Hospital District No. 1*, 714 F. Supp. 1377 (D.C. La. 1989).

50. *Glover v. ENCOR (Eastern Nebraska Community Office of Retardation)*, 3 IER Cases 135 (D.C. Neb. 1988), 867 F.2d. 461 (8th Cir. 1989).

51. *Schmerber v. California*, 384 U.S. 757 (1966).

52. O'Connor v. Ortega, 480 U.S. 709 (1987).

53. Temple, T.E. "Employers Prepare: Hope for AIDS Victims Means Conflict in Your Workplace." *Labor Law Journal* 41 (1990): 694–99.

54. Lotito, M.J. "AIDS In the Workplace: A Practical Guide for Employers." *The Practical Lawyer* 35 (1989): 35–40.

55. Lutgen, L. "AIDS in the Workplace: Fighting Fear with Facts and Policy." *Personnel* 64 (1987): 53–7.

56. Colosi, M.L. "AIDS: Human Rights Versus the Duty to Provide a Safe Workplace." *Labor Law Journal* 39 (1988): 677–87.

57. Whitty, M.D. "AIDS, Labor Law, and Good Management." *Labor Law Journal* 40 (1989): 183–87.

58. Banta, W.F. *AIDS in the Workplace: Legal Questions and Practical Answers*. Lexington, Mass.: Lexington Books, 1988.

59. Johnson, J.A. (ed.) *AIDS in the Workplace: A Policy Development and Resource Guide for Human Service Organizations*. Memphis, Tenn.: Shelby House, 1989.

Substance abuse in the workplace: Drug testing and the health care industry

Karen H. Henry
Managing Partner for the Labor
and Employment Law Department

Stephen W. Parrish
Associate
Weissburg & Aronson
San Francisco, California

V IRTUALLY EVERY manager will encounter the problems associated with alcohol or drug abuse in the workplace, and the health care supervisor is no exception. In light of the increased visibility of the problem and the public's focus on detection and prevention, health care supervisors may become involved in substance screening and testing procedures adopted by their hospitals.

Drug testing presents employers with many serious legal ramifications, resulting from the assertion of individual rights. Because employers must be sensitive to the issues involved and potential consequences before implementing any testing program, this article will describe some of the legal issues and outline practical problems encountered.

NATURE OF THE PROBLEM

The extent to which alcohol and drug abuse exists in our society is a matter of

Health Care Superv, 1988, 7(1), 1–10
© 1988 Aspen Publishers, Inc.

some dispute, but regardless of the statistics used, it is clear that the problem is significant. Consider the following:

- A generally accepted estimate is that two-thirds of adult Americans consume alcoholic beverages, and as many as one-fourth use illegal drugs or other substances on a regular basis.[1]
- Alcoholism affects an estimated 10 million Americans, and the drug addiction rate is estimated at 2% to 3% of the general population.[2]
- As recently as 1985, it was estimated that more than 45,000 people were killed in automobile accidents in which alcohol played a role.
- According to the National Institute on Drug Abuse, nearly two-thirds of people entering the work force have used illegal drugs—44% in the previous year—and companies that have tested new applicants report that 15% of those applying for nonexempt positions and 9% of those applying for exempt positions have been rejected because of positive test results.[3]

The economic cost to employers brought about by substance abuse is high. According to published reports, lost productivity alone amounts to at least $130 billion per year.[4] In 1980, health service charges relating to substance abuse totaled approximately $9 billion—of which approximately $3 billion was paid for by private third party individuals, including group health insurance payers.[5] Alcoholics also have an absenteeism rate of 3.8 to 8.3 times the nonalcoholic employee and are at 2 to 3 times greater risk of being involved in industrial accidents.[6] An estimated 40% of industrial fatalities and 47% of industrial injuries can be attributed to alcohol abuse alone.[7]

Substance abuse affects the health care workplace as well, presenting the added concern of its impact on patient care. Alcohol and drug abuse rates among both physicians and nurses are comparable to those for the general population.[8] An estimated 120,000 of the 2,400,000 registered and licensed practical nurses abuse alcohol or drugs, and 75,000 are believed to be chemically dependent at any given time.[9] According to figures maintained by the National Council of State Boards of Nursing, of approximately 3,400 disciplinary actions taken against nurses in 1986, 38% involved the use of drugs.[10]

Against this background, civil courts have long held employers accountable for the torts committed by employees in the course of their duties while substance impaired. Some courts, however, have extended liability to employers for accidents that occur after employees have stopped working. For example, the Texas Supreme Court permitted the one survivor of two accident victims to maintain a wrongful death action against an employer who had sent home an employee who appeared to be intoxicated. Although the accident occurred while the employee was driving home, the court reasoned that the employer had a duty to take action as a "reasonably prudent employer" to prevent the employee from causing an unreasonable risk to others.[11] Similarly, a California court upheld a jury verdict for injuries caused by two employees who had consumed alcohol on the employer's premises after work. The evidence showed it was customary for the employees to drink with their supervisors on the employer's premises after work. The injured party was awarded over $220,000.[12]

The primary tool previously available to

employers for dealing with substance abuse was discipline and termination *after* the employee's performance had been affected by alcohol or drugs. However, because impairment is difficult to prove by subjective observations, and because of greater awareness of the financial and social impact of substance abuse, employers in both the public and private sectors recently have begun to look at drug and alcohol testing as a method for identifying and eliminating substance abuse in the workplace.

Testing employees for substance abuse is limited by a myriad of legal restraints, including constitutional provisions guaranteeing an individual's right to privacy, statutes forbidding discrimination on the basis of handicap, and common law theories of liability derived independently from any constitutional or statutory provision. The extent to which these limitations will affect an employer depends on the state where the employer is located, whether the employer is public or private, and the nature of the testing program.

In general, drug testing is conducted in the following circumstances: before employment as part of the application process; when reasonable suspicion of drug or alcohol use exists, particularly after an accident; as part of a routine physical examination; or randomly at the discretion of the employer. Each approach carries with it different risks and practical problems. From a legal perspective, preemployment testing or screening of applicants is the safest option, because the individual affected by the testing is not yet an employee vested with the full range of employment rights. The primary legal concerns in preemployment testing involve possible invasions of privacy and discrimination laws.

Drug testing of current employees presents more difficulties. Some programs are based on "cause," defined as testing that is performed only when an employer has a reason to believe that the employee may be under the influence on the job. Some courts refer to cause in the sense used in criminal cases, i.e., based on "probable cause," whereas others have referred to the need to have a "reasonable suspicion" or an "objective basis." Testing of current employees is riskier than preemployment testing for several reasons, outlined below.

Finally, random testing at the discretion of the employer is not based on individual suspicion and is the riskiest of drug-testing policies. Random testing implicates all of the legal issues discussed below because it is not based on evidence of drug use, may very well appear to be unreasonable, and the employer may have difficulty establishing that the substance use is job related or has affected job performance.

LEGAL RESTRAINTS ON TESTING

Constitutional right to privacy

Federal protection. The Fourth Amendment of the United States Constitution, which prohibits unreasonable search and seizure, has been interpreted to prohibit taking blood from a body [13] and compelling a person to provide a urine sample.[14] This federal constitutional privacy right applies only to "state" action and, thus, it generally does not limit private employers unless they act in concert with a government agency, such as a police department.[15]

The extent to which the Fourth Amendment limits the government's ability to test its employees remains uncertain, with the courts balancing the government's legitimate concern over the effects of substance use in the workplace against the competing interest of the employee's reasonable expectation of privacy. Thus, in one case, a circuit court of appeals affirmed the right of the government to test employees for drug use when they seek transfers into "critical" positions in the United States Customs Service.[16] Another court upheld a policy requiring municipal bus drivers to submit to blood and urine tests when involved in an accident or when suspected of having been under the influence of drugs. The paramount concern for public safety overrode any bus driver's reasonable expectation of privacy.[17]

The extent to which the Fourth Amendment limits the government's ability to test its employees remains uncertain, with the courts balancing the government's legitimate concern over the effects of substance use in the workplace against the competing interest of the employee's reasonable expectation of privacy.

At the other end of the spectrum, a public employer's testing policy was found unconstitutional because it required public bus drivers to submit to random drug and alcohol testing in the absence of reasonable suspicion.[18] Yet drug testing policies not based on cause, however defined, have been upheld in some cases. The Third Circuit Court of Appeals held that a New Jersey statute requiring jockeys to submit to random testing without any reasonable suspicion of drug use was constitutional, citing a prevail-ing public interest in the safety and integrity of horse racing.[19] Another circuit court found random urine tests of prison guards to be reasonable because of the important interest in prison security and the less obtrusive nature of urinalyses as opposed to that of blood testing.[20] Another court viewed random testing differently, holding that a police department requiring all recruits to undergo surprise urine tests violated the recruits' constitutional rights against unreasonable search and seizure, rejecting arguments that testing was necessary to foster continued public confidence that police officers are themselves respectful of the law.[21]

State constitutional provisions. The constitutional provisions of at least ten states recognize a constitutional right of privacy independent of the Fourth Amendment of the United States Constitution. The California Constitution, for example, not only prohibits unreasonable searches and seizures (like the Fourth Amendment), but also has been interpreted to protect a citizen's "right to be left alone," although this does not include the right to possess controlled substances.[22,23] A California superior court recently issued an injunction prohibiting a hospital from random drug testing of its current employees, citing the California Constitution's guarantee of the right to privacy. However, this ruling did not apply to testing of employees reasonably suspected of being under the influence of narcotics, nor did it apply to job applicants.[24]

Specific legislation affecting testing

There is no significant federal legislation governing drug testing, although pending legislation would permit testing of certain employees in the railroad and aviation industries, where the public's interest in safety is especially strong. At the state level, several bills are pending, but only two states have actually enacted drug testing statutes.

Vermont recently passed a law prohibiting substance abuse testing of employees in the absence of probable cause and requiring employers to provide employee assistance programs. An initial positive test result would have to be confirmed by a second test using specified procedures to ensure greater accuracy. Also, confidentiality is mandated; laboratories administering tests are subject to strict standards; and random testing of applicants for positions is prohibited, with testing being limited to individuals who have received conditional offers of employment. By contrast, new legislation in Utah allows employers to use substance abuse for a variety of reasons, including security of property, information, and maintenance of productivity and quality assurance. Employers are authorized to terminate employees refusing to take such tests, and employers are specifically absolved from liability when they rely on a false-positive test if the reliance is reasonable and in good faith.

Local regulation of substance abuse testing is equally sparse. San Francisco, California, enacted a city ordinance, applicable to current employees, that prohibits random testing and authorizes testing only if there are reasonable grounds to believe an employee is impaired and poses a clear and present danger to the employee or to others.[25] More recently, the Los Angeles City Council approved a policy that would permit its personnel department to develop a substance abuse screening program for new job applicants applying for municipal employment in "safety-sensitive jobs." The council also proposed that standards be developed for testing current employees based on a "reasonable suspicion" standard.

Other statutes, such as state confidentiality of medical information acts, may provide additional requirements to be met by employers adopting policies for substance testing. These statutes may prohibit the disclosure of confidential medical information by health care professionals, including the results of drug tests, to the employer without the employee's consent. This type of statutory constraint exists, as a minimum, in California, Connecticut, Maine, Maryland, and Wisconsin.

Equal employment laws

Federal legislation. Legislation prohibiting discrimination against handicapped individuals, and requiring employers to offer rehabilitation to the handicapped, impacts an employer's response to drug and alcohol abuse in the workplace. The Federal Rehabilitation Act of 1973 includes alcoholism and drug addiction within its scope. It requires employers to make reasonable accommodation and to provide an opportunity for rehabilitation to employees who have at least acknowledged substance abuse problems.[26] Employers are not, however, obligated to employ handicapped individuals if they cannot perform their jobs properly or if they present a threat to the property or safety of others.[27]

In several cases, employees have sought to challenge substance abuse programs or policies on the grounds that they disproportionately impact members of racial or ethnic minorities. Because the courts have upheld such policies on the basis of business necessity, employers must ensure that rules relating to substance abuse are job related and that no alternative procedure is available that would have a lesser impact on a protected class.[28]

State legislation. The extent to which state discrimination legislation affects policies on substance abuse will vary from state to state. Most states have statutes prohibiting discrimination against employees in both the public and private sector. In some states, such as Illinois and Ohio, both alcoholism and drug addiction are considered handicaps. In others, such as California, Maryland, and Texas, alcoholism and drug addiction are not considered handicaps. A common theme of state legislation and court decisions is to require employers to make some accommodation, and each state's laws must be carefully examined to determine the extent of that duty and to whom it applies. Furthermore, although some states may provide that alcoholism is a handicap, it does not necessarily follow that drug addiction will be treated similarly.

Whether or not alcoholism and drug addiction are considered handicaps, other related limitations may be imposed by state law. For example, California has enacted an alcohol rehabilitation act that requires certain employers (those employing more than 25 persons) to "reasonably accommodate" an alcoholic employee by providing the employee with an opportunity to participate in an alcohol rehabilitation program. However, this statute does not prevent an employer from terminating an employee whose conduct or performance is unsatisfactory while under the influence of drugs.[29]

Wrongful discharge litigation

Employment terminations based on the results of drug tests also may give rise to litigation when the drug use has no demonstrable impact on the employee's performance or when the employee has refused a drug test. The common law doctrine that employment is terminable at will has given way in recent years, with many states now recognizing that under certain circumstances the employment relationship may only be terminated for "good" or "just" cause.

One of the early cases recognizing an exception to the "at will" doctrine was *Tameny v. Atlantic Richfield,* in which the California Supreme Court held that an employee could bring suit to protest termination where the employer's action was in violation of a fundamental principal of "public policy."[30] The employee in *Tameny* alleged that his termination resulted from his refusal to engage in conduct that would violate federal antitrust laws. What will constitute public policy is unclear and will depend on the state, but it will usually involve some policy defined by statute or by judicial decision. This could include a discharge on grounds that violate, for example, the constitutional or statutory provisions discussed above, such as invasion of privacy or the employee's refusal to submit to a drug test that is conducted in violation of a statute prohibiting testing.

Wrongful discharge may also be based on an express or implied "contract" between an employer and employee that discharge would only be made for good or just cause.[31] In Michigan, for example, an employee handbook, containing a "good cause" provision was held to be an express promise binding on the employer. Similarly, the Illinois Supreme Court recently held that a hospital's employee handbook, providing that an employee would not be discharged without notice and investigation, created an implied contract that the employee would only be discharged for good cause.[32]

Civil tort liability

Many theories may hold an employer liable to an employee for making employment decisions based on the results of substance abuse tests, or based on other manifestations of suspected or proven substance abuse, whether on or off duty.

Invasion of privacy. The courts have recognized a common law right to privacy, independent of constitutional guarantees, which is actionable in the courts. As one example, a federal court of appeals recently affirmed a jury verdict in excess of $400,000 based on a common law right of privacy violated by the employer's requirement that he take a polygraph test because of suspected use of drugs outside of the workplace.[33]

Defamation. Employees also have been able to recover damages for defamation when the employer has disclosed derogatory statements, such as poor performance evaluations or reasons for termination. In one reported decision, an employee ordered to undergo a drug test successfully sued his employer for disseminating the drug test result, which subsequently proved to be false. The employee recovered $200,000 in damages.[34] In another case, however, it was not defamatory to require an employee to submit to a test as part of the employer's internal investigation, even though the employee's test result proved negative.[35] It should also be noted that the reporting of suspected drug use to law enforcement officials or to employer representatives with a need to know may be privileged, thus allowing a defense to defamation claims.[36] The degree to which the privilege exists, however, may vary from state to state.

Intentional infliction of emotional distress. Employers may be liable for intentional infliction of emotional distress if otherwise permissible discipline is imposed in an "extreme and outrageous manner." For example, one federal court permitted an employee to maintain a cause of action for

---

> *The courts have recognized a common law right to privacy, independent of constitutional guarantees, which is actionable in the courts.*

---

intentional infliction of emotional distress where the employee claimed that a police investigation of the alleged drug use had been instituted by his employer for malicious reasons.[37] However, no cause of action for intentional infliction of emotional distress should result where established policy requires drug tests as part of a routine physical.[38]

Collective bargaining agreements

Another important and more practical limitation on the right of employers to implement drug testing programs is the National Labor Relations Act (NLRA), which requires employers to bargain on conditions of employment before instituting unilateral changes. In addition, a federal district court has held that because a policy for drug testing constituted a material alteration of working conditions, the unilateral implementation of the policy was a breach of the collective bargaining agreement.[39] Therefore, unionized employers must carefully examine their union contracts and their NLRA bargaining obligations before adopting testing programs.

Unemployment compensation

Terminating an employee for drug use does not automatically preclude an award of unemployment insurance benefits. In a recent decision in Virginia, an employee discharged for a positive marijuana test was entitled to unemployment benefits because the test was not related to any misconduct connected with his work.[40] However, where an employer has an express written policy to test on reasonable suspicion, an employee's refusal to submit to a test could preclude unemployment benefits.[41]

PRACTICAL CONSIDERATIONS CONCERNING TESTING

When a policy is developed regarding substance abuse that includes testing, various practical considerations will arise. Some of these considerations reflect the legal constraints discussed above, whereas others result from problems with the reliability and validity of the testing methods currently used.

The easiest and most reliable substance to test for is alcohol. Levels of alcohol can be tested by blood, urine, or breath samples, all of which are capable of measuring blood alcohol concentration (BAC) and have a high level of accuracy. Testing is nearly universal in impaired driving cases, where a BAC of 10% is the generally accepted definition of legal impairment. Drug tests, however, are not as accurate. Most drug tests available on the market are capable only of measuring the presence of a substance and cannot determine the degree of impairment,

when the drug was used, and, in most cases, what substance has been used. Thus, a positive test result may mean nothing more than the fact that the employee has ingested something in the past.

Recent experience has shown that drug use and screening tests may be unreliable. For example, experts estimate that "false positives," which falsely indicate presence of a drug, can exceed 25% for certain tests, and some laboratories may have an even higher false-positive error rate.

Particular over-the-counter nonprescription drugs will also prompt a positive result. Reliable tests are available, but often at greater expense to the employer.

An employer also must be careful to ensure that proper test procedures are followed and that the entity conducting the test is properly qualified. Many states certify laboratories engaged in drug testing, and qualified laboratories will have formal and strict protocols to be followed. Another area of concern is the "chain of custody" of the urine or blood samples tested. The employer, in cooperation with the testing laboratory, must establish a forensic protocol that includes a rigorous chain of custody to ensure that the identity and integrity of the urine or blood sample is preserved.

Another practical consideration for any employer is what to do once test results are received. Although employers clearly have an obligation not to disseminate test results beyond those with legitimate need to know, employers who become aware of dangerous conditions in the workplace also owe an affirmative duty to employees to remove the hazard. Under some worker's compensation laws, an employee may be entitled to increased compensation for the "serious and willful misconduct" of the employer when the employer has actual knowledge that a condition in the workplace is likely to cause serious injury. Therefore, an employer who becomes aware of employee drug use that could detrimentally affect performance and result in a hazard to other employees may be obligated to take affirmative action to remove that employee, even at the risk of incurring liability for wrongful discharge or other torts discussed above. Of course, an employer who obtains knowledge of an employee's substance abuse through observation or means other than testing will still be in the same predicament.

Employers also need to be aware that they should not arbitrarily choose which results they will act on and which they will ignore. In addition, for similar test results and similar circumstances, employers should make the same decisions in each case, taking care not to make exceptions in individual cases unless compelling reasons exist. Otherwise, claims of discrimination or bad faith could easily result.

Finally, the health care employer may have a specific duty to report the results of substance testing to state professional licensing boards. Several states, including Virginia, New York, and Washington, require mandatory reporting for most health care professionals. Virginia, for example, specifically requires reporting of substance abuse.[42] Some states require reporting only on a profession-by-profession basis. Illinois, for example, requires nurses serving as administrators to report any *suspected* substance abuse by another nurse.[43] California, on the other hand, has a discretionary approach; nursing directors are asked to report suspected substance abuse to the California Nursing Board for the purpose of channelling nurses into a board-sponsored diversion program

•   •   •

Substance abuse seriously impacts all employers. An effective tool in detecting and eliminating drug and alcohol abuse in the workplace—testing—raises legal, constitutional, and practical considerations that must be thoroughly examined before any testing program begins. However, where the employer is sensitive to the conflicting interests between its legitimate needs and the individual rights of employees, conflict can be minimized, and concrete efforts to control substance abuse can be successfully implemented.

REFERENCES

1. Elliott and Heines. *Disciplinary Data Bank: A Longitudinal Study*. Chicago: National Council of State Boards of Nursing, April 1, 1987: *Alcohol & Drugs in the Workplace: Costs, Controls and Controversies*. Washington, D.C.: BNA Special Report, 1986.
2. Ibid.
3. American Management Association. *Drug Abuse: The Workplace Issues*. New York: AMA, 1987.
4. Harwood. *Economic Costs to Society of Alcohol and Drug Abuse and Mental Illness: 1980*. Durham, N.C.: Research Triangle Institute June, 1984; *Alcohol & Drugs in the Workplace: Costs, Controls and Controversies*. Washington, D.C.: BNA Special Report, 1986.
5. Ibid.
6. *Alcohol & Drugs in the Workplace: Costs, Controls and Controversies*.
7. Ibid.

8. Smith, D.E., and Seymour, R. "A Clinical Approach to the Impaired Health Professional." *The International Journal of the Addictions* 20(b) (1985) 713–22; Buxton, Jessup, and Landrey, "Treatment of the Chemically Dependent Health Professionals." In *The Addictions,* edited by H. Milkman, and H. Shaffer, 1985.

9. *Book of Reports.* Chicago: National Council of State Boards of Nursing, 1987.

10. Elliott and Heines, *Disciplinary Data Bank.*

11. *Otis Engineering Corporation v. Clark,* 668 S.W.2d 307 Tex. (1983).

12. *Rodgers v. Kemper Construction Company,* 50 Cal. App.3d 608, 620 (1975).

13. *Schmerber v. California,* 384 U.S. 757, 76 (1966).

14. *Allen v. City of Marietta,* 601 F.Supp. 482, 488-89 N. D. Ga. (1985).

15. *U.S. v. McGreevy,* 652 F.2d 849 (9th Cir. 1981).

16. *National Treasury Employees Union v. Von Rabb,* 816 F.2d 170 (5th Cir. 1987), *application for stay denied mem.,* 107 S. Ct. 3182 (1987).

17. Division 241, *Amalgamated Transit Union v. Suscy,* 538 F.2d 1264 (7th Cir. 1976) *cert. denied* 429 U.S. 1029.

18. *Amalgamated Transit Union, Local 1277 v. Sunline Transit Union,* 663 F. Supp. 1560 (C.D. Cal. 1987).

19. *Shoemaker v. Handel,* 795 F.2d 1136 (3rd Cir. 1986) *cert. denied* 107 S. Ct. 577

20. *McDonnell v. Hunter,* 809 F.2d 1302 (8th Cir. 1987).

21. *Feliciano v. City of Cleveland,* 661 F.Supp. 578 N.D. Ohio (June 12, 1987).

22. Cal. Const. Art. I, § 1; *White v. Davis,* 13 Cal. 3d 757, 774 (1975).

23. *National Organization for the Reform of Marijuana Laws v. Gain,* 100 Cal. App.3d 586 (1979).

24. *Farley v. Estelle Doheny Eye Hospital,* Los Angeles Superior Court, Case No. C-629354 (1987).

25. San Francisco Ordinance 527-85, Article 33A, amending Part II, Chapter VIII of the San Francisco Municipal Code.

26. *Walker v. Weinberger,* 600 F.Supp. 757 (D.D.C. 1985).

27. 29 U.S.C. § 706(7)(B); *Tinch v. Walters,* 573 F.Supp. 346, 348 (E.D. Tenn. 1983), affirmed 765 F.2d 599 (6th Cir. 1985).

28. 42 U.S.C. § 2000 *et seq.; Griggs v. Duke Power Company,* 401 U.S. 424 (1979).

29. Cal. Labor Code § 1025-1028.

30. *Tameny v. Atlantic Richfield,* 27 Cal.3d 167 (1980).

31. *Toussaint v. Blue Cross,* 292 N.W.2d 880 Mich. (1980).

32. *Duldulao v. St. Mary of Nazareth Medical Center,* 505 N.E.2d 314 Ill. (1987).

33. *O'Brien v. Papa Gino's of America, Inc.,* 780 F.2d 1067 (1st Cir. 1986).

34. *Houston Belt and Terminal Railway Company v. Wherry,* 548 S.W.2d 743 (Tex. Civ. App. 1977).

35. *Strachan v. Union Oil Company,* 768 F.2d 703 (5th Cir. 1985).

36. E.g., California Civil Code § 47; *Tidemann v. Superior Court,* 83 Cal.App.3d 918 (1978).

37. *Norman v. General Motors Corporation.,* 628 F.Supp. 702 (D. Nev. 1986).

38. *Satterfield v. Lockheed Missile and Space Company,* 617 F.Supp. 1359 (D.S.C. 1985).

39. *Brotherhood of Locomotive Engineers v. Burlington Northern Railroad,* 620 F. Supp. 163 (D.Mont. 1985).

40. *Blake v. Hercules,* No. 0818-86-3 (May 19, 1987).

41. *In the matter of Vernon Ables, Schultz Steel Company,* PB-454, Case No. 86-05446 (May 7, 1987).

42. Va. Code § 54-325.1 (Supp. 1986).

43. Ill. Ann. Stat. ch. 111, ¶ 3435.1 (Smith-Hurd Supp. 1986).

44. Cal. Admin. Code, tit. 16, R. 85, § 1442 *et seq.* (1985).

Part IV
Organized (and Organizing) Labor

Health care union organizing: guidelines for supervisory conduct

Karen Hawley Henry
Partner
Littler, Mendelson, Fastiff & Tichy
San Francisco, California
(Offices in California and
*   Baltimore, Maryland)*

FRONT-LINE supervisors play a crucial role in union organizing campaigns and National Labor Relations Board (NLRB or board) elections because, to the employees, the supervisor is the individual who most directly personifies "the employer." To be most effective, health care supervisors must possess a solid knowledge of the legal framework that regulates union organizing campaigns and the guidelines that govern supervisory conduct. Today the need for knowledgeable and effective supervision is even greater because the frequency of unionization drives at health care institutions has increased over the past ten years and will probably continue to increase in the future.

This article is designed to introduce the major issues involved in union organizing efforts and resulting NLRB campaigns and to provide guidelines for the conduct of

Health Care Superv, 1985,4(1),14–26
© 1985 Aspen Publishers, Inc.

employees and supervisors during such efforts and elections. The legal framework will be discussed first. Guidelines for supervisory action before, during, and after a union's organizing campaign will then be outlined. Practical pointers as to what employees and supervisors can and cannot do are also provided.

The information contained in this article will not apply to every situation that may arise at every health care institution. Definite variations and quirks in the law or in the facts do exist. Furthermore, the outcome of a union organizing drive presents high stakes for health care institutions. (After losing an election, a union can legally try another election one year later, and again a year after that, and so on. An employer, however, need lose an election only once. After that, the union is certified as the exclusive collective bargaining agent of the employees, and it becomes difficult for employees to remove the union at a later date.) Therefore, supervisors and managers should always seek the advice of competent legal counsel if there is any question as to the legality or the advisability of any campaign activity. This article should not be used as a substitute for the advice of a labor attorney.

INCREASE IN ORGANIZING ACTIVITIES

Unionization at health care institutions is on the rise. In 1970, 15.7 percent of all hospitals nationally had at least one collective bargaining agreement. By 1980, that proportion had risen to 27.4 percent, an increase of almost 75 percent during the decade.[1] Similar increases are seen in the number of NLRB elections involving health care employers. There were 254 such NLRB elections in 1973, but by 1981 the number had jumped to 656.[2]

There is no indication that the trend toward more elections will soon reverse itself. On the contrary, a number of factors may further increase unionization efforts at health care institutions. First, national and state health care cost containment measures have caused health care employers, and hospitals in particular, to implement layoffs and other belt-tightening measures affecting employees. Employee anxieties resulting from such employer actions, and the general health care climate, lead some employees to seek the support and protection that they erroneously attribute to labor unions. In addition, the percentage of the labor force involved in heavy industry—traditionally the most fertile ground for union organization—is declining, while the percentage of the labor force in the service industry is increasing. Unions need members to survive and therefore are seeking organization of service employees.

Health care institutions are especially attractive targets because of their large numbers of employees and because a substantial percentage of health care institutions are still non-unionized. Also, for a number of years the courts and the NLRB have been in disagreement over what constitutes a proper *bargaining unit*—a group of employees with common employment interests—in the health care industry. This lack of certainty may have inhibited organizing efforts. The major legal issues affecting the determination of appropriate bargaining units may be on their way to resolution; if so, union organizing campaigns at health care institutions could be encouraged.

LEGAL FRAMEWORK OF UNION ORGANIZATION

Overview of the NLRA and coverage of health care institutions

The NLRB is charged with enforcing the National Labor Relations Act[3] (NLRA or *the act*). The NLRA regulates aspects of the relationships among employers, unions, and employees. In general, the jurisdiction of the NLRB covers labor disputes "affecting interstate commerce."[4,5] The United States Code (U.S.C.) defines *labor dispute* as follows:

The term "labor dispute" includes any controversy concerning terms, tenure or conditions of employment, or concerning the association or representation of persons in negotiating, fixing, maintaining, changing, or seeking to arrange terms or conditions of employment, regardless of whether the disputants stand in the proximate relation of employer and employee.[6]

In 1974, the NLRA was amended to include nonprofit health care institutions as "employers." The current definition of a health care institution

is ". . . any hospital, convalescent hospital, health maintenance organization, health clinic, nursing home, extended care facility, or other institution devoted to the care of sick, infirm, or aged persons."[7] The act covers both nonprofit and proprietary for-profit facilities. As a further prerequisite to coverage, the employer must meet other jurisdictional standards set by the NLRB; for example, nursing homes, visiting nurse associations, and related facilities must have gross revenues above $100,000 per year, and proprietary and nonprofit hospitals and other health care institutions must have gross revenues of more than $250,000 per year. Federal, state, municipal, and other public hospitals are exempt from coverage.

The National Labor Relations Act guarantees employees the right to join unions and to engage in concerted activities and the right to refuse to join unions or to engage in other concerted activities.

The act's regulation of organizational activities

The act guarantees employees the right to join unions and to engage in concerted activities and it also protects the right of employees to refuse to join unions or to engage in other concerted activities. Section 7 of the act (§157) states:

Employees shall have the right to self-organization, to form, join, or assist labor organizations, to bargain collectively through representatives of their own choosing, and to engage in other concerted activities for the purpose of collective bargaining or other mutual aid or protection and shall also have the right to refrain from any or all of such activities . . .[8]

Employers are prohibited from taking actions that impair these employee Section 7 rights. Specifically, among the unfair labor practices described in Section 8 of the act are two unfair labor practice prohibitions against the following types of employer activity:

. . . to interfere with, restrain, or coerce employees in the exercise of the rights guaranteed in section 157. . . . [§8(a)(1)]; (and) by discrimination in regard to hire or tenure of employment . . . to encourage or discourage membership in any labor organization. . . . [§8(a)(3)].[9]

Because private health care institutions are "employers" under the act, employees at health care institutions have the right to form and join unions, and a health care employer may not take actions that unlawfully prevent or discourage unionization.

Initial recognition of a union

A union can achieve employer recognition in three different ways.[10] Most commonly, a union becomes "certified" by the board after the union wins a secret ballot election conducted by the board. Additionally, an employer may voluntarily agree to recognize a union. Finally, the board may order an employer to recognize a union when the employer has committed flagrant unfair labor practices that have made futile any attempt at an impartial election.[11] Before an employer is ordered to bargain, the union is required by the board to show that it had majority support at some time during its demand for recognition.[12]

Supervisors will generally not be involved in a decision by management to voluntarily recognize a union, and supervisory behavior alone is rarely egregious enough to constitute the flagrant unfair labor practices that can lead to a bargaining order. Supervisory conduct, however, is crucial in the most common method of union recognition—the NLRB-conducted secret ballot election.

Recognition by election

A summary of the board's process and procedure for conducting representation elections (RC Cases) follows.

- First, a petition for an election must be filed with the NLRB. The petition must be accompanied by a "showing of interest"—proof that at least 30 percent of bargaining unit employees support the petition.[13] This is usually done by collecting "authorization cards"—cards signed by employees stating either that the employee wishes to have the union as his or her collective bargaining representative, or that the employee supports the petition for election. Service of a petition on an employer gives official notice of union activity. The employer's actions may then be closely scrutinized by the board, and otherwise lawful conduct may now be seen as unlawful interference with employees' right to freely choose or reject a union.

- The board next conducts a hearing concerning a number of issues pertinent to the election. Most hearings focus primarily on questions concerning the scope of the bargaining unit—which employees should be included and which ones should be excluded from the unit. Other issues to be determined include (1) whether the board has jurisdiction over the employer, (2) whether the petitioning union is a labor organization, (3) whether there is any reason an election should not be held (for example, when a current union contract already covers the employees), and, (4) whether the election date should be delayed.

  Employer and union may, at any time before or during the hearing, stipulate to any of the issues to be resolved at the hearing. The parties may also agree to skip the hearing and stipulate to an election.

- If the parties do not stipulate to an election, the board will examine the evidence obtained at the representation hearing and will either direct an election or dismiss the petition. Both parties are entitled to file posthearing briefs with the board.

- Formal notices of the election, provided by the board, must be conspicuously posted by the employer at least three working days prior to the election. On election day, a conference is held between the board agent and the parties. The ground rules of the election are stated and the parties agree on the placement of the voting booths and the method for calling employees to vote, among other items.

  Polling is generally conducted at the work place. Each side is permitted to have an equal number of observers, who must be nonsupervisory employees, present in the polling area. The observers mentally record the conduct of the election and challenge any voter who the observer feels is ineligible. If the union receives a simple majority of the votes cast (50 percent plus one vote), it wins the election.

Objections to the election

A victory or defeat by the union does not always end the organizing period. Objections to the conduct of the election or to conduct affecting the results of the election may be filed by the losing party. If the objections are found to have merit, the election can be set aside and a new election ordered. Employer conduct that can lead to the setting aside of an election is discussed below.

Unfair labor practices

When an employer commits unfair labor practices, a second election may be held even though a majority of the employees voted against the union during the first election. Section 8(a) of the NLRA lists the various types of unfair labor practices an employer can commit,[14] that is, interfering with employee rights to organize and engage in concerted activities [§8(a)(1)]; dominating a labor union [§8(a)(2)]; discriminating in hiring or setting terms of employment based on union membership [§8(a)(3)]; discharging or discriminating against an employee because he or she filed charges or gave testimony under the act [§8(a)(4)]; and, refusing to bargain collectively with employees [§8(a)(5)].

Changes in working conditions

After a petition for an election is filed, an employer cannot make changes or threaten or promise to make changes in wages, hours, or working conditions,[15] unless the employer can show that these changes would have been made even in the absence of the petition.[16] In general, an employer should not treat employees any differently merely because a union election is forthcoming.

Misrepresentations

Campaign statements that are factually inaccurate may lead to the set-

ting aside of an election. The board has changed its position frequently on this issue,[17] but its current standard holds that elections will not be set aside solely because of misleading campaign statements or misrepresentations of fact.[18] The board has stated its belief that employees are mature individuals, capable of recognizing and discounting campaign propaganda.[19] However, the board will intervene when voters are unable to recognize documents as propaganda because they are forged, or when official board documents are altered to give the impression that the board is not neutral.[20] Because the rules applicable to misrepresentation have changed so frequently, however, employers are well advised to use caution in this area.

Refusal to give certain information to the union

Within seven days after the stipulation or direction of election, the employer is required to furnish the union with a list of the names and addresses of all eligible voters, called the *Excelsior* list.[21] Failure to provide an accurate, complete list in a timely manner may lead to the setting aside of an election.[22]

The Peerless Plywood rule

Both employer and union may campaign during the 24-hour period immediately preceding the election, but may not make speeches to groups of workers during this period.[23]

Prohibiting solicitation and distribution

Although nonemployees may be prohibited from soliciting and distributing on the employer's premises if the union has an opportunity to reach employees in other ways,[24,25] an employer must allow employee supporters to solicit members and to distribute literature, within certain limits:[26]

- Oral solicitation by employees may be prohibited only during work time[27] (rest breaks and meal periods are generally not work time).
- In health care institutions, solicitation also may be prohibited in "immediate patient care areas."[28]
- Distribution by employees may be prohibited during working time and in work areas.[29]
- Both solicitation and distribution by an employer, however, may take place during work time and in work areas.[30]

Overriding these general principles is the rule that an employer must not discriminate against unions by allowing other outsiders to solicit or distribute material that has no union purpose, while refusing unions that same right.[31]

Preelection polling

Questioning employees about their support of the union during an election campaign may lead to the setting aside of an election.[32] If certain safeguards are observed, however, preelection polling by the employer may

Questioning employees about their support of the union during an election campaign may lead to the setting aside of an election. If certain safeguards are observed, however, preelection polling by the employer may take place.

take place.[33] Polling is lawful if the purpose of the poll is to determine the truth of the union's claim of majority, this purpose is communicated to the employees, assurances against reprisal are given, the poll is by secret ballot, and the employer has not engaged in unfair labor practices or otherwise created a coercive atmosphere.[34] Preelection polling can be very risky, however, because it can lead to recognition of a union without an NLRB election.

Other employer conduct

Elections may also be set aside when employers engage in the following conduct: appeals to racial prejudice, use of violence or threats of violence,[35] extended conversation in the polling area,[36] and threatening employees with closure of business.[37]

PRACTICAL GUIDELINES FOR SUPERVISORS

The remainder of this article contains a discussion of what actions supervisors may take within the legal limits of the NLRA during a union campaign. For purposes of this discussion, the organization campaign will be divided into four general phases:

1. prepetition;
2. postpetition;
3. election day; and
4. postelection.

Pre-petition supervisory conduct and preventive action

"Unions rarely organize employees; rather it is the administration's poor employee relations record (uppermost in that grouping is the first-line supervisor) that drives employees into unions."[38] The employer who wishes to maintain and foster a direct relationship with employees, therefore, must take the initiative to establish an environment where a union is unnecessary, not waiting for the first signs of organization before taking action. Key among these actions is the need to strengthen the supervisor-employee relationship, and the ability of supervisors to effectively handle their role as the link between employees and the employer. Other general guidelines for establishing a work environment that is satisfactory to employees are as follows.

- Good communication is essential. Supervisors must be willing to actively listen to employee complaints. If not, employees may find someone else (perhaps a union representative) who is willing to listen. In addition, praise for a job well done is crucial to employee satisfaction. The importance of good communication was stressed by Charles McConnell of the Hospital Association of New York State: "Many employees—quite likely the majority—would prefer to be loyal to the organization, but the organization's seeming indifference to upward communication can discourage such loyalty."[39]
- Employees also appreciate an employer who is consistent in enforcing rules and who gives ample notice and seeks employee input prior to implementing changes in working conditions.
- Employees need to have an understanding of the circumstances affecting their employer, the steps that are being taken to meet these challenges, and the way in which any resulting impact on employees will be handled.
- Supervisors should not be reluctant to discuss unionization with their employees, but should avoid philosophical discussions of the advantages and drawbacks of unions in general. The stress of any discussions must be that in *our* hospital, a union is not needed, and why. If appropriate, the health care institution may be portrayed as a "family" that does not need the intervention of an outside third party (the union) to solve its problems.[40]

If employee support for unionization is low, outside unions will most likely not attempt an organization drive. Such drives are expensive, and unions hesitate to enter them unless there is a good chance of winning support from a majority of the employees. The bottom line is that a union will have little or nothing to offer employees if the employees already believe that the employer is responding to their needs.

Postpetition

Management must develop an overall strategy for dealing with the employer's election campaign, and supervisors must participate in implementing the strategy by actively campaigning. Such a campaign may consist of meetings,[41] individual discussions, distribution of literature, and other methods of communication. Supervisors must be aware that their actions during an organizational campaign are limited by law, and that their conduct may be objectionable and may lead to the setting aside of an election.

Section 8(c) of the act, the "freedom of speech" provision, describes the general boundaries of permitted and prohibited campaign conduct. Section 8(c) states,

The expressing of any views, argument, or opinion, or the dissemination thereof, whether in written, printed, graphic, or visual form, shall not constitute or be evidence of an unfair labor practice under any of the provisions of this Act, if such expression contains no threat of reprisal or force or promise of benefit.[42]

Section 8(c), therefore, guarantees employers and unions the right to actively campaign, within limits, during an organizational drive. Furthermore, as a practical matter, such campaigning must be done regardless of the employer's record or the employee relations climate that existed prior to the petition's filing. A primary reason for campaigning by an employer is that unions do not engage in full and frank disclosure concerning unionization. For example, they generally do not reveal union security obligations, requirements binding employees to union bylaws and rules, and so on. As a result, this information, which can have a very direct impact on employee support of unionization, will not be forthcoming unless it and other issues are presented by the employer.

With the foregoing general comments in mind, an illustrative list of permitted and prohibited supervisory actions during an election campaign follows. The list is simply an elaboration of the earlier discussion of objectionable employer campaign conduct (see Section II–D–5).

Permitted campaign conduct

Under Section 8(c), supervisors *can* express opinions or present arguments to employees and discuss the union and the election with them. Supervisors, therefore, may discuss

1. advantages of remaining non-union:
   - current wages and benefits;
   - comparison of current wages and benefits with wages and benefits at unionized facilities; and

- comparison of existing benefits to benefits offered by the union;[43] and
2. disadvantages of unionization:
    - expensive dues;
    - possibility of fines for union members;
    - loss of income during strikes;
    - possibility of being *required* to serve on a picket line;
    - possibility that a strike will interrupt hospital services and may therefore endanger the health and lives of patients;
    - inability to discuss problems directly with supervisor and employer;[44] and
    - possibility that the union will demand union shop (mandatory dues) provisions.

With regard to discussing the union and the election with employees, supervisors may provide the following information:

- Signing a union authorization card does not mean that the employee has promised to vote for the union in the election.
- The outcome of an NLRB election is determined by a majority of the employees *actually voting*—not by a majority of the total number of employees eligible to vote. (For this reason, and also because employees who do not support the union may be the ones most likely to avoid voting or to forget about voting, it is important that all employees be encouraged to exercise their right to vote.)
- Voting in NLRB elections is

done in private booths, where the employees mark their choice in absolute secrecy.[45,46]

- The law permits an employer to permanently replace anyone who engages in an "economic" strike—a strike not motivated by employer unfair labor practices.[47]
- A local union is subject to governance by the international union through bylaws.
- Truthful information about the union and its leaders may be given to employees.[48]
- No union can force an employer to pay more than it is willing or able to pay.[49]

Prohibited campaign conduct

Supervisors must realize that a communication is not protected by the freedom of speech provisions of the act if it contains an express or implied threat of reprisal or force or an express or implied promise of a benefit. Conduct that shows hostility toward pro-union employees or that shows favoritism toward employees who do not support the union is prohibited.

Supervisors thus cannot

1. promise that pay and benefit increases will be forthcoming if the union loses the election;
2. promise pay increases or special favors to anti-union employees;
3. threaten employees supporting the union with loss of job, reduction of income, discontinuance of privileges or benefits,

discipline, layoff, and/or re-classification;

4. ask employees certain questions. For example, a supervisor cannot ask an employee
   - how he or she will vote;
   - what he or she thinks about the union;[50]
   - whether he or she belongs to a union; or
   - whether he or she knows the internal affairs of the union;

5. question prospective employees about past union affiliation;

6. state that the employer will not deal with the union or will shut down if the union wins the election;[51]

7. spy on union meetings[52] (do not even drive past the meeting place);

8. forge campaign materials;[53]

9. alter official board documents;[54]

10. enforce an invalid solicitation–distribution policy;

11. use a third party to threaten, coerce, or intimidate employees; or

12. visit employee homes for the purpose of campaigning (although an employer cannot visit employee homes to campaign, a union may do so).

Election day

When the day of the union election comes, the supervisor may still speak to employees individually and may pass out literature, but must avoid "captive audience" speeches to groups of employees on work time.[55]

The NLRB has held that "the final minutes before an employee casts his vote should be his own, as free from interference as possible."[56] Thus, in the voting area, prolonged conversation with employees can lead to the setting aside of an election.[57] Even shaking hands or conversing about nonelection matters with employees waiting to vote must be avoided. On one occasion the NLRB set aside an election in which employer officials were merely present near the voting area.[58]

Postelection

As the key communication link between management and employees, the supervisor plays an important role in ensuring that the normal operations of the health care institution will not be disrupted during the postelection period, regardless of the outcome of the election.

The supervisor should seek to downplay election results and events of the campaign period, helping others to put the past behind them and to get on with the task at hand—keeping the hospital or health care institution running smoothly.

If the employees have chosen to be represented by a union, direct channels of communication with employees still must be kept open to the fullest extent possible. Knowledge of the legal requirements for dealing with a union is essential, as is a complete understanding of the terms of any collective bargaining agreement that is negotiated.

If the union has lost the election, supervisors should deal with all employees in the normal manner: honestly, and without regard for whether the employee did or did not support the union.

•   •   •

A union organizing campaign is not something that supervisors at health care institutions should dread. The employer who campaigns with honesty and conviction, armed with a basic understanding of the legal framework that regulates conduct during an organizational campaign, should be able to maintain a healthy working environment before, during, and after a union election.

REFERENCES

1. Becker, E.R., Sloan, F.A., and Steinwald, B. "Union Activity in Hospitals: Past, Present, and Future." *Health Care Financing Review* 3, no. 4 (1982): 1–13. These figures come from responses to surveys conducted by the American Hospital Association of all AHA-registered hospitals. The figures quoted above include both public and private hospitals. For federal hospitals, 51.9 percent had a collective bargaining agreement in 1970, 86.1 percent in 1980. For nonfederal hospitals, the figures are: 1970—13.3 percent, 1980—23.8 percent. It is interesting to note, though, that private proprietary hospitals registered only a very small gain in the number of institutions with collective bargaining agreements, from 10 percent in 1970 to 11.5 percent in 1980.
2. *NLRB Annual Reports.* Washington, D.C.: Government Printing Office. Figures for 1981 are the most recent available.
3. 29 U.S.C. §§151–68 (1982).
4. NLRB v. Jones & Laughlin Steel Corp., 301 U.S. 1 (1937).
5. 29 U.S.C. §151 (1982).
6. 29 U.S.C. §152(9) (1982).
7. 29 U.S.C. §152(14) (1982).
8. 29 U.S.C. §157 (1982).
9. 29 U.S.C. §158(a) (1982).
10. 29 U.S.C. §159 (1984). In general, Section 9 of the act covers the process by which a labor union becomes recognized as the exclusive representative of a unit of employees for the purpose of collective bargaining.
11. NLRB v. Gissel Packing Co., 395 U.S. 575 (1969).
12. Conair Corp., 261 N.L.R.B. 1189 (1982), *enforced in part, denied in part.* See Conair Corp. v. NLRB, 721 F.2d 1355 (D.C. Cir. 1983) (bargaining order improper when union never attained majority status); but see United Dairy Farmers Coop Ass'n v. NLRB, 633 F.2d 1054 (3d Cir. 1980) (nonmajority bargaining order permissible). Recently, however, the NLRB has determined that a bargaining order would not be issued unless a union had demonstrated majority support. Gourmet Foods, Inc., 270 N.L.R.B. 113 (1984).
13. 29 C.F.R. §101.18 (1984). It is generally believed that an outside union usually will not attempt an organization drive unless about 65 percent of the employees support the union in the early organization stages.
14. 29 U.S.C. §158(a) (1982).
15. Coty Messenger Service, Inc., 272 N.L.R.B. 42 (1984). See Brenol Electric, Inc., 271 N.L.R.B. 231 (1984).
16. Lancer Corp., 271 N.L.R.B. 228 (1984).
17. Hollywood Ceramics Co., 140 N.L.R.B. 221 (1962). See generally, Shopping Kart Food Mkts., Inc., 228 N.L.R.B. 1311 (1977); General Knit of California, 239 N.L.R.B. 619 (1978); and Midland National Life Insurance Co., 263 N.L.R.B. 127 (1982).
18. Midland National Life Insurance Co., 263 N.L.R.B. 127 (1982).
19. Shopping Kart Food Mkts., Inc., 228 N.L.R.B. 1311 (1977).
20. Midland National Life Insurance Co., 263 N.L.R.B. 127 (1982).
21. Excelsior Underwear, Inc., 156 N.L.R.B. 1236 (1966).
22. All-Weather Architectural Aluminum, Inc., 692 F.2d 76 (9th Cir. 1982).
23. Peerless Plywood Co., 107 N.L.R.B. 427 (1953).
24. NLRB v. Babcock & Wilcox, 351 U.S. 105 (1956).

25. For a general discussion of solicitation and distribution policies, see Henry, K. *The Health Care Supervisor's Legal Guide*. Rockville, Md.: Aspen Systems, 1984, pp. 62–64.

26. An employer's policy prohibiting all solicitation conducted without the "prior express written approval of the executive director" was found to be unlawful and led to the setting aside of the election in St. Joseph's Hospital, 262 N.L.R.B. 1385 (1982).

27. Republic Aviation Corp. v. NLRB, 324 U.S. 793 (1945).

28. Beth Israel Hospital v. NLRB, 437 U.S. 483 (1978). Accord, NLRB v. Baptist Hospital, Inc., 442 U.S. 773 (1979). Operating rooms, patient rooms, and treatment areas are "immediate patient care areas," whereas cafeterias, lobbies, gift shops, etc., are usually not.

29. Stoddard-Quirk Mfg. Co., 138 N.L.R.B. 615 (1962).

30. McGraw Edison Co., Halo Lighting Div., 259 N.L.R.B. 702 (1981). See Livingston Shirt Co., 107 N.L.R.B. 400 (1953).

31. NLRB v. Babcock & Wilcox, 351 U.S. 105 (1956); but see, for liberalization of rule applicable to health care institutions, Rochester General Hospital, 234 N.L.R.B. 253 (1978).

32. NLRB v. West Coast Casket Co., 205 F.2d 902 (9th Cir. 1953). A poll conducted by a *union*, however, does not lead to the setting aside of an election. Louis-Allis Co. v. NLRB, 463 F.2d 512 (7th Cir. 1972).

33. Struksnes Constr. Co., 165 N.L.R.B. 1062 (1967).

34. Id. A recent Ninth Circuit (California and other western states) decision has extended the right of an employer to poll its employees concerning their support or lack of support for an *incumbent* union. Mingtree Restaurant, Inc. v. NLRB, 736 F.2d 1295 (9th Cir. 1984). Prior to conducting such a poll, the employer must possess a sincere doubt of the union's majority status, backed by substantial objective evidence of a loss of union support.

35. Swan Coal Co., 271 N.L.R.B. 140 (1984).

36. Milchem, Inc., 170 N.L.R.B. 362 (1968).

37. Brenol Electric, Inc., 271 N.L.R.B. 231 (1984).

38. Metzger, N. *The Health Care Supervisor's Handbook*. Rockville, Md.: Aspen Systems, 1982, p. 105.

39. McConnell, C. *The Effective Health Care Supervisor*. Rockville, Md.: Aspen Systems, 1982, p. 292.

40. Greensboro News Co., 272 N.L.R.B. 28 (1984). The statement by an employer that "[we could not] talk about financial or family problems if we had a union. . . . everything would have to go through proper channels . . ." was found to be lawful. In McGraw Edison Co., Halo Lighting Div., 259 N.L.R.B. 702 (1981), the following language in an employer letter to employees was found to be lawful: "[the] presence of [a] union results in a tense working relationship." But see Hahn Property Management Corp., 263 N.L.R.B. 586 (1982). The employer interfered with an election when it told employees that a union victory would result in an adversary relationship and in cessation of direct communication between employees and management.

41. Livingston Shirt Corp., 107 N.L.R.B. 400 (1983). An employer may hold meetings of employees during working hours without having to give equal time for union scheduled meetings.

42. 29 U.S.C. §158(c) (1984).

43. Daniels Cadillac, Inc., 270 N.L.R.B. 86 (1984).

44. Greensboro News Co., 272 N.L.R.B. 28 (1984).

45. 29 C.F.R. §102.69(a) (1984).

46. NLRB Casehandling Manual §1130.43 (1984).

47. NLRB v. Mackay Radio & Telephone Co., 304 U.S. 333 (1938). See Purolator Products, Inc., 270 N.L.R.B. 87 (1984).

48. A truthful answer to an employee's question about the union is allowed. Thus in General Electric Co., 264 N.L.R.B. 953 (1982), a supervisor did not interfere with the election by replying in the affirmative to employee's question as to whether, under the union's national contract, employees who ran out of work during the shift would be sent home.

49. Purolator Products, Inc., 270 N.L.R.B. 87 (1984).

50. Electric Hose & Rubber Co., 262 N.L.R.B. 186 (1982).

51. Nebraska Bulk Transportation v. NLRB, 608 F.2d 311 (8th Cir. 1979).

52. Consolidated Edison Co. v. NLRB, 305 U.S. 197 (1938). See Hamilton Nursing Home, 270 N.L.R.B. 203 (1984).

53. Midland National Life Insurance Co., 263 N.L.R.B. 127 (1982).

54. Id.

55. Peerless Plywood Co., 107 N.L.R.B. 427 (1953).

56. Milchem, Inc., 170 N.L.R.B. 362 (1968).

57. Antenna Dept. West, 266 N.L.R.B. 909 (1983).

58. Performance Measurements Co., 148 N.L.R.B. 1657, supplemented, 149 N.L.R.B. 1451 (1964).

Issues concerning an employee strike

Andrew Banoff
Baruch College
Health Care Administration
   Program
Mount Sinai School of Medicine
New York, New York

A HOSPITAL faced with an employee strike is put in a delicate position. The institution's main function is to provide quality health care, and this requires many highly trained employees. Therefore, a strike can have far-reaching effects on the hospital's objectives.

Labor laws regarding strikes and negotiations have evolved into a complex array of requirements for both management and unions. The issues in an employee strike are as complex as the law and need to be evaluated in this context. The purpose of this article is to provide a historical and up-to-date analysis of these issues and the practical problems they pose.

HISTORY

After the Great Depression, the U.S. government began to enact legislation to aid the nation's recovery. The foundation of the country's labor

Health Care Superv, 1987, 5(4), 54–60

code was the National Labor Relations (Wagner) Act of 1935. The purpose of the act, as stated in the preamble was: "to define and protect the rights of employees and employers, to encourage collective bargaining, and to eliminate certain practices on the part of labor and management that are harmful to the general welfare."[1] Health care facilities were not exempted from this law, because the rule for inclusion was the impact on interstate commerce rather than the issue of for-profit status.

The next step in the evolution of labor law was the passage of the Labor-Management Relations (Taft-Hartley) Act of 1947, which amended the Wagner Act. The expansion of union membership in the industrial sector had created new problems regarding union–management relations and had made new legislation necessary. Unlike under the Wagner Act, health care facilities were excluded.

The implications of the exemption of nonprofit hospitals from the Taft-Hartley Act were clear. In the absence of any state statute which specifically included nonprofit hospitals, such hospitals had no obligation under the law to recognize or deal with their employees on a collective basis. Additionally, hospital management could engage in direct action to halt or limit union activity.[2]

The Taft-Hartley Act is still the nation's central piece of labor legislation. Unfortunately, it led to a fragmented labor law system in the health care industry because there was no coordinating force in this area.

National sentiment for a consolidation of health care facility labor laws grew during the 1960s and early 1970s, resulting in the 1974 amendments to the Taft-Hartley Act.[3] Essentially, the amendments extended coverage to the health care industry, with certain specific changes designed to provide for a continuum of health care. These changes focused on strike and contract notice times, mediation, emergency disputes, bargaining units, etc.

There is now an established set of rules and regulations regarding labor–management relations, including health care facilities. There are also several other laws that relate to this subject that should be mentioned briefly:

- The Labor Management Reporting and Disclosure (Landrum-Griffin) Act of 1959 was enacted to eliminate or prevent improper practices on the part of labor organizations, employers, and consultants with regard to the Taft-Hartley Act of 1947.
- Equal employment opportunity laws were designed to protect workers from discrimination in the work place. The most significant of these were the Civil Rights Act of 1964, the Equal Pay Act of 1963, the Age Discrimination in Employment Act, and the Rehabilitation Act of 1973.
- The Fair Labor Standards Act, initially enacted in 1938 and frequently amended, was designed to ensure national wage and hour standards.

These laws, in conjunction with the Taft-Hartley Act and its amendments, provide a forum to evaluate disputes, conflicts, and negotiations between management and employees. Before analyzing the practical impact of a health care strike, it is necessary to look at some of the specific strike requirements of these laws.

STRIKE REQUIREMENTS

The amended National Labor Relations Act established specific procedures that must be followed before engaging in a strike or picketing activity. When a contract is being modified or terminated, written notification must be given 90 days in advance to the other party involved and 60 days in advance to the Federal Mediation and Conciliation Service (FMCS). A 10-day notice of intent to strike or picket must be given to health care institutions to give them time to prepare for continued patient care or alternative arrangements. Striking during any of these "cooling-off" periods deprives employees of their status and makes them subject to discharge or other discipline by the employer.[4]

In addition, during economic strikes health care employers may temporarily or permanently replace strikers in order to maintain operations. This is among the key issues that need to be evaluated by hospital administration. Vacant positions must be offered to the strikers after the strike if they apply for reinstatement. However, strikers who are guilty of misconduct during the strike do not have to be rehired.[5]

The other main area of action subject to specific requirements is picketing. Picketing rules apply not only to the union and the employees on strike but to all others as well. Specifically, legal action has been taken against organizations for sympathy or informational picketing without providing appropriate advanced notices. Furthermore, recognitional and organizational picketing are prohibited when the employer has lawfully recognized another union, a valid election has been held within the past 12 months, or a representation petition has not been filed within 30 days of such picketing.[6]

The bargaining unit is another important area to be considered. Union and management must both work within very strict guidelines to pursue their conflict. The National Labor Relations Board (NLRB) has identified five fundamental groupings of appropriate units for hospitals: registered nurses, professional employees, technical employees, business and clerical employees, and service and maintenance employees. The National Labor Relations Act also excludes certain individuals from eligibility in bargaining units in hospitals: independent contractors, supervisors, managerial employees, and confidential employees.

THE STRIKE

The remainder of this article will be devoted to analyzing the issues to be dealt with during the actual strike. These can be separated into two main areas: hospital operations and contract negotiations.

Hospital operations

The main function of a hospital, remaining its main concern during a strike, is to provide quality health care to its patients. When employees

---

The main function of a hospital, remaining its main concern during a strike, is to provide quality health care to its patients.

---

are on strike this can be especially difficult in a non-profit setting. "In the hospital setting, the rationale for a strike is . . . to disrupt the institution, inconvenience patients and staff, and put pressure on the community that the institution serves so that the community will compel the institution to agree to the union's demands."[7] This is unlike private industry where the rationale to strike is to deprive management and shareholders of income and profit. Since there is clearly a conflict between the hospital's purpose and the union's rationale, the hospital is faced with some very difficult questions. The first of these is the decision whether to remain open during the strike. If hospital administration feels that it cannot meet its objective with certain employees on strike, then it should not risk the welfare of its patients.

Closing the institution will hamper the union's efforts but will also have a negative impact on the hospital's public image.

If the hospital decides to stay open then it has a different situation to deal with. The striking employees can dramatically influence patient care. Therefore, it is advisable to reduce the number of patients in the hospital as much as possible. Patients must be categorized as eligible for discharge, potentially eligible for discharge, and definitely not eligible for discharge. The first category should be discharged prior to the beginning of the strike. The remaining patients should be condensed into a smaller number of units to make coverage easier. Potentially dischargeable patients should be kept together if possible.

Once the number of patients has been reduced it is important to keep the census low. Therefore, all elective admissions should be cancelled. The hospital must be prepared to handle emergency admissions and to continue the operation of its emergency department. If the hospital is an emergency medical services (EMS) receiving hospital, that agency should be informed of the pending strike so as to avoid additional patients if at all possible. This should also be conveyed to the other area hospitals. It is important to remember, though, that the hospital cannot refuse care to anyone who arrives for treatment under any circumstances.

The other main concern during the strike will be to ensure adequate staff for the remaining patients. These will be the more acute patients, so special consideration must be given. The main resources at the hospital are supervisors, nurses, house staff, and attending physicians. All of these personnel, as well as other nonunion employees, have to cover for those on strike, performing functions that are undoubtedly not in their job descriptions. The other possibility that must be considered is the hiring of temporary or permanent replacements for the strikers. This can also be used as a bargaining chip when dealing with the union.

Picketing will probably arise as an operational issue during the strike. As discussed previously, this is legal if certain requirements are met; these requirements have several main purposes: "to ensure that striking employees stay on strike, to discourage "strike-breaking" by nonemployee replacements, to prevent deliveries from reaching the employer, and to induce the public to side with the strikers."[8]

Picketing can have drastic effects on operations and must be dealt with carefully. Peaceful strikes and picketing are subject to regulation by the NLRB. Once activity becomes violent, however, the states have authority to maintain peace through the exercise of local police power.

Two final points must be made in regard to hospital operations. First, a hospital is never exposed to greater public scrutiny than during a strike. The image portrayed by the media can have far-reaching effects on the hospital's standing in the community.

Therefore, administration must be very cautious in this regard. Finally, almost all strikes have similar characteristics, and there are people available who have worked through such a crisis. Thus, it may be advisable for a hospital to hire a labor consultant to help out during a strike.

Contract negotiations

While the majority of our staff will be concerned with the scaled-down operation of the hospital, certain members of management will be involved in negotiations with the union. This is likely to occur in three distinct phases: internal negotiation, external arbitration, and formal litigation. In any context, a negotiating team should be created for the hospital. This will consist of (at a minimum) the administrator, the assistant administrator for support services, and the personnel manager. One person should be the chief negotiator, and this could be any of the foregoing or a labor attorney engaged for the purpose. This person must represent the consensus of the hospital's position.

Prior to any negotiations, the hospital should agree upon a framework for dealing with the union. This includes the degree to which concessions will be made, a time frame for concessions, and as many foreseeable outcomes as possible. Naturally, these decisions must be based on the current situation, including the current rate of inflation, comparable salaries and benefits at similar institutions, the ability to meet all concessions, economic status of the organization, and productivity of the staff. Negotiations that result in an environment in which the hospital cannot survive are useless.

The National Labor Relations Act provides one basic rule for any negotiations, and that is to bargain in good faith. There are no standards for concessions, and neither side is expected to agree to something that they do not want to agree to.

The law requires an employee to recognize and bargain in good faith with a certified union, but it does not force the employer to agree with the union. Management is free to yield to union's persuasions, but it does not have to be persuaded, provided always that management has given the union opportunity—in good faith—to persuade."[9]

Therefore, the hospital negotiating team can work within its framework and still abide by the law. The hospital can also put into effect contract changes that it has discussed with the union during negotiations. However,

---

Before the hospital institutes any unilateral changes, it must be certain that such changes do not discriminate against strikers.

---

before the hospital institutes any unilateral changes, it must be certain that such changes do not discriminate against strikers.

The second level of negotiation is accomplished through arbitration. Once it is clear that the two sides cannot reach agreement on their own, they have an opportunity to settle their differences through arbitration. This process is voluntary and it is a preferred alternative to the courts. Arbitration is faster and less expensive than court, and arbitrators are experts in labor negotiations. It is important to note that the FMCS is the largest arbitration agency and has certain powers regarding health care. If the director of the FMCS feels that a continued strike will substantially interrupt the delivery of health care, he or she may appoint an impartial board of inquiry that is responsible for submitting recommendations for settling the dispute. Decisions by an arbitrator are binding and will hold up in court.[10] However, if there are unusual circumstances the FMCS may require the case to be settled by litigation.

Once the strike has been settled, the hospital must get back to normal operations with its new contract. Elective admissions, full services, and normal staff levels will be reinstated. This will take some time, as the effect of the strike is not readily forgotten. Two specific issues must be dealt with: discipline of strikers who violated labor law, and rehiring of strikers for vacant positions. First, management has the right to discipline employees for strike-related offenses, but this will only add to the after-effects of the strike. Second, management must rehire these employees unless they have broken strike rules. Most likely, one stipulation of the settlement will be that no action be taken against strikers. Finally, management should take this opportunity, with their newly acquired wisdom, to formulate a strike contingency plan.

•   •   •

The National Labor Relations Act and its amendments and other labor laws provide an overall structure in which a variety of union and employer relationships can be established. There are many requirements for contract negotiations, strikes, and other conflicts. A hospital that is faced with a strike must operate within the context of these laws as they pertain to the health care industry. Failure to do so would only add further to the dilemma of a strike.

Continued quality patient care and the settlement of the dispute as quickly as possible with a workable contract are the two main concerns to contend with during the course of a strike. It is important to remember that

negotiating a contract with a labor organization flows from the requirements under the law to bargain in good faith, but much of the outcome of such bargaining is determined by the structure of the union-management relationship and the personalities involved in collective bargaining. The mere fact that there are provisions in the law will not organize employees, nor will such provisions guarantee the negotiation of a sound collective bargaining agreement.[11]

REFERENCES

1. National Labor Relations Board, Office of General Counsel. *A Guide to Basic Laws and Procedures Under the National Labor Relations Act.* Washington, D.C.: Government Printing Office, 1978, p. 1.
2. Pointer, D., and Metzger, N. *The National Labor Relations Act: A Guidebook for Health Care Facility Administrators.* New York: Spectrum Publications, 1975, p. 18.
3. Lasky, P., ed. *Hospital Law Manual: Administrators Volume 1A, Labor.* Rockville, Md.: Aspen Publishers, 1983, p. 39.
4. Kramer, S., and Ellert, W. "Strikes, Solicitation and Bargaining: The National Labor Relations Board Applies the Act to the Health Care Industry." In *Handbook of Health Care Human Resources Management,* edited by N. Metzger. Rockville, Md.: Aspen Publishers, 1981, pp. 597–99.
5. Pointer and Metzger, *The National Labor Relations Act,* 138.
6. Ibid.
7. Lasky, *Hospital Law Manual: Administrators Volume 1A, Labor,* 88.
8. Ibid., 93.
9. Pointer and Metzger, *The National Labor Relations Act,* 191.
10. Teple, E., and Moberly, R. *Arbitration and Conflict Resolution,* Washington, D.C.: The Bureau of National Affairs, 1979, p. 439.
11. Pointer and Metzger, *The National Labor Relations Act,* 181.

From grievance through arbitration: a supervisor's perspective

Donald J. Petersen
Professor of Management
Loyola University of Chicago
Chicago, Illinois

THE GRIEVANCE procedure has been aptly described as the "heart of the collective bargaining process." Collective negotiations, of course, normally result in a written agreement. However, an agreement is a static document presumably intended to cover all aspects of labor–management relations, a task that no document can accomplish completely. For one thing, contract negotiators cannot possibly foresee all future contingencies or changes that might occur over the life of the agreement. Yet it is sometimes necessary to apply such a document, drafted at a given point in time, to current problems. Second, the substance of any contract is words, and words carry different connotations and have different meanings to each person. Whether intended or not, words often provide the grist of future disputes regarding the interpretation or application of the collective agreement. Moreover, at times, the negotiators place vague and ambiguous language

Health Care Superv, 1984,2(4),48–67
© 1984 Aspen Publishers, Inc.

in the agreement such as "overtime will be distributed as equally as possible," "just cause" and "reasonable time will be granted union stewards for adjusting grievances." While this type of language often permits the parties to reach agreement, it may also lead to future disputes about meaning. And, of course, the omission of contract language (i.e., the contract is silent) may also present problems for contract administration. In fact, it is sometimes said that there are more grievances concerning what is missing from the contract than what is actually in the contract.

When there is a disagreement as to how the contract is interpreted or applied, some mechanism must exist for permitting employee or union protest. That mechanism is the grievance procedure.

In most cases, the grievance procedure consists of a set of appeals to higher levels of management which, in about 90 percent of hospital collective bargaining agreements, terminates in binding arbitration.[1] Typically, hospital contracts call for a four-step procedure (arbitration being the fourth step), but there is a definite trend toward compacting the process into three steps. In an overwhelming number of contracts, the first step involves the supervisor as management's representative.

THE SUPERVISOR'S ROLE IN THE GRIEVANCE PROCEDURE

Many experts believe that the most effective grievance procedure exists when as many grievances as possible are settled at the first step, or at the supervisor level. The supervisor is the closest hierarchical link to the subordinate, and grievances are normally handled most expeditiously at this point. As grievances proceed through steps of the grievance procedure, many employees feel they lose control of their grievances and management–union decision making appears to be more formal and remote.

If the supervisor is a key figure in the grievance procedure, what should his or her role be? How can a supervisor become more effective in handling grievances, and what does "effective" mean in this sense? To some members of higher management, effective grievance handling means that a supervisor has "few grievances," that is, the grievance rate for each supervisor is low. A paucity of grievances equates with good labor relations in a department, at least according to such thinking. The grievance rate is not, however, a particularly good measure for that purpose. Grievances may flood the grievance procedure prior to contract negotiations, after contract negotiations, before a union election (of officers), or in response to a political upheaval within the union. On the other hand, there have been cases in which unions have filed numerous grievances against supervisors to discredit them in retaliation for alleged mistreatment of employees, or as a means of control.[2] By way of contrast, a low grievance rate could mean a weak union, docile employees, poor

---

A low grievance rate does not necessarily indicate good union–management relations; nor does a high grievance rate mean that poor relations exist.

---

union leadership, etc. Therefore, a low grievance rate does not necessarily indicate good union–management relations; nor does a high grievance rate mean that poor relations exist.

Rather than concentrating on the grievance rate as an index of how the grievance process is functioning, a preferred approach may focus on:

- giving the supervisor *authority* to settle as many grievances as possible;
- acting promptly in processing grievances; and
- handling grievances fairly.[3]

Supervisor authority—key to successful grievance handling

Although the collective agreement may specify the supervisor as the first step in the grievance procedure, too often this step is meaningless. This happens because management may instruct supervisors to simply write "grievance denied," as a response to a complaint and then refer it to the personnel or industrial relations department. This is done because it is felt that supervisors are not competent to handle contract interpretation matters, and because it is feared that an adverse past practice or precedent may be established by an incorrect

grievance answer. Of course, some supervisors are only too happy to abdicate their industrial relations responsibilities in order to devote attention to the "real" mission of their departments.

There is no excuse for failing to train supervisors in the techniques of grievance handling.[4] This can—and possibly should—be done in-house. Training programs should focus on such areas as interpretation of the agreement, contract negotiations, and prior grievance and arbitration settlements. University courses can be used to round out the educational process. Management should stress the importance of grievance settlement at the supervisory level and indicate in the strongest terms that supervisors are expected to handle grievances. This will help reduce the possibility that supervisors will automatically "kick grievances upstairs."

In the absence of supervisory authority to settle grievances, supervisors may be perceived by the union and employees alike as powerless "rubber stamps." The supervisor not only loses credibility with his or her subordinates, but also misses out on the chance to be a positive force in improving labor relations.

One way (besides training) to reduce management fears about giving grievance settlement authority to supervisors is to make their decisions nonbinding (non–precedent setting) in future cases. In this way the incorrect resolution of a grievance will not create the calamity it may otherwise cause.[5]

Internal and external factors influencing supervisory grievance handling

Given that a supervisor has the authority and the management support for grievance settlement, there are still other factors that impinge on the supervisor's effectiveness in accomplishing settlement. Some of these factors are within the supervisor's control, such as leadership style and approach to grievance processing. These factors may be referred to as "internal factors." The other set of factors impinging on supervisor grievance-handling success may be referred to as "external factors." These include such considerations as provisions in the collective agreement dealing with the definition of a grievance, timeliness and the union steward.

Leadership style and grievance-handling effectiveness

One area in which a supervisor may influence grievance handling is the leadership style with which the employees are approached. A useful way of classifying leadership is in terms of the so-called autocratic or democratic styles.[6] Autocratic leaders tend to believe that their subordinates are basically lazy and irresponsible, that they prefer to be directed, have little ambition and are motivated by monetary rewards. In short, such leaders have little confidence in the abilities of their employees and believe that motivation can be achieved only through threat of punishment or promise of reward. Democratic leaders, in contrast, hold opposite assumptions regarding their employees.

A study by Walker and Robinson concluded that autocratic leaders have significantly lower grievance rates than do democratic leaders, and also have significantly lower rates of discipline-related and overtime-related grievances. They also found that autocratic leaders had significantly fewer grievances settled at the *lower steps* in the grievance procedure than democratic leaders.[7]

It must be remembered, when analyzing such claims, that the study was done in a work environment that was highly favorable to the autocratic style of leadership and that included: (1) good leader—member relationships, (2) structured job-related tasks and (3) strong leader position power.[8] However, an autocratic leadership style will also be appropriate in an opposite type of environment, for example, (1) if poor leader—member relationships exist, (2) if there are unstructured job-related tasks and (3) if the supervisor is in a weak leadership position.[9] In virtually any other situation, a democratic leadership style may be more effective. Certainly the democratic style of leadership met a major test of grievance procedure effectiveness, in other words, producing more settlements in the early steps of the grievance procedure.

In order for the reader to test his or her own leadership style, a questionnaire is provided in Figure 1. There

After each question, check the column that most accurately describes your activities. Be sure to make one choice for each question.

	Usually	*Often*	*Sometimes*	*Seldom*
1. I supervise my subordinates closely in order to get better work from them.				
2. I provide my subordinates with my goals and objectives and sell them on the merit of my plans.				
3. I set up controls to assure that my subordinates are getting the job done.				
4. I believe that, since I carry the responsibility, my subordinates must accept my decisions.				
5. I make sure that my subordinates' major workload is planned for them.				
6. I check with my subordinates daily to see if they need any help.				
7. I step in as soon as reports indicate that the job is slipping.				
8. I have frequent meetings to keep in touch with what is going on.				
9. I back up spontaneous but unauthorized decisions made by my employees.				
10. If necessary, I push my people to meet schedules.				

Figure 1. Leadership style on the job. Score all questions except number 9 as follows: -2 for usually (that you checked); -1 for often; 1 for sometimes; and 2 for seldom. Reverse the process for question 9: Score 2 for usually; 1 for often; -1 for sometimes; and -2 for seldom. Total your score. On the scale below, indicate the type of superior you could best work with:

-20	0	$+20$
Theory X (Autocratic)	Neutral	Theory Y (Democratic)

are no right or wrong answers. A key to scoring is also included.

Few supervisors will be either "all" autocratic or "all" democratic. Most fall somewhere between but usually tend toward one end of the scale or the other. Once a supervisor is aware of autocratic and democratic style, it may be easier to assess how each style helps or hinders the grievance settling process.

Clinical versus judicial approach to grievance handling

Various experts have suggested that a supervisor's approach to grievance handling can be a significant determinant of effectiveness. They suggest two approaches. One is the clinical approach, which advocates a problem-solving method of settling grievances. The other, called the judicial approach, suggests that grievances be treated in accordance with the strict provisions of the collective agreement.

The two approaches are not mutually exclusive. While it is often useful to treat grievances as problems to be solved rather than annoyances, good-faith attempts to settle grievances cannot be at variance with the terms of the collective agreement. Therefore, one approach cannot prevail over the other.

Contract limitations on grievance handling

As noted, the contract itself (an external factor) can also exert a strong influence on the grievance procedure. While all contract terms can, of course, become possible grievances, of particular interest are those parts of the agreement dealing with definitions of a grievance and the time limits imposed on filing grievances.

While some contracts do not attempt to define grievances at all, others contain detailed descriptions as to what constitutes a grievance. The latter may specify that a grievance must be based on an alleged violation of some specific provision of the contract. If an employee cannot point to such a provision, the grievance must fail (i.e., it becomes nonarbitrable). With a detailed definition

of what constitutes a permissible grievance, a supervisor has little choice but to deny (i.e., take the judicial approach) a grievance that does not meet contractual restrictions. Management should raise this defense at each step in the grievance procedure or it may lose its opportunity to do so if the grievance reaches arbitration. In any case, the complaint does not go away. It must therefore be treated apart from the formal grievance procedure.

Frequently the contract will specify time limits for filing grievances, as in the following example of such a provision contained in Hospital Employees Labor Program (HELP). "All grievances, except those hereafter specified, must be presented in the first step of the grievance procedure within twenty (20) calendar days from the date the cause for the grievance occurs or the employee or union has knowledge of the cause for grievance.[10] Under such a clause the grievant or the union has a specified number of days in which to file a grievance. Failure to observe the time limit may result in the union or grievant losing the opportunity to have the grievance reviewed on its merits. Once again, objection must be raised to the grievant's timeliness at each step in the grievance procedure in order to render the grievance procedurally nonarbitrable. Arbitrators will not consider the defense of untimeliness at the arbitration stage unless management raised that defense in the earlier grievance steps. While a grievance filed without regard to timeliness effectively disposes of it-self, the complaint may resurrect itself later on.

There is some evidence to suggest that grievances are more easily resolved prior to being committed to writing. Both discussion and compromise are facilitated during this early phase, but once a grievance is written the parties feel compelled to observe contractual time limits and move it through the formal steps in the grievance process. One problem with the practice of oral discussion of grievances is that they often become bogged down for long periods. Yet oral discussion of complaints can facilitate settlement at the earliest steps in the grievance procedure.

The role of the steward

Another external factor that influences the effectiveness of supervisory handling of grievances is the union steward. Unions have the controlling authority with respect to grievance and arbitration rates, and possibly even control the speed of settlement. Stewards play an important part in this total process. On the average, they devote more than half of their union-related activity to processing grievances.[11]

There are some data to support the notion that there is a positive relationship between lower grievance rates and a good industrial relations climate.[12] A union steward may be less inclined to file grievances, encourage members to file or even file grievances over the objections of union members, when that climate is positive.[13] Thus stewards enjoy a great deal of discretion in filing and processing grievances.

A basic question is whether union cooperation in grievance handling occurs because the industrial relations climate is positive, or whether effective grievance processing helps create such a positive industrial relations climate. Unfortunately, no studies exist to indicate the line of causation.

Each supervisor can help create a better working climate with his or her union steward by building trust and confidence through honest dealing. It

Each supervisor can help create a better working climate with his or her union steward by building trust and confidence through honest dealing.

is critical for supervisors to keep their words. Supervisors need to be sensitive to the pressures that stewards face; sometimes they find themselves confronting a membership that wishes them to file grievances that have no merit. It is also important to permit a steward to "save face." A supervisor creates trust and confidence when he or she "gives in" on grievances when the union is obviously correct. Building such a relationship takes time, and turnover of union officials seems to be a factor in making settlement of grievances difficult early in the procedure.[14]

TOWARD EFFECTIVE GRIEVANCE HANDLING

While internal and external factors may profoundly influence a supervisor's grievance-handling effectiveness, there are some measures (in addition to those already suggested) which can also facilitate grievance processing. An important prerequisite, as previously noted, is for a supervisor to be given—and to accept—the authority and responsibility for settling grievances. Once these important conditions have been established, a number of other steps can be taken to make grievance handling more effective.

Investigation, not evaluation

It is important that grievances be approached as problems to be solved, not mere annoyances in the workday. When a grievance is received, therefore, an immediate answer is not normally necessary. Schedule a meeting for later in the day or for the following day. Allow time to thoroughly investigate the grievance without first concluding that it lacks merit. This means that the contract must be consulted, past practices, if any, determined and negotiations history reviewed, if appropriate. In discipline or discharge cases, one will need various kinds of information such as production records, absentee or tardiness records, and past disciplinary-action records. The personnel or industrial relations department may be consulted to help find the information needed, and also to give advice regarding the possible disposition of the case. Obviously, it is important to have all the facts available at the grievance meeting.

Interviewing witnesses

Frequently, in cases dealing with discipline (and other cases as well), the testimony of witnesses is critical in determining what actually happened. For example, disciplinary action imposed for incidents of fighting, insubordination or theft often hinges on what various witnesses saw and heard. It is necessary to interview opposing witnesses as well as those on the side of the hospital. It is important to find out what each witness has to say without being critical or threatening, and without suggesting what one might want them to say. Notes of testimony should be taken and kept. Later, should the story of a witness be changed, the notes can be used to refute that testimony.

One may also want to prepare questions to ask during the grievance meeting. The answers of witnesses should be known in advance, based on the interviews. In general, it is better not to ask questions when the answers are not known.

Weingarten considerations

The National Labor Relations Board (NLRB), in its *Weingarten*[15] decision, ruled that an employer has the obligation to permit an employee to ask to have a union steward present when he or she has reason to believe that an interview may result in disciplinary action. A supervisor's failure to allow an employee representation may violate that employee's due process rights and render the disciplinary action invalid if the case reaches arbitration or is scrutinized by the NLRB. It is not necessary, however, that the grievance meeting be delayed just because the employee wishes a particular steward who is not available.

The importance of listening

Because it is helpful in grievance handling to bring out the facts, one must find out and understand what the real problems are. Therefore, one must listen carefully to what is being said, without interrupting. A helpful approach after hearing the grievance is to attempt to summarize or report what is heard to make certain it is understood, and also to let the employees know that it is understood.

Rules of conduct

The supervisor should set up rules for the conduct of the grievance meeting. While it is not necessary to keep grievance meetings rigid or formal, without some basic ground rules for hearing conduct, the process can "get away" from the supervisor. Only one person should be allowed to talk at a time. Interruptions should not be permitted. It may be preferable to consider allowing the union to complete its case before presenting any rebuttal testimony or evidence.

Follow-up

Finally, the supervisor must follow up on the disposition of each grievance. If the union prevails, the supervisor should check that the situation has been corrected as agreed to (has the grievant been paid, have methods changed, etc.). A failure to give what was promised in a grievance can appear to be welshing, and can tear down trust and confidence between the supervisor and the union. Even when the hospital's position is upheld, it is wise to study the grievance to determine how similar problems can be avoided in the future. This is part of good preventive labor relations.

THE DECISION TO ARBITRATE

Despite the parties' efforts to resolve a grievance during the first steps of the procedure, there are times when they cannot do so or will not be able to do so. There are, of course, two alternatives available: (1) the union can withdraw the grievance, in effect accepting management's final position on the matter; or (2) it can appeal the dispute to binding arbitration.[16] (Management can also insist that a grievance be arbitrated. However, this is rarely done because, if the union fails to demand arbitration, it is management's final answer that prevails in the matter.) Attached to either of these alternatives are various costs. If the union chooses the first, it loses that grievance (even if withdrawn without prejudice). On the other hand, arbitration involves bringing in a third party who may or may not be familiar with the bargaining history, practices or the relationship between the union and hospital management. Arbitration also increases monetary costs to the parties, such as arbitrators' fees, attorneys' fees and payment for witnesses (while they are away from their jobs). In fact, there have been estimates made that an arbitration may cost, on the average, $4,440.[17] Naturally, costs are not the only possible considerations facing the parties. There is also the danger that an arbitration award may erode an important management right or union benefit. For those reasons and more, the decision to arbitrate should not be taken lightly.

STRATEGIC AND POLITICAL REASONS FOR ARBITRATING

There are times when both sides have considerations apart from either the monetary or contractual implications of a grievance when making the decision to arbitrate. Sometimes the political or strategic consequences of a grievance may override even these considerations. For example, if, unknown to management, a union steward has promised his or her constituency that a particular grievance will be fought "all the way." Upper union leadership probably would not want to appear to be abandoning its representative by failing to support him or her, even if convinced that the case had no merit. Management may, at times, also hold the same perspective with regard to its supervisors.

Since unions are political institutions, there are usually various factions within them. Some factions may support the incumbent leadership and some may not. If a member of a rival faction had a grievance, perhaps even a frivolous one, the union leadership could hardly afford to refuse to arbitrate the grievance if by doing so it would provide grist for the rival faction to criticize its "militancy," or "concern for the membership." Unions have also been known to let the arbitrator take the blame for a negative decision rather than risk failing to process a politically sensitive grievance.

Some unions even have a policy of arbitrating *all* discharge cases regardless of their merits. In other situations, one can almost predict that arbitration will follow the discharge of a union representative. Still other unions, sensitive to the implications of the duty of fair representation, not to mention the Civil Rights Act, will be likely to arbitrate the grievances of minorities and women. A union may even arbitrate to stir up interest in the union itself, that is, to let the membership know it is actively supporting them. Unions have also filed grievances, and have even arbitrated some of them, for the purpose of harassing a supervisor as a means of revenge or control. The author has reported that as many as 25 percent of all grievances submitted by unions reach arbitration for primarily political or strategic reasons.[18]

The supervisor should be aware that not all grievances are filed or arbitrated on their merits alone. One must try to study the behind-the-scenes implications of each dispute and learn to ask questions like "Who is involved?" "Who stands to gain or lose from this grievance?" "Is a union election coming up?" "How strongly entrenched is present union leadership?" "Who is the grievant and what is his or her role relative to the union?" A supervisor cannot always hold off grievances by asking these questions, but he or she can better understand the union's position and perhaps plan a personal strategy accordingly.

SELECTION OF AN ARBITRATOR

When it is decided that a grievance will be submitted to arbitration, an obvious first step is the selection of the arbitrator. The parties' ability to select an arbitrator is one of the major advantages of arbitration over the courts. In court matters, the parties have no opportunity to select their judge, but in arbitration the parties enjoy considerable flexibility in choosing an arbitrator. There are several ways that an arbitrator can be selected. Usually the collective bargaining agreement specifies the method. Some hospital contracts state that the parties must first attempt to agree on an arbitrator, but failing a

mutually agreeable choice they will contact an agency that maintains rosters of qualified arbitrators, such as the American Arbitration Association or Federal Mediation and Conciliation Service. [Note: The American Arbitration Association is a private, not-for-profit organization that charges the parties for supplying a panel of arbitrator names and vitaes. The Federal Mediation and Conciliation Service is a federal government agency that provides a similar service, among other duties, at no cost.] These agencies will send five to seven arbitrators' names along with their background and qualifications. The parties review this information and attempt to select one person whom they believe would be most sympathetic to their case. They will sometimes attempt to "research" the arbitrators' backgrounds by contacting associates or attorneys, or by reading cases published by the arbitrators. In this way the parties believe they are enhancing their chances for success. However, most unions and hospital selectors demand an experienced arbitrator.

Frequently, after researching the arbitrators' background, the parties will alternately strike the names of arbitrators whom they do not, for whatever reasons, want to hear the case. The remaining arbitrator is the one chosen. Another method of selecting an arbitrator is to rank each arbitrator as one, two, three, etc., with one being most preferred. The arbitrator with the lowest average rank to both sides is the individual picked.

HOW ARBITRATORS SERVE THE PARTIES

There are three common methods by which arbitrators serve the parties. These include ad hoc, ad hoc and board, and permanent umpireships. The collective bargaining agreement normally defines the method that a particular hospital and union will use.

Under an ad hoc arrangement, the parties are free to choose whichever arbitrator they wish, by whatever means their contract specifies (as primarily discussed). However, there is no obligation for the parties to ever use that arbitrator's services again if either or both sides are not satisfied. On the other hand, if the parties are convinced the arbitrator did a good job, they are free to select that person

There are probably more advantages than disadvantages to the ad hoc approach to arbitrators serving the parties, and it is the most preferred method of arbitration.

again and again. There are probably more advantages than disadvantages to this approach, and it is the most preferred method of arbitration according to surveys of arbitration procedures. Chiefly, it allows hospitals with relatively few arbitrations the convenience of appointing an arbitrator only as needed, and it further permits the use of arbitrators with special qualifications, such as background in a technical area, when the need arises. The main disadvantage of the method is that an arbitrator who is called to hear only one case cannot become totally familiar with the collective bargaining history of the parties and the background of the dispute. This disadvantage can be offset, however, if the parties take the time to provide the arbitrator with needed details.

The ad hoc and board system, though once widely favored, is falling into disuse. In this method, the parties select one ad hoc arbitrator and each side has its own individual "arbitrator." The latter are usually not arbitrators in the strictest sense, and they typically decide for their side. The neutral arbitrator then casts the decisive "vote" in the case. It is said that this method permits the partial arbitrators (i.e., the "board") to provide the neutral arbitrator with relevant background information that might otherwise be missing. However, any such information should be brought out in the hearing itself so that both sides have a chance to respond and clarify. If this is done, there is little or no reason to prefer an ad hoc and board system over the ad hoc one.

The third type of arbitration system calls for a "permanent" arbitrator. Actually, most permanent umpires serve only for the duration of a collective agreement. Some permanent arbitration systems specify one arbitrator who hears all of the hospital's cases, or a rotating panel of three to five arbitrators who do the same. Obviously, it makes little sense for the parties to use a permanent umpireship unless their volume of cases is sufficient to justify such an arrangement. Moreover, the main advantage of a permanent umpireship (i.e., the arbitrator becomes well acquainted with the parties' background, collective bargaining history, peculiarities of the industry, etc.), can also be a disadvantage if the arbitrator becomes biased or begins "splitting" awards. It is an old wives' tale that arbitrators maintain their acceptability by giving each side something in their decision. By the time a grievance reaches the arbitration stage, undoubtedly the parties have discussed various compromise solutions. They have rejected these for one or another reason, and now desire an answer to the issue at hand.

ROLES THE SUPERVISOR PLAYS IN THE ARBITRATION PROCESS

Though supervisors are seldom directly involved in the selection of an arbitrator, they nonetheless may play a significant role in the arbitration process. Normally their role is twofold: (1) as investigators and evidence gatherers and (2) as witnesses in the arbitration hearing. The former role has already been discussed. When a supervisor is to be a witness in an arbitration hearing, he or she will generally be interviewed by the attorney representing the hospital or by the chief presenter of the case. The purpose of this interview is to learn what

the supervisor can or cannot testify to at the hearing. No ethical attorney will ever tell a supervisor to change a story or to fabricate testimony. Indeed, witnesses are usually placed under oath to tell the truth during an arbitration hearing.

However, even when a supervisor is telling the truth at a hearing the testimony must also come across as forceful and convincing. Normally, it is easier to testify on direct examination when the sympathetic hospital presenter is asking the questions. Snags may occur when the supervisor is confronted on cross-examination by an attorney whose manner may be abrasive and whose questions may have a "bite" to them. Naturally supervisors will attempt to testify in a way that makes their side look good. One should testify to only those things that were actually seen or heard. When a supervisor testifies as to what another employee said or what another employee supposedly saw, it becomes "hearsay" evidence. While an arbitrator may accept such evidence, it is seldom given any weight and may even damage the credibility of a witness.

A witness is also more effective if he or she avoids giving "opinion" testimony (unless, of course, called as an expert witness, such as a physician or a consultant). Comments such as "the grievant was angry," "the grievant was sleeping" or "the grievant is habitually absent" are examples of opinion testimony and evidence. While they may be said with all good intent, they remain unconvincing to an arbitrator. Drawing conclusions is the job of the arbitrator, not of the witness. Instead of saying, "The grievant was angry," it would be better to say that "the grievant was talking in a loud manner, slamming his fist down on the table." It is preferable to say that the "grievant has been absent on ten occasions each month for the last six months," rather than testifying that the "grievant is habitually absent." In short, a witness should simply relate the "facts" and not draw conclusions.

There are many arbitration cases that hinge on questions of the credibility of witnesses. In such a case, the arbitrator must resolve the dispute largely around which side's testimony was believable and which was not. Discipline and discharge cases often involve this type of question. A witness who contradicts his or her own testimony will usually cast doubt upon it. For example, a witness may be asked on direct examination, "When did you witness the fight?" and replies "At ten minutes to six." But on close questioning on cross-examination, the witness is asked, "How can you be so sure of that time?" This may have the effect of rattling the witness. The opposing attorney follows up by asking, "Are you sure it wasn't five after six when the shift was already over?" The witness answers, "It could have been after six." Now the arbitrator is not sure of the truth. Had the witness said, "When I heard the noises of the fight, I remember glancing at my watch," the testimony would be much more convincing.

Also, when a witness takes an un-

necessarily long time before answering a question, it suggests to the arbitrator that the witness must be thinking what the answer *should be* instead of simply telling the truth. This is not to say the witness is not entitled to think through the question, but when long pauses are frequent, as are requests to repeat a clear question, the arbitrator wonders about the veracity of the witness. Another common problem that witnesses experience relates to their belief that they are obliged to know the answer to every question. A witness knows only what he or she knows; if asked about a subject about which one has no knowledge, one should simply admit that lack of knowledge. Credibility may be more seriously damaged by a fabricated reply than by an honest answer of "I don't know."

On cross-examination, questions are sometimes tough and are even asked in a caustic or sarcastic manner. One should not rise to the bait by becoming angry or defensive. A witness is responsible only for his or her own answers and not for the opposing counsel's demeanor.

THE HEARING

An arbitration hearing may come as a surprise to a person who has never attended one. Normally it is conducted in a more formal manner than a lower step grievance meeting but less formally than a court proceeding. The arbitrator usually begins the arbitration hearing by asking whether there are joint exhibits the parties want to submit. The arbitrator then will inquire whether they wish to make opening statements. The party with the burden of proof is obliged to make its opening statement first, as well as to present its witnesses and evidence first. In discipline and discharge cases that burden is on the employer, but in all other issues the burden falls on the union.

Following the opening statements, the party with the burden of proof presents its witnesses. As previously noted, witnesses are sworn and examined by their own counsel and then subjected to cross-examination. When evidence is introduced through a witness, there can be objections to its introduction (there can, of course, also be objections to what a witness says during examination). Usually arbitrators do not follow the technical rules of evidence, on the theory that the purpose of the arbitration is designed to bring out the truth of the matter, not to indulge in the technicalities of a court proceeding. It is each arbitrator's decision as to where he or she will draw the line in observing those rules and in determining what evidence will be admitted. Even though an arbitrator takes certain evidence, this does not necessarily mean it will be given weight. Normally the arbitrator will not give credence to such so-called evidence as unsupported allegations, lie detector results, hearsay evidence, opinion evidence and offers of compromise made during the lower steps of the grievance procedure.

Following the presentation by the party with the burden of proof, the other side gives its case. This side's witnesses are also subjected to cross-examination with the same rights of objection to the introduction of evidence and statements by witnesses. At the close of their case, there may be rebuttal witnesses by the other side and rebuttal of the rebuttal witnesses.

When each side has concluded, the arbitrator allows the parties the option of making closing statements or filing briefs. A brief is a written summary of the background of the case and the arguments of the parties. Should one or both parties elect to file briefs, the arbitrator will set a date when the briefs are due. When the briefs are received, the hearing is declared closed. The arbitrator normally has a fixed time in which to submit the decision. This time can be fixed by the contract or determined by the rules of the appointing agency (i.e., American Arbitration Association, AAA, or Federal Mediation and Conciliation Service, FMCS). Under AAA rules the arbitrator has 30 days following the hearing, should oral summation be used, or 30 days after receipt of briefs, to render the award. FMCS rules allow 60 days.

TYPES OF ARBITRATION DISPUTES

There are two types of arbitration cases. These involve so-called interest and rights disputes. Interest disputes are concerned with those situations in which the parties cannot agree on the terms of an upcoming collective bargaining agreement. When they have bargained to a point of impasse, rather than facing the prospect of a strike, the parties may call on an arbitrator to review their respective positions and make a final determination as to what the unresolved parts of the new collective agreement should be. It is emphasized that in the absence of contractual provisions stating otherwise, an arbitrator cannot be brought in to hear and decide an interest dispute type of case unless there is *mutual agreement* by the parties to make such an arrangement.

On the other hand, a rights dispute case involves a question concerning the interpretation or application of the *current* or *existing* collective agreement. Normally, arbitration of such disputes can be invoked by the action of either *one* of the parties. Mutual agreement to arbitrate is not, therefore, necessary. Obviously, most arbitration cases involve rights disputes.

Rights disputes themselves can be subdivided into discharge and discipline cases and other cases involving contract interpretation. The former kinds of cases involve the interpretation of the "just cause" language in the agreement. Other contract interpretation cases can run the full gamut of the contract's provisions.

STANDARDS OF CONTRACT INTERPRETATION

It is helpful for a supervisor to be aware of the standards of contract interpretation that arbitrators normally use to resolve arbitration cases involving rights disputes.[19] Supervisors with such knowledge can not only better understand an arbitrator's award, they can also use such knowledge to check their own positions concerning a grievance involving rights disputes.

Probably the most common tenet of contract interpretation is the one that states that unambiguous contract language prevails above all other standards. If the contract language is clear, the arbitrator should go no further to resolve the dispute. Even past practice or the precedent of a prior arbitration award should not be given weight in the face of clear and unambiguous contract language. For example, the author decided a hospital arbitration involving a situation in which a supervisor was permitting his employees 25 to 30 minutes for their breaks instead of the 10 minutes specified in the contract. When the supervisor was told to discontinue this practice the union grieved, contending that past practice had been established for allowing longer breaks. Had the author decided in the union's favor he would have denied the clear language of the contract and in doing so could have exceeded his authority.

Other standards of contract interpretation come into play when language is not clear and precise. For example, what does "Overtime will be distributed as equally as possible" really mean? In the absence of some additional clarifying language, an arbitrator will have to try to apply vague language to a specific situation.

How does one do this? In such a case, the standard of past practice may be helpful. Past practice means a usual and customary way of doing things. The party arguing past practice will attempt to demonstrate that a certain procedure for effectuating the language in question has been established in the past, and therefore it must be demonstrative of how the parties understand and apply the agreement. It should be noted, however, that just because the parties did something a certain way once or twice, this does not mean that it is a "practice." A past practice usually requires that the parties both acquiesced in the practice and that it has been in effect for some considerable period of time.

The parties' negotiation history can also be a useful standard of contract interpretation when language is ambiguous or imprecise. Most hospitals maintain notes and minutes as to what was proposed, accepted or rejected, and by which side. For example, when a party has attempted to introduce certain language into the contract and that proposal is rejected, it is clear to the arbitrator that the party's subsequent interpretation of the collective agreement could not be as it was in the proposal. Arbitrators do not wish to give through arbitration that which was not obtained at the bargaining table.

Frequently, language concerning a certain subject, for example seniority, will exist in more than one place in the collective agreement. Suppose that statements in two or more sec-

tions of the contract are at odds with one another. The standard of interpretation an arbitrator might apply in such a situation is the one that says: "Specific contract language prevails over general contract language." This means that the arbitrator will place more emphasis on that section of the contract that specifically deals with the subject matter in dispute than the one that treats the matter in general terms.

Finally, arbitrators may also use precedents established by other arbitration decisions in a dispute involving contract interpretation. Arbitration, unlike the law, does not adhere to the doctrine of *stare decisis* (i.e., arbitrators are not bound by the decisions of their colleagues). The main reason for this is the fact that an arbitrator is hired to interpret a *particular* contract with its own unique terms and language. It may differ in many ways from other contracts. While arbitrators may learn much from the general approach taken by their colleagues to certain kinds of cases, it is the wisest policy to ignore other rulings unless the award concerned the same contract language, the language in question had not been changed, and it involved a similar factual situation. Under these circumstances, precedent may be entitled to great weight.

THE OPINION

The most important part of the arbitration award is the reasoning the arbitrator used in reaching the decision. That reasoning is contained in the "opinion" section of the arbitration award. It is of paramount importance that the arbitrator specifically address the issues the parties have presented and each of the arguments raised by the parties. Otherwise the

---

It is of paramount importance that the arbitrator specifically address the issues the parties have presented and each of the arguments raised by the parties.

---

losing party may be tempted to raise the grievance again, reasoning that, as the arbitrator did not consider the argument it may thus have some merit.[20] Both union and management representatives also prefer that the arbitrator write the decision for the presenters of the case and for the grievant.[21] They believe that they can explain the award to the grievant if there is any misunderstanding.

In any event, arbitrators are often "rated" by the parties on the basis of the reasoning (or lack thereof) demonstrated in the opinion. Even the losing side may be favorably impressed with an arbitrator who has forcefully and logically defended the decision. The parties have already made a subjective evaluation of the worth of their cases and a party expecting to lose an arbitration is not unduly dismayed when the award meets its expectations.

ENFORCEMENT OF THE ARBITRATION AWARD

Arbitration is often referred to as the "terminal step" in the grievance procedure. There are no appeals beyond arbitration. The arbitrator's decision is final and binding on the parties because their contract usually so specifies and the award is enforceable by injunction in federal district court under Section 301 of the Taft-Hartley Act for those employees covered by that act (including hospitals), or by state law (if such exists).

Vacating an arbitrator's award in court may be a difficult undertaking as there are only three common-law grounds for setting an arbitration decision aside: (1) the existence of fraud, (2) the fact that the arbitrator did not allow a full and fair hearing or (3) the fact that the arbitrator exceeded his or her powers.[22] Regarding the first, the moving party would have to establish that the arbitrator took a bribe to influence the decision. There has never been a major case of such fraud that has been documented. Moreover, arbitrators usually go out of their way to allow the parties the fullest opportunity to present their arguments and proofs. Perhaps the only viable way to vacate an arbitration award is to establish that the arbitrator exceeded his or her authority. Normally this means that the arbitrator, in interpreting or applying disputed contract language, actually modified the clear terms of the collective agreement. Collective bargaining agreements may specify that an arbitrator must not "add to, delete from, modify, or change the language of this agreement." When the arbitrator does so, he or she runs the risk of seeing the award set aside in court.

However, most parties would not attempt to vacate an award even if they thought they had sufficient grounds. If a party tries to overturn a case following a loss, this may prompt the other side to take similar action upon losing the next case, and so on. Once the parties establish such a pattern of conduct, where does it end? Arbitration loses its effectiveness under such circumstances and ceases to be the "supreme court" in the grievance procedure. Instead, it becomes just another step on the road to the courts. Fortunately, the parties are well aware that, by destroying the arbitration process, they leave themselves only the alternatives of a labor court or crippling strikes.

• • •

An important prerequisite for effective supervisory grievance handling is for management to allow supervisors both the authority and responsibility for adjusting grievances at the first step. Management must properly train supervisors in the techniques of processing grievances and must stress the importance of their taking that responsibility. One way to foster the settlement of grievances at the supervisory level is to make grievance settlements by supervisors nonbinding for future cases.

A supervisor's leadership style may also influence the effectiveness of grievance processing. While an autocratic style can act to reduce the grievance rate, it also works against settlement of complaints during the earlier steps in the grievance procedure. An effective leadership style may depend on the quality of relations between the employees and supervisor, the nature of the work and the supervisor's power (or lack thereof).

A supervisor can improve grievance-handling effectiveness by:

- investigating grievances thoroughly before deciding what to do;
- concentrating on being a good listener;
- setting up rules for the conduct of a hearing;
- remaining aware of *Weingarten* obligations; and
- following up on grievance settlement.

The supervisor should also accept the possibility that some grievances will reach arbitration and that not all of them will get there because the grievances are meritorious. Important strategic and political reasons may propel a dispute through the various steps of the grievance procedure. An alert supervisor will look behind the scenes to assess the possible motivation for each grievance that reaches arbitration.

Supervisors should be aware of the principles of contract interpretation that arbitrators use in resolving "rights" disputes. Some of the major ones are:

- clear contract language prevails over any other standard;
- specific language takes precedence over general contract language;
- past practice and precedent are useful methods for resolving issues when contract language is ambiguous or contradictory.

Finally, in addition to investigating grievances and gathering evidence, supervisors may also play a key role as witnesses at arbitration hearings. Testimony by a supervisor will be more forceful and believable when he or she avoids giving hearsay evidence, offering opinion, or taking long or frequent pauses before answering.

REFERENCES

1. Juris, H., et al. "Employee Discipline No Longer Management Prerogative Only. *Hospitals* 51 (May 1977): 71.
2. Kuhn, W. *Bargaining in Grievance Settlement.* New York: Columbia University Press, 1961.
3. Lawshe, C.H., and Guion, R.M. "A Comparison of Management-Labor Attitudes toward Grievance Procedures." *Personnel Psychology* 4, No. 1 (1951): 5–7.
4. Petersen, D.J. "Grass Roots Problem Solving." *Personnel Administration* 35 (May–June 1972): 20–23.
5. Gilliam, D.W. "Discussion." In *Proceedings of the Thirty-Fourth Annual Meeting*, edited by B.D. Dennis. Madison, Wisc.: Industrial Relations Research Association, 1981, p. 334.
6. McGregor, D. *The Human Side of Enterprise.* New York: McGraw-Hill, 1960, pp. 35–57.
7. Walker, R.L., and Robinson, J.W. "The First-Line Supervisor's Role in the Grievance Procedure." *Arbitration Journal* 32 (December 1977): 289.
8. Ibid., 291.
9. Ibid.
10. Chicago Hospital Council. *Analysis of Collective Bargaining Agreements in Chicago Area Hospitals, 1975–76.* Chicago: Chicago Hospital Council, 1975, p. 48.
11. Graham, H., and Heshizer, B. "The Effect of Contract Language on Low-Level Settlement of Grievances." *Labor Law Journal* 30 (July 1979): 431.
12. Nash, A. *The Union Steward: Duties, Rights*

and Status. Ithaca: New York State School of Industrial and Labor Relations, 1977, pp. 6, 11.
13. Gandz, J., and Whitehead, J.D. "The Relationship between Industrial Relations Climate and Grievance Initiation and Resolution." In *Proceedings of the Thirty-Fourth Annual Meeting*, edited by B.D. Dennis. Madison, Wisc.: Industrial Relations Research Association, 1981, pp. 325–326.
14. Dalton, D.R., and Todor, W.D. "Antecedents of Grievance Filing Behavior: Attitude/Behavioral Consistency and the Union Steward." *Academy of Management Journal* 25, no. 1 (1982): 166.
15. N.L.R.B. v. Weingarten, Inc., 76 Labor Cases 10,662 (Feb. 19, 1975).
16. Graham and Heshizer, "The Effect of Contract Language," 431.
17. Petersen, D.J., Rezler, J., and Reed, K.A. *Arbitration in Health Care.* Rockville, Md.: Aspen, 1981, pp. 15–16.
18. Petersen, D.J. "Why Unions Go to Arbitration: Politics and Strategy vs. Merit." *Personnel* 48 (July–August 1971): 44–49.
19. Rezler, J., and Petersen, D.J. "Strategies of Arbitrator Selection." 70 *Labor Arbitration Reports* 1308.
20. Petersen, D.J., and Rezler, J., "Arbitration Decision Writing: Selected Criteria." *Arbitration Journal* 38, no. 2 (1983): 24.
21. Ibid., 26–27.
22. Petersen, Rezler and Reed, "Arbitration in Health Care" 7–9.

Index

Notes

Notes

Notes

Notes

Notes

Notes

Notes

Notes

Notes

Notes

Notes

Notes

Notes

Notes

Notes

Notes